The
ESSENTIAL
TOURING
CYCLIST

The
ESSENTIAL
TOURING
CYCLIST

Richard A. Lovett

Photographs by Vera Jagendorf
Illustrations by Elizabeth Halsey

Ragged Mountain Press
Camden, Maine

To Pat and Dick Lovett, for nurturing the spirit of adventure. And to John and Helen Holland, for the encouragement to share it.

Published by Ragged Mountain Press

10 9 8 7 6 5 4 3 2 1

Copyright © 1994 Ragged Mountain Press, an imprint of TAB Books. TAB Books is a division of McGraw-Hill, Inc.

All rights reserved. The publisher and author take no responsibility for the use of any of the materials or methods described in this book, nor for the products thereof. "Ragged Mountain Press" and the Ragged Mountain Press logo are trademarks of McGraw-Hill, Inc. Printed in the United States of America.

Library of Congress Cataloging-in-Publication Data
Lovett, Richard A.
    The essential touring cyclist / Richard A. Lovett.
       p.   cm.
    ISBN 0-07-038849-0 (acid-free paper)
    1. Bicycle touring.   I. Title.
  GV1044.L68   1994
  796.6'4–dc20   94-5926
                                  CIP

Questions regarding the content of this book should be addressed to:
Ragged Mountain Press
P.O. Box 220
Camden, ME 04843

Questions regarding the ordering of this book should be addressed to:
TAB Books
A Division of McGraw-Hill, Inc.
Blue Ridge Summit, PA 17294
1-800-233-1128

The Essential Touring Cyclist is printed on recycled paper containing a minimum of 50% total recycled paper with 10% postconsumer de-inked fiber.

Printed by Fairfield Graphics, Fairfield, PA

Design and Production by Dan Kirchoff

Edited by J.R. Babb and Tom McCarthy

CONTENTS

▼

ACKNOWLEDGMENTS

▼

My thanks to the many people who contributed to this book: Elizabeth for her many excellent drawings and willingness to sweat the details, to Vera not only for photographs but also for input into many sections of the book, and to Robert Grott for being our guinea pig and model on the road. I also thank Dick and Pat Lovett and Kelly Scott for reading and commenting on drafts, and the Eastside Bike Gallery in Portland, Oregon, (especially Sarah Perrault and David Feldman) for fielding innumerable technical questions. Thanks also to the following equipment manufacturers whose products appear in photos: Bridgestone, Madden, Blackburn, Avocet, Pearllzumi, REI, Yakima, Outdoor Research, MSR, and Giro. Thanks also to Greg Siple of Bikecentennial. And finally, thanks to Jim Babb, Tom McCarthy, and the other folks at Ragged Mountain Press.

INTRODUCTION

▼

Your bicycle slips gently along a winding ribbon of asphalt, smooth as glass. Pedaling seems effortless, as natural as breathing. Crossing a small creek, you watch the water leap over rocky ledges. A farmer waves at you from a field of new-mown hay, then for the next half mile you are overwhelmed by the sweet aroma of curing alfalfa. It is the last hour before sunset, when the motorized tourists have gone to ground and what little traffic remains is as benign as the warm glow of the sun, which bathes everything in gold and gives you a shadow 50 feet long.

Such is bicycle touring at its finest. Unless you wish it so, it is not a gasping effort, straining to climb hill after hill. There may be hills, but you don't have to race over them. The essence of touring is spontaneity and flexibility. If you tire, you stop. If you encounter the dream tailwind and you feel as though you could go on forever, you milk the day for all it's worth. But always you are immersed in the scenery, surrounded by sights, sounds, and smells denied those who travel in the fleeting, insulated world of an automobile.

There are as many styles of bicycle touring as types of vacation. Some are athletic challenges; others are relaxed excursions with time to bask in the sun, read a book, or share the camaraderie of a campfire. It's even possible to mix touring with fine wines and rustic B&Bs, with someone else carrying your baggage. Here are the possibilities:

- *Posh, Catered Touring.* For a fee you'll be put up in inns or motels and given meals, a guide, and a van to carry your baggage. This is tour-

ing at its most luxurious, combining cycling with southern mansions, California wineries, or New England fall colors.

- *Van-Supported Touring.* This is similar to catered touring, except you do the catering yourself, persuading a friend to drive the van, or taking turns driving. You can stay in motels or rough it by camping.

- *Organized Touring.* These camping tours are conducted by bike clubs, state tourist departments, or budget-minded touring companies. They provide baggage transport and arrange group camping on school lawns, country fairgrounds, or in parks.

- *Credit-Card Touring.* For this form of lightweight touring, you need a credit card and little else. As on catered tours you stay in inns or motels and eat in restaurants, and carry what little baggage you need.

- *Light Touring.* In mild climates you can do short self-contained tours with little more than you'd carry on a credit-card tour.

- *Self-Contained Touring.* With everything you need for a week (or longer), your load will weigh 40 to 60 pounds, depending on weather and how good you are at paring out unneeded luxuries. With low gears this type of touring isn't as difficult as it sounds. It pays back the extra effort with a flexible schedule that gives you the ultimate in cycling freedom.

Know Your Author

Some people take up a sport as an act of deliberate volition; others drift into it by a series of steps so gradual they seem to have been born to it. I was the latter: As a preschooler on training wheels, my greatest ambition was to bicycle into the unexplored country three blocks away. From those beginnings it was simply a matter of extending my range and learning from experience—sometimes good, sometimes bad. By the time I was in my early 30s, I'd done a half-dozen shorter bicycling trips before I struck out solo cross-country. It was a life-changing adventure, recorded in my book, *Freewheelin': A Solo Journey Across America.*

Over the years I've introduced a number of friends to touring, watching them transform from beginners to seasoned veterans as they planned and carried out their first trips. *The Essential Touring Cyclist* offers you the same tutorial, combining the cycling lore I've learned from dozens of sources into a single volume that will serve as the foundation for your first trip.

My collaborator, photographer Vera Jagendorf, is the other type of cyclist, one who took up the sport by a sudden act of decision. Not previously an active cyclist, in 1986 she bought a touring bike and set off a month later on a mostly solo, 2,500-mile trek across the West.

Who Are You?
Cycle touring isn't just for macho kids with perfect bodies. It's for anyone with a sense of adventure who is drawn to backcountry America or to poke along a seacoast unimpeded by the sense-deadening shell of an automobile. It's for people who want to discover a "real" America with as few barriers as possible—and it doesn't matter if you're 21, 41, or 61 if you're in sound physical condition and willing to take some time to prepare. You don't even have

to be all that athletic. I've known people as much as 80 pounds overweight who successfully completed mountainous 500-mile tours. Gearing and patience are more important than raw strength.

The Essential Touring Cyclist is aimed at beginners, although it will be useful to experienced cyclists whose background does not include touring. It assumes you know how to ride a bicycle and are familiar with the basic operation of shift levers and brakes.

Families can tour if they keep distances and conditions within the abilities of their children (or within the ability of the parent to pull a trailer or do most of the work on a tandem). Many people with disabilities can also tour, although it may take special equipment.

Using This Book
This book's progression is logical but not completely linear. There's no reason you can't be buying camping gear at the same time you're training—no reason that part of your training for a long tour can't include a couple of short ones.

To make it simple, I've divided the book into two parts, Cycle Touring 101 and Cycle Touring 102, with a "midterm" and "final" for each. Think of it as two semester-long courses, because six to eight months is about what it takes to go from beginner to being ready to start your first week-long tour.

Cycle Touring 101 deals mostly with preparation and training—things you'll do around home or on day rides, without going out overnight. Cycle Touring 102 takes you on the road for overnight tours, culminating with the prospect of an adventure of a week or longer.

Cycle Touring 101

GETTING STARTED

I thought the matter over, and concluded I could do it. So I went down and bought . . . a bicycle. The Expert came home with me to instruct me. . . . We got up a handsome speed, and presently traversed a brick, and I went out over the top of the tiller and landed, head down, on the instructor's back, and saw the machine fluttering in the air between me and the sun. It was well it came down on us, for that broke the fall, and it was not injured.

Five days later I . . . was carried down to the hospital, and found the Expert doing pretty fairly. In a few more days I was quite sound. I attribute this to my prudence in always dismounting on something soft. Some recommend a feather bed, but I think an Expert is better. . . .

—Mark Twain, "Taming the Bicycle"

This book assumes that you already have more experience than Mark Twain did in his initial encounter with his two-wheeled adversary. When starting a new endeavor, however, it's often reassuring to be reminded of how much you already know—not to mention how much bicycle technology has progressed from the high wheelers of Twain's era.

If you bought this book, you've already made an initial commitment to the possibility of taking a cycling vacation. But if you're like most people at this stage, you have a welter of questions: What type of bike should I get? Do I really need those funny-looking cycling shorts? How much should I train? And how do I deal with dogs, cars, potholes, headwinds, or any of the other obstacles that experienced cyclists take in stride?

Cycle Touring 101 will reduce the intimidation factor inherent in these and similar questions. We'll begin by looking at equipment, keeping in mind the fact that while the latest and greatest in specialized equipment may be appealing, it isn't necessary for an enjoyable touring experience. If you already have a well-maintained bicycle, odds are you can use it for your first tour with only a few changes in gearing and accessories. And you can certainly use it for training.

In addition to equipment and training, we'll also look at basic cycling skills such as riding in traffic, negotiating railroad crossings, and working together in a group to overcome headwinds. Finally, we'll look at fine-tuning your bicycle for added comfort, and we'll briefly catalog common aches and pains and ways to prevent them.

The only prerequisites for this course are curiosity about cycling and a sense of adventure. For a midterm exercise, you can buy a bicycle and equip it for touring, or you can retrofit the one you already own. For a final exam, take the bike out on the road for a 30- to 50-mile day trip.

CHOOSING AND EQUIPPING A BICYCLE

▼

Bicycling can easily be dominated by gadgetry. Each year brings a new set of latest-and-greatest inventions. Some quickly become passing fads, but a few take the sport by storm and rapidly set new standards.

Cyclists with money to burn can get sucked into trying them all. Club rides sometimes look like showrooms on wheels, with everyone decked out in the latest miracle fabric, riding sleek new machines that look as though they've never seen rain or a chip in the paint.

As a touring cyclist, you can pronounce yourself above all that. Your equipment concerns are far more practical: Does it work? Is it comfortable? Reliable? Can you fix it or replace it if it breaks down in the middle of nowhere?

Avoid any gadget that hasn't been around at least a couple of years unless it's something you can't live without. The last thing you want is to stop in some small-town bike shop and have the mechanic study your misbehaving component and say, "I've heard about these, but this is the first one I've ever seen."

If you haven't paid much attention to bicycle technology for a while you've missed a virtual revolution and will be surprised by the number of new gadgets developed in the past few years.

Not that such revolutions are anything new.

There was a time when high-wheelers were the height of fashion. Later, coaster-braked, balloon-tired 1-speeds, or 3-speed "English racers" dominated the popular image of "bicycle." Then the 10-speed boom of the early 1970s brought drop handlebars, narrow saddles, and that strange French word *derailleur*.

The modern revolution is no less far-reaching. Very few 10-speeds have 10 speeds anymore—12, 15, 18, and 21 are more common. Similarly, the mountain-bike boom and explosion of "hybrid" frame styles following in its wake dominated the market virtually overnight, and continue to do so today.

Other changes are more subtle. Click-stop "index" shifting went from avant-garde to standard in only a few years. Brake cables are hidden beneath the handlebar winding tape, and freewheels have become easy-to-remove "cassettes" or cartridges.

This chapter won't turn you into a techno-freak gearhead. Rather, it will examine the basic styles of bicycles and components and assess their strengths and weaknesses for touring. If keeping abreast of the latest developments also appeals to you, subscribe to one of the bicycling magazines for a wealth of information each month.

Types of Bicycles

Touring doesn't require a special bicycle. Such machines are nice, but you can tour just fine on your old college 10-speed (with a few equipment upgrades) or a mountain bike. You can even do light-duty touring on a racing bike. For this reason, the first time you tour, concentrate on buying camping equipment—racks and panniers—rather than a new bicycle. If you find you like touring, decide then whether you want to further customize your existing bicycle or buy a new one.

There are five basic kinds of adult bicycles: racing, mountain, sport bikes, dedicated touring, and crossover. Some differences, such as the type of tires or handlebar styles, are immediately obvious; others are more subtle, showing up best if you compare the various bikes side by side.

Racing Bikes

Racing bikes are lightweight, with narrow, high-pressure tires. Everything about them is designed for going fast, on pavement, with no baggage. The thin tires, for example, reduce both rolling resistance and the weight of the wheels, making quick starts and sharp turns easier. The first time you ride a racing bike, the highly responsive steering will probably feel unsteady, but it won't take long to get used to it.

To increase speed and responsiveness, racing frames are stiff, with the seat post and head tube closer to vertical than on other bicycle types. This keeps the frame from wasting energy by flexing when it hits bumps, but it also transmits the bump more directly to your body, which can be uncomfortable in the long haul.

Racing bikes aren't designed to carry gear and may become unstable when loaded down with panniers. But an entry-level racer can be good for light touring; I've used one for week-long organized tours, and some credit-card touring with up to 20 pounds of baggage. I've even successfully navigated short stretches of gravel with such a load, though the thin tires increase the risk of flats.

Racing bikes are fast and fun to ride for short distances, but be wary about sitting on one for long hours, day after day. They're unlikely to be sturdy enough—or stable enough—for self-contained touring.

Mountain Bikes

Mountain bikes—by far the most common bicycle sold in the last few years—are at the opposite end of the sturdiness spectrum. Built for rugged gravel roads or breakneck charges up and down steep trails, a good mountain bike will easily take the strain of a heavy pack.

But the traditional mountain bike is best designed for touring under Third World conditions. The fat tires, even if you replace the traditional

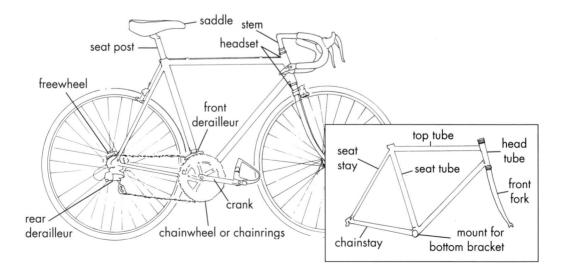

knobby with a thinner road tire, often run at low enough pressure to slow you down appreciably, and the standard straight handlebar gives you only one hand position, something that can get tiring after a few hours.

A mountain bike can be improved for on-pavement touring by substituting lighter wheels and higher-pressure tires, and by changing handlebar style or adding bar extenders. Some newer mountain bikes also have frames closer to traditional road-bike frames than earlier models.

Mountain bikes are at their best for heavy touring, when you need the strength and stability. They're at their worst on van-supported or organized tours, when they slow you down and give you little but a softer ride and less pressure on your hands in return. If your only bicycle is a mountain bike, use it for your first touring experiments, but unless you plan to do a lot of off-pavement touring, you'll want to shift to a touring or crossover bike.

Sport Bikes

Sport bikes are the descendents of the traditional 10-speed. Although not many seem to be selling today, there are a lot of them on the road.

Sport bikes look like racing bikes except that the angles of the head tube and fork will be a bit farther from vertical to give a softer (but less efficient) ride. Expect heavier rims and slightly fatter tires than on a racing bike, but by no means the dramatically fat tires of a mountain bike. There will also be slightly more rake to the fork, contributing to a stabler, more shock-absorbing ride.

Sport bikes are a little better on gravel than racing bikes, but aren't designed to go off-pavement for extended periods. They don't truly *excel* at any form of touring—slower than racing bikes for van-supported or organized tours, and not quite as nicely designed for loaded touring as a dedicated touring bike. But they make an excellent multipurpose compromise. I've done many tours on such a

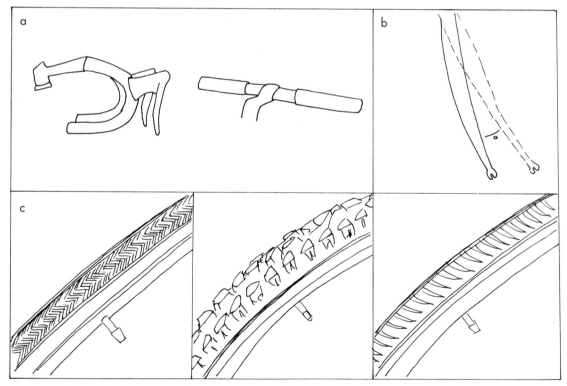

(a) Handlebar types, (b) Fork types: raked and not highly raked, (c) Tire types.

bicycle, including going cross-country. And, the price is right: Since these bikes aren't currently stylish, you might pick up a good used one inexpensively.

Dedicated Touring Bikes

A dedicated touring bike is the best design for long-haul touring on pavement. Manufacturers' goals have always been stability, comfort, and the ability to carry heavy weight. There never have been many of these bikes on the market.

At first glance, a touring bike looks much like a sport bike, but it has some important differences. Its wheel base will be longer for added stability, the frame angles even farther from vertical, and the rake of the fork more pronounced. A touring bike will also accommodate slightly wider tires than will a typical racing or sport bike.

In addition, it should have a number of useful touring-oriented details, the most important being eyelets and braze-ons for front and rear racks. There may also be mounting attachments for three water-bottle cages instead of the traditional two, with the third cage attached to the front of the down tube, where the long wheelbase leaves plenty of room.

Think of a touring bike as a truck on two wheels. On a test ride, it will feel sluggish compared with a sport or racing bike, slower on the turns, but also very stable, happily maintaining its course on a straightaway with a minimum of steering effort. All these are functions of the frame geometry.

A touring bike will have drop handlebars, a triple crank, and (hopefully) a wide-range gear cluster rather than the narrow "corncob" cluster found on racing bikes. The bike may even come with a rear rack already attached.

When loaded with panniers, it should remain stable, or possibly become even more stable than ever, handling as though this is what it was created to do—after all, it was.

The rims will be strong, the tires probably 700 x 32c (the metric equivalent of 1¼ inch). Brakes will likely be cantilevers, designed to stop you plus 40 to 60 pounds of gear. These bikes will do anything sport bikes can do, though not quite as nimbly. On gravel, they'll outperform sport or racing bikes, but won't do nearly as well as mountain bikes.

Crossover Bikes

Crossover bikes blend mountain-bike and road-bike features into a mix that is sometimes called "hybrid." The mix, however, varies from manufacturer to manufacturer. Some crossover bikes are little more than road bikes with upright handlebars. Others are more like mountain bikes, with triple cranks and 26-inch wheels—but drop handlebars. Some use tires similar to what you'd find on a dedicated touring bike; others use wheels between a road bike and mountain bike, taking perhaps a 1.4-inch tire. The choices can get confusing, changing from year to year as manufacturers tinker with designs.

The usefulness of such a bike for various forms of touring depends on its mix of road- and mountain-bike features. If it's basically a road bike except for the handlebars, it will function like a conventional road bike. But if it's designed more like a dedicated touring bike except for the handlebars or a slightly fatter tire, it can be excellent for loaded touring. It might even have specific touring features such as front and rear braze-ons or a third water-bottle cage, and many people will find the hybrid design more comfortable than a pure road bike.

If the bike can take a fatter tire, perhaps 1.9 inches, it will also allow you to traverse a wide range of gravel or dirt roads, even with a load, making it the best choice for wide-ranging conditions.

Don't limit your shopping only to crossover bikes claiming to be designed for touring. Bikes designed for commuting can also make excellent touring bikes, since many of the desired features are similar.

It's in the Details

In marketing, "detailing" usually refers to paint stripes, decals, and other pieces of purely cosmetic trim. In biking, the details that matter are in the frame design, making the difference between bicycles that can carry camping equipment and those that can't.

If you want to do fully loaded touring, check the bike frame for the following details.

1 Eyelets for attaching a rear rack. Except for expensive racing bikes, most bicycles have these, but don't assume. Look for two threaded

eyelets above or behind the slot ("drop-out") on each side of the rear axle. You can mount a fender to one set, a rear rack to the other. Without them, there's no reasonable way to mount either accessory, and the bike is *not* designed for touring.

2 Seat-stay braze-ons for mounting a rear rack. These are a second set of threaded eyelets, welded to the seat stays, near the top. On steel frames you can mount a rear rack without them, with a clamp that holds it to the stays, but you won't be able to carry as much weight.

3 Front ("fork") eyelets. If you plan to use front fenders or a front rack—or want the option to do so—you'll want these. You can buy clamps that function as substitutes, but eyelets are your best indicator that the manufacturer intended its machine to carry front panniers. If the bike has no front eyelets and the frame is made of anything other than steel, don't use clamps before consulting a good bike shop about whether or not the frame can handle the stress.

4 Braze-ons for Low Rider front panniers. Like rear-rack braze-ons, these are welded eyelets on the outside of the fork, approximately at its midpoint. They're not essential, but simplify the task of mounting a Low Rider front rack.

Customizing Your Bicycle

When you buy a bicycle, it comes with stock components—gear clusters, wheels, tires, crank, saddle, handlebars, etc. Don't assume this is a take-it-or-leave-it proposition. If you tell the shop what you want when you're buying the bicycle, you can negotiate the changes as part of the purchase price. You might get a discount if the shop can sell the unwanted components to someone else. A shop might even offer to swap components at close to the difference in retail prices, especially if the components you want are low-demand items that it would love to get rid of.

Expect to pay a labor charge for the substitutions, but it might not be large if you're willing to wait for the shop to assemble a bike to your order rather than modifying one of the assembled bicycles on display. Manufacturers ship bicycles in a partially disassembled state, and some component changes involve labor that would have to be done anyway. The time to get what you want—at a significant savings compared to what it would cost later—is when you buy the bike.

Don't be intimidated by the thought of overriding the manufacturer's equipment choices. Bike manufacturers attempt to rig their machines for the average user, and as a touring cyclist you aren't average. Among other things, the bicycle almost certainly won't come with the ideal set of gears for real-world hills, especially for touring in mountains.

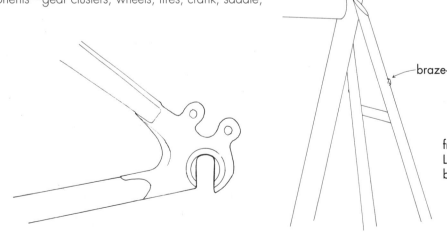

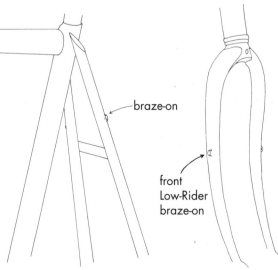

braze-on

front
Low-Rider
braze-on

Gearing

The importance of proper gearing is obvious—so much so that until recently bicycles were identified by the number of gears: 10-speeds, 5-speeds, 3-speeds, 1-speeds. (To calculate the number of speeds, multiply the number of chainrings in the front by the number of gears in the rear.)

Today, with the abundance of multispeed models, what matters isn't so much the number of gears as their range. It's also useful to have gears spaced uniformly across that range with a minimum of overlap, and to have a shifting pattern that allows you to upshift or downshift by one gear without floundering around trying to figure out which one it is.

For touring, you're mostly interested in the low and middle gear ranges. Many bikes, even some that are sold for touring, don't have low enough gears. It's easy, however, to modify them. Just ask your shop to swap gear clusters, chainrings, or both. You might also have to change derailleurs or bottom brackets (the bearing where the crank passes through the frame), but probably only if you're making extreme changes such as changing from a double to a triple crank.

In discussing gearing, it helps to be at least vaguely familiar with a mathematical construct called "gear inches." You don't have to know precisely what this means, only that it's proportional to how far you go per pedal revolution and is therefore a measure of how "high" or "low" a gear really is.

Any good bike shop will have several pages of charts showing the number of gear inches for any combination of wheel size, front gear, and rear gear. But the formula is simple:

$$\text{inches} = \binom{\text{wheel diameter}}{\text{in inches}} \times \frac{\text{(teeth in chainring)}}{\text{(teeth in rear cog)}}$$

If the number is big, you're looking at a high gear: *i.e.*, a large chainring and a small rear cog. Low gears are produced by small chainrings and big rear cogs.

The lowest gear you want depends on how much baggage you're carrying and the hilliness of the terrain you're visiting. But don't ignore the low gears even if you plan to do all of your touring on a tabletop; a strong wind can kick you all the way down into your hill-climbing gears, especially if you're dragging bulky panniers directly into it. Unless you're stronger than average, plan on a low gear of 30 inches or smaller, no matter what kind of touring you plan.

For loaded touring in hilly terrain, I like a gear range of at least 21 to 100 inches, but if you never plan on carrying much baggage, you can probably get away with a range of 27 to 100. The upper end isn't all that important because you'll rarely use it, but the lower end is: You want a low enough "granny" gear to allow you to comfortably pedal uphill at a pace barely faster than a walk.

If your bike shop can get the cogs, I recommend an 18-inch gear as your lowest. You may never need it—and other cyclists may joke that you look as though you're geared to climb telephone poles—but such a gear allows you to maintain a

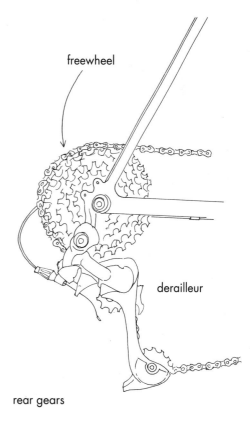

freewheel

derailleur

rear gears

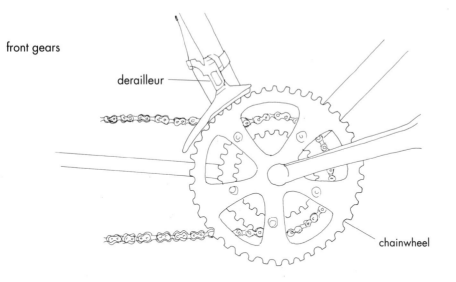

front gears

derailleur

chainwheel

pedaling cadence of 80 rpm at a pace of 4¼ mph. Carrying baggage, there are plenty of hills where that's precisely what you'll want. Smaller gears are theoretically possible, but they're overkill—you'd probably topple over at the slow speeds involved.

If all of this sounds horribly confusing, just tell your bike shop the gear range you want and ask for a freewheel/chainring combination that provides it. Eighteen -or 21-inch low gears aren't a common request, so expect disbelief and possibly an effort to talk you out of it. Stand firm. For self-contained touring, a low-low gear is a lifesaver.

Designer Gears

The preceding is all you really need to know about customizing your gearing. But if you can handle the mathematics, it's fun to work out a complete gearing pattern yourself. That way you'll know exactly what you're getting. Don't be fanatical about perfection; slight variations from ideal are something you'll never notice.

Construct a chart showing the number of gear inches for each possible combination of front and rear gears. It takes some number crunching, but it's the simplest way to translate this talk of gear inches into real-world implications. With a computer spreadsheet program, or even a pocket calculator, you can generate endless numbers of these charts. Using the formula from page 19, here's one for a typical off-the-rack touring bicycle with 21 speeds:

In addition to showing you what gears are available, such a chart helps you figure out the shifting pattern. Trace the numbers in descending order, thinking about what you'd do to make each shift in real life. In the chart, for example, you get your

	Rear Cog (Freewheel) Size						
Chainring	13	15	17	19	21	24	28
30	60	52	46	41	37	33	28
40	80	69	61	55	50	43	37
50	100	87	76	68	62	54	46

Wheel size (inches):   26

highest gear, 100 inches, on the 50-tooth chainring in front and the 13-tooth cog in back. To downshift one gear, you'd stay on the 50 and shift to the second smallest gear in the back—all quite sensible.

For the next gear, you've got two similar choices: downshifting yet again on the large chainwheel to the 76-inch gear, or shifting to the middle chainwheel for the 80-inch gear. The difference between these two isn't much; you'd probably just stay on the 50-tooth chainring rather than shifting both derailleurs. Similarly, for the next downshift, you have two even more similar choices—the 68 or the 69—followed by the 62 or the 61, and the 54 or 55.

Gear overlap is intentional. This gearing pattern is called "crossover gearing," and is common, perhaps universal, on new bicycles. It's designed under the assumption that going fast, you'll use the 50-tooth chainring. When you slow down, you'll downshift along the rear cog until eventually, somewhere in the middle of the range, you'll switch ("cross over") to the middle chainring, upshifting appropriately on the rear cog to maintain a single-gear transition. Farther down the gear range, you'll cross over yet again from the middle chainring to the small one. The overlap allows you to cross over at any of several gears, making the shifting pattern easy to remember.

The simplicity of crossover gearing is a virtue, but it throws away nearly half the gears on the bicycle used in the chart, converting a 21-speed to an 11-speed. Furthermore, like most off-the-rack bicycles, this one doesn't have a low enough granny gear for serious hill climbing, especially with a full load of camping equipment.

How can you improve this gearing pattern? Begin by substituting a smaller granny gear in the front—28 is a common size; 26 or 24 are even better for heavy touring. Some cranks, called

"microdrive," even accept 20-tooth chainrings, but this is new equipment and there's no telling if it will be the next rage or go the way of the dodo.

If this doesn't give you a low enough gear, swap the rear cluster for something with a wider range. The largest cog you're likely to find is a 34; the smallest you'll need is a 13. Figure out what size you want as your largest, and hold out for it, even if the cluster has to be ordered specially. A 13–34-tooth cluster, for example, combined with a 24-tooth chainring, adds two gears at the lower end, including that wonderful 18-inch hill-climber. With a 20-tooth granny gear, a 13–28 does the same—better because the gaps between gears in the middle of the upper range are smaller.

Even with its expanded gear range, our sample bicycle has only 13 effective speeds. The rest are still lost to overlap. Some duplication is necessary because certain gear combinations—those combining the smallest chainring with the smallest rear cog (or the biggest chainring with the biggest cog)— twist the chain sharply enough to cause it, the freewheel, and the derailleur to wear out faster than normal. The world won't end if you find yourself in one of these "prohibited" gears, but it's nice to have a duplicate to shift into.

Only a few of the gears are duplicated by necessity, however. The rest of that duplication is a function of the crossover pattern. The solution is to change the middle chainring to produce a pattern called "half-step gearing."

Half-Step Gearing

First, a caveat: Half-step gearing is currently badly out of vogue. Because of that, mountain-bike derailleurs aren't made for it, though some racing-bike derailleurs will still accommodate it quite happily. To go to a half-step system you might have to

high-stress gear combinations

switch your front derailleur along with your gearing.

The trick to half-step gearing is to reduce the size differential between the middle and largest chainrings, usually by increasing the size of the middle chainring. Properly done, this allows you to shift back and forth between them to halve each of the rear cog's gear intervals. Half-step gearing gives you a lot of gears for fine tuning—particularly nice for loaded touring, when the weight of your baggage makes you particularly sensitive to small changes in road gradient.

For the gear cluster described in our chart on page 20, you can create a good half-step pattern by swapping the 40-tooth middle chainring for a 46. For other gear clusters, the ideal middle chainring might be slightly different.

Below is the gearing pattern that results using a 24-tooth chainring as a granny gear, and a 13–34 tooth rear cluster. The result is a bike with 17 non-overlapping gears, with the remaining overlap mostly where it's necessary to prevent equipment-punishing high-angle gear combinations.

Notice how the shifting pattern has become one of alternating between the big and middle chainrings, all the way down the scale. That's why half-step gearing isn't popular—50% of the gear changes involve shifting both derailleurs. But that isn't all that difficult, especially with fingertip shifting. And if you're feeling lazy you can always run up and down the back gears without shifting in front, just as you would with crossover gearing. The intermediate gears are still there when you need them.

The problem with half-step gearing isn't getting chainrings of the proper size. That's easy. The problem is that most front derailleurs that can handle a triple crank aren't designed for half-step gearing. The difficulty lies in the "cage" surrounding the chain. On a typical triple-crank derailleur the cage is asymmetrical, with its inside plate hanging lower than the outside one. With the large middle chainrings used for half-step gearing, that lower edge hits the middle chainring when you try to shift across it to the big one.

Elliptical Chainrings

Another gearing feature currently out of style is the use of elliptical chainrings, the leading brand of which was Biopace.

Elliptical chainrings vary from true round, so the amount of strength you need to turn the crank changes during the pedal stroke. Pedaling with one is akin to smoothly upshifting and downshifting with each half revolution.

Even in their heyday, elliptical chainrings were controversial. One reviewer compared the sensation of using one to stepping off a curb you didn't know was there. Racers hated them because they bounced on the saddle while pedaling at a high cadence. But people with lower cadences—which includes beginners and most touring cyclists—often liked the effect because it gives you a slight rest break at the weakest point in each stroke. By allowing you to use a lower cadence than would otherwise be comfortable, elliptical chainrings can also help you to stretch the range of a low gear that isn't really low enough.

Even if they someday come back in style, it's best not to get elliptical chainrings on your first bike because they can interfere with learning a good, quick pedaling cadence.

Chainring	Rear Cog (Freewheel) Size						
	13	15	18	21	24	28	34
24	48	42	35	30	26	22	18
46	92	80	66	57	50	43	35
50	100	87	72	62	54	46	38

Wheel size (inches): 26

Wheels, Tires, and Tubes

Wheels come in a dizzying variety of widths, numbers of spokes, and spoking patterns—enough that wheel-building is an esoteric art about which the average cyclist knows little.

Little, however, is all you really need to know. If you buy a good bicycle it will have adequate wheels. Of most interest to you will be the wheel's diameter, the width of tires it can accommodate, and the type of tubes it's designed for.

In the United States, wheels come in two diameters, 26 inch and a slightly larger metric size called 700C; older bikes might have 27-inch wheels. Currently, 700C is the standard for road bikes, 26 inch for mountain bikes. Fat tires are more readily available for 26-inch wheels, skinny ones for 700C.

The differences in wheel diameter are large enough that the tires aren't interchangeable. Nor is it likely you could replace your wheels with ones of

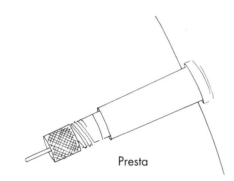

Presta

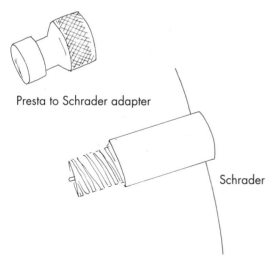

Presta to Schrader adapter

Schrader

a different diameter; your brakes are positioned for the size of wheel that came with the bike, and probably can't be sufficiently readjusted. Other factors will also limit your choice of tire size, namely the clearance between the tire and the frame, and the width of the rim. You'll have some flexibility, but you won't be able to put everything on any given bicycle.

Tire widths range from less than 1 inch for the skinniest racing tires to upwards of 2 inches for mountain-bike knobbies. Small changes can make dramatic differences. A 700 x 32c (a 700C tire that's 32 mm wide) gives you significantly more "float" on gravel than even a 700 x 28c, and a 1.4-inch (equivalent to 700 x 35c) is more stable yet. Wider tires also improve the smoothness of the ride, even on pavement.

Extremely fat tires are for trail riding, not touring. On pavement, they slow you down. Even for a tour with a lot of gravel you don't want anything fatter than 1.7 or 1.9 inches. On pavement, 700 x 32c is fine, with 1.4 inch acceptable if you want more freedom to take gravel shortcuts.

Tires should be kept inflated to the manufacturer's recommended pressure. Check them daily; unlike automobile tires, bicycle tires can lose several pounds of pressure daily. You might have been told you can run them at slightly lower pressure for a smoother ride; the cost of doing so is wasted energy, increased tire wear, and potential damage to your wheels if you hit a bump. Cheap tires, I might add, are no bargain. They wear out faster and often can't be inflated to high pressure, causing the same problems as underinflation of better tires.

Rims. Most modern wheels have aluminum alloy rims. Old or inexpensive bicycles might have wheels with steel rims. Replace these with alloy, even though it's costly. Steel rims brake very poorly when wet.

All rims are designed for one of two types of tubes: Schrader or Presta. Schrader valve stems look like conventional automobile stems, fitting the same tire gauges and pumps, and they can be pumped up at a gas station. (You may have been warned against doing this for fear of bursting your tires, but that's not likely as long as you use common sense.)

Presta tubes have metal valve stems held in place by thin nuts. The valve itself opens by unscrewing a threaded pin. Presta valves are better for use with hand pumps because they're less likely to leak air when you connect or disconnect the pump.

Presta valve stems are narrower than Schrader, and the valve stem holes in the rim are sized accordingly. This means than in an emergency, a Presta tube will fit a Schrader rim, but not vice versa. But if you find yourself desperate for a tube in a small town where the only ones available are Schrader, it is the work of only a few seconds with a circular file to (permanently) convert the rim to Schrader.

If you like to top off your tires at gas stations, you can still do so with Presta, using a $1 adapter that threads onto the valve stem. I've known people who put such adapters on both wheels and leave them there.

Non-Pneumatic Tires. Periodically, an enterprising manufacturer markets a tire that never needs to be inflated. Such non-pneumatic tires will never go flat. Theoretically, they also should be less prone to catastrophic cuts, freeing you from the need to tour with spare tubes, a spare tire, or even a pump. (But I don't know if I'd ever trust *any* tire enough not to carry a backup on a long tour.) Historically, however, efforts to produce non-pneumatic tires have been plagued by technical problems: The tire is too hard, too soft, too heavy, or slippery on wet pavement.

A recent attempt by the Green Tyre Company of Britain has produced a passable tire that overcomes most of these obstacles, but it's an absolute beast to install. When I test-rode a set of them, they performed reasonably well, though they were softer than the 100-pound pneumatic tires I was accustomed to and felt a bit sluggish on the road. I compared the two sets of tires on the same 21-mile loop and found that on the pneumatic tires I was nearly 2 mph faster. The comparative sluggishness may be less for the fatter-tire versions, where the pneumatic-tire competition itself is significantly softer.

Non-pneumatic tires will be most appreciated by bike commuters or people who *really* hate flats. People who like to go fast should use conventional tires and resign themselves to occasionally fixing a flat.

Quick-Release Hubs

These days, any good bike comes with quick-release wheels, which allow you to fix a flat quickly by removing a wheel without a wrench. They also help you pop the wheel off to load a bike into a car trunk or the back of a hatchback, where it otherwise wouldn't fit.

Make sure you know how to use quick-release hubs. The release lever should be tight when folded closed, parallel to the wheel's plane—not sticking out where it might be bumped or interfere with a pannier. Ideally the lever should be angled up and back, reducing the chance of something snagging it and accidentally releasing the wheel. This might be difficult if your front or rear rack is in the way, but do the best you can, checking periodically to make sure the lever is tight. That's a good idea, anyway, especially if you've left the bike unattended where some street urchin with nothing better to do can maliciously flip your quick-releases.

The best way to learn the proper tightness for quick-release levers is with a hands-on demonstration: Ask your bike shop to show you the difference between too loose and too tight. If the quick-release lever is misadjusted, fix it by flipping it open and tightening or loosening the nut on the other end of the spindle. A wrench is not needed.

Some bikes have wheel-retention devices to keep the wheel from coming loose if the quick-release pops open. These are designed primarily to reduce the manufacturer's liability if a quick-release opens at the wrong time—unlikely if it's properly tightened. Wheel-retention devices serve their function, but do so by robbing the quick release of its convenience.

adjusting nut

quick-release hubs

Saddles

The part of the bicycle you sit on is the "saddle," not the "seat."

Bike saddles have long been controversial. One faction argues that the most comfortable saddles are firm but carefully contoured to support weight in precisely the right places; an opposing group sings the praises of padding. The advent of gel-filled saddles has produced a new generation of cushioned saddles while doing nothing to resolve the dispute.

The case for a soft saddle is obvious. When you first sit on it, it feels far more comfortable than a hard one. But the detractors of gel argue that it's shape that matters, not cushion. A cushy saddle, they say, may actually make you more uncomfortable in the long run by allowing you to sink so deeply into it that your weight is improperly distributed, possibly onto portions of the anatomy not meant to bear it.

Many hard-saddle advocates recommend leather saddles, which are rock hard but gradually shape themselves to conform to your posterior. I'm dubious about using a leather saddle for touring, though. If it gets wet, you may have trouble drying it.

As far as the gel controversy goes, don't feel like a wimp if you decide you want some padding. Gel-filled saddles are nice; some even have springs.

More important than the padding dispute is knowing that there's a difference between men's and women's saddles. Women's saddles tend to be wider, with the "anatomical" supports for the bones of the pelvis placed farther apart than on men's.

They may also have a depression on top to take the pressure off sensitive portions of the anatomy. Ask the shop which gender saddle comes on your bike, and realize that unisex means men's. Insist on a gender-appropriate saddle.

Choosing a saddle is difficult, and the only way to be sure it fits is to take it on a long test ride. Saddles aren't outrageously expensive, though, so if you do get a bad fit, you can replace it relatively easily.

Toe Clips

Toe clips hold your feet properly on the pedals and increase your pedaling power by allowing you to pull upward on one pedal while you push down on

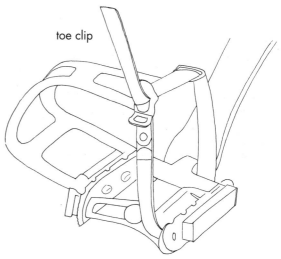

toe clip

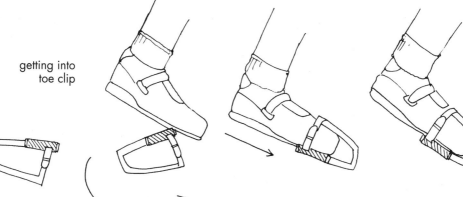

getting into toe clip

Other Components

the other. They have easily reachable straps that can be loosened or tightened as you ride. Loosen them in the city for frequent starts and stops. Tighten them in the country or for steep hills.

Toe clips often frighten beginners, who fear their feet will be trapped in them if they fall. In a serious crash this isn't likely; as long as you aren't wearing cleats, even a tightly snugged toe clip is easy to get out of—just pull the foot up and back. Try it a few times on a quiet backroad, adjusting the strap to various tightnesses and seeing how much effort it takes to get your foot out. Most likely, you'll be cutting the circulation off to your toes long before escape becomes difficult.

Another beginner's fear is more realistic: If you've never used toe clips, you might topple over a couple of times when you forget to take your foot out of the strap. Practice a few times in a parking lot before venturing onto the road.

Getting your foot into the clip is also an art. Put one foot in before you start to move, letting the other clip drag until you're going fast enough to coast. Then, position the remaining foot on the pedal with the spindle more or less directly under your arch. (The ideal location depends on your shoe size and the tightness of the clip.) Raise your foot slightly until the pedal, overbalanced in front by the weight of the clip, starts to roll forward. Catch its front edge with the sole of your shoe and gently flip it backward. Bingo! Your toe should slide right into the clip. With practice, you can do this as one smooth motion without even having to stop pedaling.

Chainrings, gear clusters, saddles, and tires aren't the only components on your bicycle, of course, but they're the ones you're most likely to tinker with. Others of interest are brakes, shift levers, handlebars, and cranks.

Brakes. There are two common styles of brakes: side-pulls and cantilevers. (For details, see the discussion of brake adjustment on pages 157–158.) Racing bikes generally come with side-pulls; mountain bikes and touring bikes usually have cantilevers. Good brakes of either type have adequate stopping power.

Shift levers. The positioning of shift levers varies, but the most convenient places are where you can reach them with your hands still on the handlebars. This lets you shift both derailleurs simultaneously, simplifying the double shifts in half-step gearing. If you *really* don't like the location of your shift levers, you can change them, but it will take new parts and a fair amount of work. First, try to get used to the levers you've got.

Handlebars. The boundaries between bike types and their handlebars are crumbling, and people are mixing frame type and handlebars with an eye to comfort rather than style. In addition, prompted by the growing interest in mountain-bike handlebars with more than one hand position, manufacturers are experimenting with enough strange new shapes to satisfy anyone with an eye for novelty. And, if you don't like the handlebars that came with your bike, change them—even going so far as to swap between drop handlebars and upright ones.

Crank. Top-of-the-line cranks can cost hundreds of dollars. What you get for all that money are increased stiffness so the crank doesn't waste energy by flexing on each pedal stroke and reduced weight.

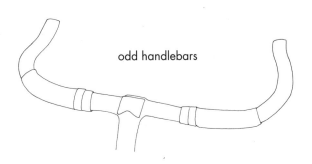

odd handlebars

Since the crank is perhaps the single most expensive component on your bicycle, you aren't likely to change it except perhaps to swap a double for a triple. High-quality bikes come with good cranks; cheap bikes come with cheap cranks. There's not much reason to put a $200 crank on a $350 bicycle.

You Don't Have to Get a New Bike

If you already have a good bicycle, you don't need to buy a new one for touring. Or, if you're willing to settle for a bike that's anywhere from a couple of years out of date to a decade old, you can buy a good used one through the classified ads or for-sale signs posted in bike shops.

Old bicycles, referred to both lovingly and sneeringly as "retro" bikes, have many advantages. For one thing, since they don't represent the cutting edge of fashion, they're a lot less likely to be stolen. Functionally, a 10-year-old bicycle isn't a whole lot different from a new one. So what if the brakes don't look aerodynamic or it doesn't click when you shift? Older drive-train components may actually be more durable than modern ones, because index shifting reduces the life of chains, freewheels, and shifters. Older bikes may also have greater tire clearance than modern ones, giving you a larger choice of tire sizes.

Customizing a used bicycle for touring is no different from customizing a new one except that you lose the advantage of being able to trade in the original components. The most expensive changes will involve the power train if the bicycle doesn't already have a triple crank. The cost will range from a few tens of dollars to several hundred, depending on which changes you have to make and how much you spend on components. But if the brakes and frame of the bicycle you're upgrading are good, when you're done you may have a touring bike equivalent to a new one that would cost much more.

Here's a list of likely changes:

- Add a triple crank.
- Change to a longer spindle in the bottom bracket so the triple's granny gear doesn't rub the frame.
- Change the front derailleur to accommodate the triple.
- Replace the gear cluster with a wide-ranging touring cluster.
- Replace the rear derailleur if it won't accommodate all of the slack chain when you shift into the granny gear, or won't handle the large cog of the new rear cluster.
- Replace the chain, or at least add or subtract links to fit the new gearing.

LIGHTWEIGHT TOURING BIKE FOR SALE

ONLY USED DOWNHILL!
NEVER SWEATED ON !!!

$____ OR BEST OFFER!

Accessories

Accessories are items that mount onto the bicycle more or less permanently but aren't involved in the bike's functioning. They range from the essential to the trivial, from fun toys to gadgets that can be more of a nuisance than they're worth.

Four Essentials

Some accessories are so important for touring that you might as well install them when you buy the bicycle, viewing their cost as part of its purchase price.

Pump. Flat tires are part of cycling, so you'll need a pump. Even if you'll always be with a friend, each of you should have your own; you may occasionally get separated. Having two pumps also gives you a backup when one breaks.

Pumps aren't a place to skimp money. Inexpensive ones can break easily and might not be rated to reach the maximum pressure of your tires.

Double-action pumps, which inject air into the tire on both strokes of the handle, are nice but not essential. What is important is a fairly large air chamber; don't get one of the mini-pumps—even if it can handle your tire pressure, it will take forever to pump the tire up.

Most pumps have spring-loaded handles to fit firmly beneath the top tube or on the front side of the down tube. The top tube is best because that saves the down tube for water bottles. Pumps come in a variety of sizes, so you should be able to get one that fits your frame without a special mounting bracket.

Presta and Schrader valves require different pump nozzles, so make sure your pump is set for the right one. Most better-grade pumps will convert easily from one to the other. Learn how to make the conversion (usually something simple, like unscrewing the pump head and reversing the orientation of one or more washers or gaskets) so you can use the pump if you switch tube types, or to help out a friend.

Water bottles. Get at least two water bottles and cages. Expensive ones aren't necessary. The best bolt directly to the frame. Your bike should come equipped with attachments for two bottles: one on the down tube, one on the seat tube.

Additional bottles can be mounted with clamps. To protect your paint, put a strip of rubber or some other soft material behind any bare-metal clamp.

Rear rack. For any form of touring, you'll need to carry some baggage—at least rain gear and a change of clothes. If you're never going to carry more than that, you can get away with a lightweight rack, but otherwise, this is another place where you shouldn't skimp. Get a sturdy aluminum rack such as those made by Blackburn, which bolt to the rear drop-out eyelets and seat-stay braze-ons.

Some racks have a flat surface on top, others are an open framework. Both carry weight nicely, but the ones with a solid top serve double duty as a partial fender. They also reduce the chance of a loose strap getting into your spokes.

These racks aren't made to sit on but they can carry a pretty healthy load through bumpy terrain.

Mirror. If you want to know what's going on behind you, get a mirror and know how to use it. It's no substitute for looking over your shoulder in city traffic, but it's great for advance warning of overtaking cars on rural roads.

I've experimented with a number of mirrors, and I prefer the type made by Rhode Gear, which fastens to the brake levers with a Velcro strap. Note that there are two types of these mirrors: one for

braze-on

drop handlebars, the other for straight handlebars. For either it's a good idea to carry a backup strap; the straps have plastic buckles that break if cinched too tightly.

Another type of mirror mounts to the end of your handlebars. These put the mirror farther out from your body than the brake lever–mounting variety, making it easier to see directly behind you. But the bar end is more vibration-prone than the brake lever, and the only time I've tried one of these, I found that the extra vibration made it difficult to see. There are a variety of designs, though, so it may be a matter of how sturdily the mirror is attached. None of them, of course, works with bar-end shifters.

A third type of mirror, discussed on page 38, mounts to your helmet.

Using a handlebar-mounted mirror takes practice. If your hips, shoulders, or a wind-billowed jacket block the view, shift your body sideways on the saddle or steer ever so slightly to the left to give yourself a better view. It doesn't take much of a turn to open up the view considerably, so learn to do this without swerving into the path of a car or bicycle that may be starting to pass you. I can give

myself a good, half-second glimpse without veering any farther off course than I would to dodge a small rock. Also, take advantage of left-hand bends in the road to give you a good clear view behind.

rear rack,
unmounted

mirror, unattached

29

Useful Additions

If you're on a budget you might be able to live without the following accessories, but they can make life on the road a lot more pleasant. Unfortunately, not everything is compatible with everything else, at least not without modification, so I've included a brief description of potential problems, and their likely solutions.

Padded seat cover. This is one of the greatest inventions of the last couple of decades, virtually guaranteed to reduce derriere pains. A thick pad of gel with some kind of low-friction nylon cover, the gel seat cover sits on your saddle, held in position by a zipper or drawstring running underneath the saddle.

These seat covers, though, are expensive and weigh about a pound. But it's money and weight well spent, and few people who buy one ever go back to riding without it.

Compatibility problems: You will need to read-just your seat height. Also, since saddles come in several sizes, make sure you get the right size pad. There's a difference between gel covers for mountain-bike seats and road-bike seats.

Cyclometer. A cyclometer is a bicycle computer that counts wheel revolutions or pedal strokes. Features vary from brand to brand, but most can function as odometer, stopwatch, cadence counter, and speedometer. Cyclometers aren't necessary but they do serve as all-round fun toys. One model even contains a startlingly accurate altimeter—just what you might (or might not) want to tell you precisely how far it is to the top of the mountain pass you've been climbing for the last hour.

Compatibility problems: Cyclometers consist of a handlebar-mounting "head" and a magnetic sensor that attaches to the hub, spokes, or fork. The head's mounting bracket may conflict with a handlebar bag, although some tinkering can fix this. The wheel sensor may conflict with your front rack or its eyelets. Get a brand designed for touring bikes, or buy a special sensor for the rear wheel, where there are fewer problems. Units with cadence counters have an additional sensor that mounts near the crank.

Padded handlebar covers. People who spend day after day leaning on handlebars often find that their hands become numb or tingle from the constant pressure. The solution is padding. So what if the racers don't think it looks chic?

Grab-Ons, the leading brand, mount by sliding over the handlebar tube. They aren't expensive, but installation is a real pain, partly because you have to remove brake levers and handlebar winding tape. Grab-Ons slide onto the bare tube (with effort). For aesthetics—and to preserve the life of the Grab-Ons—you can wind tape over the top after you're finished. If you can afford it, let the shop do the installation, even though the labor will probably cost more than the Grab-Ons themselves.

A quick-and-dirty way to install Grab-Ons is to slit them lengthwise then fit them over the handlebar from the side. Use nylon strapping tape or strong plastic tape to hold the loose Grab-On in place, then wind handlebar tape over the top to keep it from looking too sloppy. The result may have a tendency to twist, but I've ridden Grab-Ons mounted in this manner for thousands of miles.

If you've got tiny hands and find Grab-Ons to be too bulky, look for cork-backed handlebar tape. It gives you an intermediate amount of comfort without bulking up the handlebars as much.

Mountain bikers, too, can get relief from jarring by using padded handgrips.

Compatibility problems: With mountain-bike handgrips there shouldn't be much problem, but for

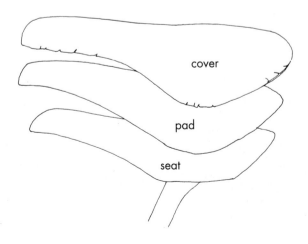

cover

pad

seat

drop handlebars, anything that clamps to them—cyclometers, aero bars, and certain types of head-lights—aren't designed to fit over the Grab-Ons. Handlebar bags may also present a problem if they mount by a metal bracket that loops over the stem and handlebars. The extra thickness of the Grab-Ons is likely to leave the bracket tilted skyward.

Solutions: Don't slide the Grab-Ons all the way to the center of the handlebars; cut off the extra length, if necessary. You won't need a big gap if all you're adding is a handlebar bag; an inch should be plenty. If you're mounting a cyclometer, decide which side of the stem you want it on and allow an additional 2-inch gap. A similar gap on the other side of the stem will leave room for a strap-on headlight.

For aero bars, you'll need to shorten the Grab-On or cut a hole in it at the point where the bar attaches to the handlebars.

All of these changes are easiest when you first install the Grab-Ons, but you can do them retroactively by peeling back the winding tape and operating on the Grab-On with a pocket knife. Use electri-

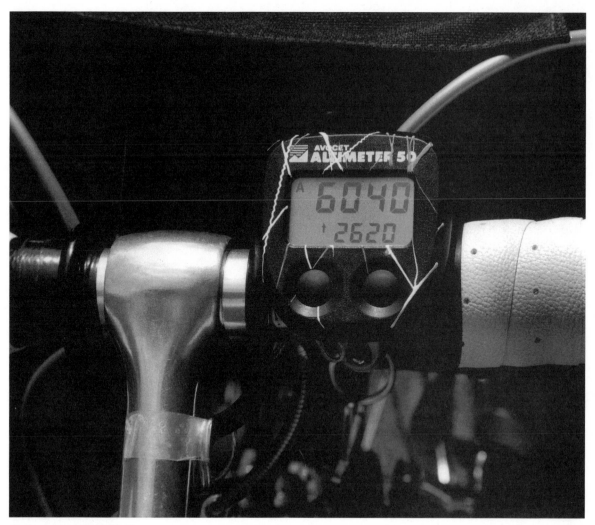

Cyclometer with Grab-Ons.

Low Rider front rack.

cal tape to reattach the loose end of the handlebar tape afterward, since you'll probably have ruined the glue.

Front rack. Depending on your bicycle and your coordination, you may not *have* to have a front rack, even with a full touring rig. But most bicycles are a lot easier to handle if you split the weight between front and rear wheels. That requires a front rack.

There are two types. One looks like the mirror image of the rear rack and mounts above the wheel. The preferred model, however, is called a Low Rider. It is a strange trapezoidal contraption that holds panniers a few inches below the top of the front wheel, which gives you a lower center of gravity for more stable steering. As long as you don't use enormous panniers, it still holds them high enough above the road that they won't drag.

Compatibility problems: Front racks can be incompatible with some front-wheel mounting cyclometers, as well as headlights that clamp to the lower end of the fork.

Solutions: See discussion on cyclometers. Get the rack first, then figure out how to make a cyclometer work around it.

Thorn-resistant tire inserts. These thick pieces of plastic go inside the tire and provide an extra layer of puncture resistance between tire and tube. They work. The leading brand is Mr. Tuffy. If you're feeling cheap, split a pair with a friend, putting them only in the rear wheels, where most flats occur. To save on installation charges, do it yourself the first time you have a flat.

Compatibility problems: None.

Aero bars and bar extenders. Aero bars are metal tubes that clamp to your handlebars and loop far out in front of you. Pads on the handlebars allow you to rest your elbows and take your weight off your palms. They're designed more to reduce wind resistance than for comfort, and they reduce your steering control, so don't use them if you're carrying baggage.

Bar extenders are a different matter altogether. They attach to the ends of mountain bike handlebars, giving you a variety of new hand positions. Unlike aero bars, they don't leave you lying forward on your elbows, so they don't rob you of steering control. There are a number of styles, designed to make your bike a lot more comfortable for long distances on the road—in short, for touring.

Compatibility problems: Bar-end mounting mirrors, handlebar bags. Anything that mounts to your handlebars may be in the way of some bar extenders or aero bars.

Solutions: Figure out what you want to mount on your handlebars, then look for a compatible bar extender.

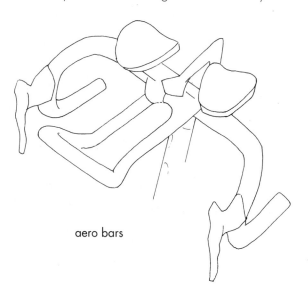

aero bars

How Much Must I Spend?

Fenders. Riding in rain, the back wheel gives you a stripe up your backside, while the front wheel picks up water and dumps it in your shoes. For some people, this is a badge of honor. For others it's a nuisance.

Loaded for touring, your panniers and the equipment on your rear rack will act as a partial fender, but there's no reason not to get true fenders unless you're offended by the aesthetics, live in a desert where it *never* rains, or fanatically count the extra ounces on your bicycle. For touring, none of these reasons makes much sense; you might as well get fenders.

Fenders come in two styles: those that mount permanently with a series of struts, and clip-ons made mostly for mountain bikers. I prefer the permanent kind, since they'll always be with you when you need them.

Compatibility problems: Your fork and seat stays may be too narrow to accommodate a fender; also there's potential incompatibility with front or rear racks. If you have a bike with a short wheel base (or if you have really big feet), the fender and your toe may meet at the front of the pedal stroke on a sharp turn.

Solutions: Some people view toe overlap as a safety hazard; others are willing to learn to live with it. Installing a fender isn't likely to be a serious problem on a touring bike, so long as you get one designed for your tire width. It will be more difficult to get fenders for a narrow-wheeled racing bike, though, since there's not much market for them.

You can buy a bicycle cheaply. Discount-store models still sell for as little as $150, but are utterly unsuitable for the rigors of touring.

The best way to tell the difference between a good bicycle and an inexpensive one is by comparing them. Go to a discount store and check out what they're selling, paying particular attention to the frame. Notice how the dropouts of the front and rear wheels look cheap and fragile compared with what you find on more expensive bicycles. Compare the welding on the frame. Strong frames are made with lugged joints (except for expensive aluminum frames for which the construction process is quite different). Cheap ones omit the lugs, increasing the chances of breakage.

To get a feel for what makes the difference between fine workmanship and average, look at bicycles you can't afford. You don't need a $1,500 bicycle, but you do need one whose frame won't break if you hit a big bump with a heavy load. Good components also reduce the frequency of repairs or minor adjustments.

Don't buy a used bicycle that looks like it's seen a lot of hard use. Unless you're an expert bike mechanic, these aren't bargains. Particularly, don't buy one with a rusty frame or one that's been repainted, possibly masking a host of flaws. If the frame is bent or cracked even slightly, reject it. Damaged frames are dangerous.

If in doubt, take a knowledgeable friend with you before making the final purchase.

All told, it costs several hundred dollars to pur-

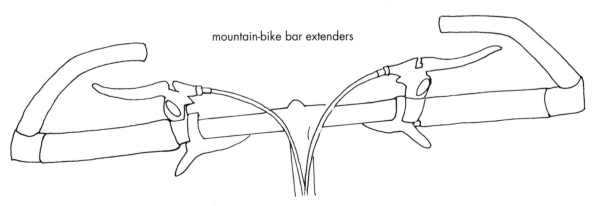

mountain-bike bar extenders

	Economy	Mid-price	Luxury
Bicycle	$0 – $350	$400 – $700	$800 – $1,300
Accessories	$75 – $90	$250 – $300	$300 – $400
Touring bags*	$85 – $110	$175 – $225	$300 – $350
Cycling clothes**	$120 – $150	$275 – $350	$550 – $900
Total	$280 – $700	$1,110 – $1,575	$1,950 – $2,950

* Not neccessary for all types of touring.
** Economy level includes only helmet, gloves, cycling shorts, and cycling shoes; mid-price improves the quality of these and adds tights and a cycling jacket; luxury includes a full suit of clothing plus goggles, Gore-Tex rain gear, aerodynamic helmet, and more.

chase and customize a touring bike. The above chart shows how to do it on three budgets: economy, mid-price, and luxury. The economy column assumes you are upgrading a used bicycle, either one that you already have, or one that you purchased. The mid-price range assumes you are buying a new bicycle and are willing to spend a little money to do it right. The luxury column assumes that budget really isn't a factor.

The same goes for accessories. The economy budget allows only the four essentials: rear rack, water bottles, pump, and mirror. It assumes, though, that you get good ones since they need to be surable. The mid-price budget adds fenders, a gel seat cover, thorn-resistant tire inserts, a cyclometer, and padded handlebar covers. The luxury column includes a top-of-the-line pump, a gel saddle, and a fancy cyclometer. The chart also includes entries for clothing and bags, which are discussed on pages 97 and 100, respectively.

EQUIPPING YOURSELF

▼

Bicycle clothing has become chic, which means it's also expensive. If you set out to be the most stylish rider in your group, you can easily spend as much on attire as for a top-notch touring bike.

Thankfully, you don't have to buy the best of everything, and if you're an otherwise outdoorsy person, several potentially expensive items—like jackets and rain gear—can be scrounged from whatever camping equipment you already have. On my first forays into touring, I had virtually no cycling clothes, and I've known people to go cross-country with no specialty clothing except a helmet and shoes.

Going to extremes, though, is no more practical than the clothes-horse, money-is-no-obstacle attitude. A student-budget approach will leave you pedaling around in blue jeans and tennis shoes, carrying a vulcanized rubber rain suit for bad weather. If you're 20 years old that might be acceptable, at least under mild conditions, but it's not much fun, and you're likely to seek out another sport without ever giving cycle touring a fair chance.

Set up a personal priority list for clothing—not according to the whims of fashion, but according to its functionality and the frequency that you'll need it.

Helmets

Bicycling without a helmet is like driving without a seat belt. You can get away with it, even for your entire life. But it might be a short life. Head injuries are far and away the leading cause of cycling deaths or disabilities, and a large percentage of them could be prevented by wearing a helmet.

I've only truly *needed* a helmet once. But when I did, I was glad I'd worn one for years. I was on a training ride on a lightly traveled backroad—the type of place where it's tempting to ride without a helmet. I'd just stood up on the pedals to power up a small rise when, suddenly, the derailleur skipped then threw the chain (my fault—I'd been trying to ignore the fact it was out of adjustment). I teetered precariously, then fell sideways, bouncing the side of my helmet off the pavement so hard I worried about whiplash. A moment later I realized that the simple fact that I *could* worry was a blessing. I wound up bruised, but able to remount my bicycle and pedal home. Without a helmet, I'd certainly have been heading for the hospital instead—perhaps worse. I won't ride 10 feet without a helmet.

In addition to protecting your head, wearing a helmet sends an important message to motorists, telling them you're a serious cyclist and expect to be treated as one. Motorists will give you greater respect simply because you respect yourself.

Typical helmets consist of a foam interior covered by a hard plastic shell. The shell is designed to distribute impact, reduce the risk of puncture by a sharp object, and allow your head to skid smoothly over a rough surface without twisting your neck. The foam is designed to crush under impact, giving you lifesaving cushion.

Pick a helmet that meets the two accepted safety standards, ANSI and Snell. You'll find this information stamped somewhere on the box and probably on a label in the helmet itself. Some ANSI- and Snell-approved helmets omit the hard shell. They're lightweight, but I'd rather have the added protection.

As long as the helmet meets the safety standards, choose it based on fit, price (which ranges from $30 to $100 plus), and your tastes for appearance. There's a considerable range in prices; what you'll get from the more expensive models is styling, aerodynamic shaping (valuable for racers, not much use for touring), and lighter weight (nice). You might also get better ventilation. (If your helmet has really big ventilation louvers, beware of sunburning a bald spot or the part in your hair through them.)

Fit is more important than price and styling. Try a lot of models and don't be surprised if the fit varies even among styles made by the same manufacturer. Before pinching pennies on a poor-fitting helmet remember that fit affects safety—especially if a poor fit discourages you from wearing the helmet in the first place.

Helmets come in a variety of colors, but basic white is the best if you care about being seen. A white helmet will show up from a long distance; a dark one, even if it's fire-engine red, will blend into the scenery.

If you crash and hit your head, replace your helmet even if there's no visible damage, unless an expert assures you it's safe. Often the manufacturer will exchange it for a new one at a nominal price.

Helmet-mounting mirrors. As mentioned previously, I prefer a handlebar-mounted rear-view mirror. But there are also mirrors that clip to your helmet or eyeglasses or mount to the helmet with Velcro fasteners. If you get a helmet-mounting type, make sure it fits your helmet. Helmet styles change, and the mirrors stocked by your bike shop could be dated. Some people swear by these mirrors, but I find them hard to use while still paying attention to what's going on in front of me.

Gloves

For long-distance touring, cycling gloves are one of the most useful inexpensive purchases you can make. The leather palms provide much-desired cushion as you lean on the handlebars, while the open mesh fabric and fingerless design allow sufficient cooling. The leather palm also serves to prevent painful abrasions in a fall, and allows you to (carefully) skim your palm against a moving tire if you've just ridden through a patch of glass and are afraid of a flat.

Gloves come with various amounts of padding, ranging from simple leather to gel-filled.

Goggles

Goggles are a luxury, but a nice one, keeping everything from dust and rain to insects out of your eyes. Good ones are expensive, but they also block the wind from drying out your eyes. Some have interchangeable lenses so you can choose between tinted and clear, depending on the weather. Inexpensive goggles are not much better than sunglasses.

Don't expect goggles to fit over eyeglasses. Eyeglass wearers will either have to switch to contact lenses or spend a small fortune to have goggles custom-made with their prescriptions. On the other hand, eyeglass wearers don't need goggles as much as other people do, since glasses themselves provide a good deal of protection.

Shoes

To increase your speed or the distance you can cover in a day, cycling shoes are, dollar for dollar, one of the best investments you can make. Unlike running shoes, which have cushioned soles, cycling shoes are firm to transfer the energy of your pedal stroke directly into turning the crank. No energy is wasted squishing and unsquishing shoe material. The soles also seem to be more durable than the waffled tread of running shoes and are easier to slip into and out of a toe clip.

When I bought my first pair of cycling shoes, after years of riding without them, I was amazed by the difference. The day I got them, I tried out both my new shoes and the old ones on a favorite 10-mile course. The results, though not scientific, were dramatic: I was 25% faster with the cycling shoes. Cycling shoes also have reinforced uppers so the toe clip won't wear holes in them.

There are two basic shoe types: touring and cleats (or clip-in shoes).

Touring shoes look a lot like running shoes except for the firmer sole and reinforced upper. Because they look like street shoes, touring shoes are passable walking shoes, allowing you to visit stores, museums, or restaurants without having to change footwear.

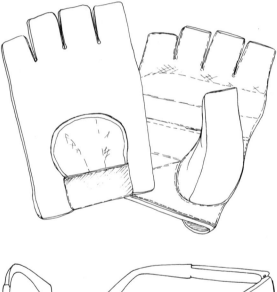

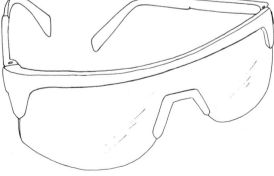

With a mesh upper and a slotted cleat bolted to the sole, cleats are at the opposite end of the comfort extreme. The slot hooks to the pedal, and when the toe clip is tightened, the shoe is secured much more firmly than a touring shoe, increasing your ability to pull and push.

Such cleats still exist, but they've been largely replaced by "click-in," "step-in," or "clipless" shoes, for which the slotted cleat is replaced by one that snaps into a specially designed pedal, with toe clips unnecessary.

Popular as these shoes are, they have a major drawback for touring: the thick cleat under the ball of the foot makes them uncomfortable for even short walks. They also have *very* stiff soles, and the cleats may make you unwelcome in restaurants or shops whose owners fear you'll scratch their floors.

A new click-in pedal, however, represents a major breakthrough, with the clip recessed into a reasonably flexible sole. The result is a cleated shoe in which you can walk normally. There might even be a snap-on dirt cover to keep grit out of the cleat mechanism.

Nevertheless, even this type of click-in shoes won't completely replace traditional touring shoes. Yes, they are more efficient, but step-in pedals can be expensive. They're also more difficult to get your foot into than toe clips, and more frightening for beginners to get out of.

With click-in shoes, the shoe has to be placed just right before it snaps into the pedal. This isn't a problem if you do most of your riding in the country but it can turn a series of stoplights into a exercise in frustration.

Getting out is simpler, but you have to remember to do it correctly. Click-in cycling shoes have their ancestry in downhill ski bindings, and their release is similar, by rotating the heel of your foot outward or inward, or from a sudden blow, as in a crash. With adjustable tension, you can choose how easily they pop free.

Part of the process of learning to use them involves a few slow-motion crashes when you habitually try to lift your foot off the pedal normally after you've stopped. There's also the ignoble fate of reaching for the ground with one foot only to topple slowly in the opposite direction, with that foot still firmly attached to the pedal.

Cleats of any kind should be adjusted to align your foot properly with the pedal. The owner's manual will give you precise tips on how to do this. For some cleats, precise adjustment is critical because even a small error can give you a sore knee, but some recent models including some with the walkable, recessed cleats, allow your foot to "float" freely over a range of motion, rather than holding it rigid. Unfortunately, this mechanism tends to be found only on expensive, high-end equipment.

Even the less expensive models, though, don't hold the foot perfectly rigid. If you decide to go the click-in route, ask how much freedom of motion you have with each brand. The larger it is, the easier it will be to get the shoe properly adjusted.

An external cleat is acceptable for organized tours or van-supported touring if you're the type of rider who likes to ride hard all day and seldom stop. But for start-and-stop touring, the recessed, click-in pedals are the only cleat I'd consider. For self-contained touring, I'd even be suspicious of them: It's hard enough to get a fully loaded bicycle moving after a rest break halfway up a hill without also having to worry about getting your shoes clicked into the pedals.

Socks. Any athletic socks can be used for cycling. I prefer the lightweight anklet variety that don't come up much higher than the tops of my shoes.

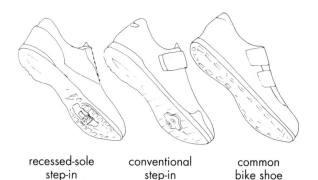

recessed-sole
step-in

conventional
step-in

common
bike shoe

Cycling Shorts

It's possible to cycle in blue jeans or cutoffs—I did for years. But many people find cycling shorts much more comfortable. Put them high on your priority list.

The distinguishing feature of cycling shorts is a sewn-in seat patch, called a chamois because years ago, that's was what it was made of (now it's imitation). Good cycling shorts are designed with the seams placed where you won't have to sit on them.

These shorts are either the stretchy, tight-fitting variety that have become so popular they are part of the public image of cycling, or baggier touring shorts, complete with pockets.

The choice is mostly one of taste. Compared with blue jeans or cutoffs, both offer much greater freedom of motion, and compared to running shorts, both have longer legs, preventing the inside of the thigh from chafing against the saddle.

The loose-fitting variety probably will have an elastic waist with a drawstring and an inner lining as on men's boxer-style swimming trunks. If you're on a budget, you could substitute any other form of loose-fitting long-legged shorts, particularly if you have a soft saddle or saddle cover and don't need the cushion of the chamois.

Form-fitting cycling shorts are made of Lycra, Spandex, or a similar fabric designed to be fast-drying and provide low friction against the saddle. The chamois material not only pads, but also wicks moisture from your body, increasing comfort and further reducing chafing.

Surprisingly durable unless you snag them on something, these shorts should last for years. They are designed to be tight, both to cut down on wind resistance and, more importantly, to prevent chafing. Try on a few pairs in the shop and ask the sales staff to tell you which ones fit.

Prices vary. Expensive shorts will be better tailored, with a more comfortable chamois material. When choosing a pair, feel the chamois material to decide if it might become abrasive with repeated washings. It's hard to guess, but you often get the quality you pay for.

If you have a fixed budget for shorts, it's better to buy two or three cheap pairs rather than a single expensive one. On a multi-day trip you'll have one to wear, one clean and dry, and another drying in the sun, instead of a single pair that gets dirtier and dirtier, day after day.

Some cycling shorts come in separate men's and women's models, cut differently in the hips and waist and with differences in the shape of the chamois. Cycling shorts that claim to be unisex are probably men's, though many women will find the fit acceptable.

If you temporarily need a pocket on Lycra-style shorts, you can stuff things like your wallet or spare change under the elastic of the leg without too much worry of it falling out. Don't put anything in there that will get sweat damaged, though, and don't ride with anything hard and sharp, such as car keys, that you wouldn't care to land on in a crash.

This style of cycling shorts is designed to be worn without underwear to reduce the risk of chafing. But for many people, the very idea of wearing such shorts makes them feel naked, so going with-

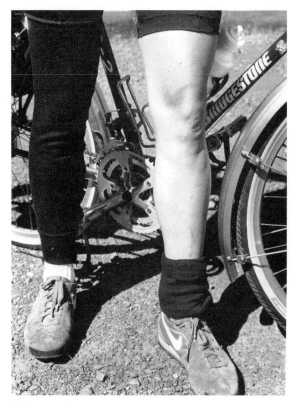

Leg warmers.

out underwear is unthinkable. If that's you, wear underwear and see if you chafe. If so, the pain will probably overcome your modesty quickly enough.

Tights

Cycling tights are another piece of functional attire you probably won't want to be without. Light and easy to carry, they provide freedom of motion you can't get with street pants, and are more durable than cotton warm-ups. Tights also dry out better when wet, and keep you surprisingly warm on chilly mornings. Wear them over your cycling shorts so you can take them off easily as the day warms up.

You don't need to buy expensive, name-brand tights; running tights work equally well and may be lower priced, especially if you get them at a discount sporting goods store.

Another option is a pair of leg warmers to cover the gap between your cycling shorts and socks. Usually made of a slightly heavier fabric than tights, they can give you a bit more warmth, for a lower price. When in use, the top end tucks under the elastic of your shorts; if the weather warms up, just shove the leg warmers down to your ankles until you're sure you won't need them again.

Shirts and Jerseys

Browse the pages of any cycling magazine, and you'll see that everybody's dressed in form-fitting cycling jerseys gaily decorated with the logos of racing-team sponsors. Since racing fashion drives much of the rest of cycling fashion, you won't be surprised to find that you, too, can buy jerseys that make you look like a traveling billboard.

But this is money you don't need to spend. T-shirts work fine; on hot days, their loose-fitting cotton or cotton blend fabric makes them more comfortable than most jerseys. On cooler days, though, the quick-drying jersey fabric is likely to have the edge over cotton. The biggest advantage of jerseys is that they reduce wind resistance. Touring, your shirt's wind resistance isn't all that important; pick shirts for comfort and visibility.

For visibility, look for bright, solid colors whenever you buy souvenir T-shirts; such mementos, even

if they aren't from bike trips, are a perfect source of cycling shirts. For slightly cooler weather, long-sleeved T-shirts are also valuable, giving you a pleasant bit of warmth on your arms. Because the best colors tend to fade quickly in the sun, you'll be needing a constant supply of new shirts, both short-sleeved and long.

If you want a jersey, of course, there's no reason not to get one. Sometimes, it's fun to feel like a racer. Also, many jerseys have elasticized pockets at the small of the back, where you can stuff a banana or your wallet—a true convenience. Some even come in cool, comfortable cotton.

If you get a racing jersey, avoid the ones that are plastered with too many logos. Even with bright colors, from a distance the effect is still a bit like Army camouflage. And be warned—any of these jerseys will show every extra ounce of fat. But then, that can make their purchase a great incentive for a diet!

Jackets and Wind Shells

On any ride longer than a few hours, include a lightweight jacket in your pack as a combination wind shell and light-duty rain repellent.

If you're on a budget, an inexpensive nylon jacket is more than adequate. Tyvek jackets are also nice. Made from a type of plasticized paper and frequently sold or given away in place of T-shirts on bicycle tours, these jackets are wind-proof, reasonably rain resistant, and surprisingly durable, considering what they're made from. Since they're designed specially for cycling, they often come in good, bright colors.

If you want to invest some money in a cycling wind shell, there are also some nice jackets made from a new generation of fabrics that are reasonably breathable, fast-drying, and somewhat water repellent. Look for ones using bright colors, so the traffic can see you on a dim, drizzly day. Pearl Izumi, for example, makes a jacket from a vivid yellow fabric that practically glows in the dark.

A less expensive, lightweight specialty item for cool-weather riding is a set of arm warmers similar to the leg warmers described earlier. They won't do anything to cut the wind on your torso, but they effectively convert a short-sleeved shirt to long sleeves.

Rain Gear

It's easy to make fabrics rainproof, and it's easy to make them breathable; it's difficult to strike a happy medium, especially if you're going to be working hard and sweating.

A fisherman's rain suit, for example, is impressively waterproofed, but you'll take a sauna in it on a bicycle. A nylon jacket is an improvement, but not a big one unless it has zippered air vents on the sides or back panel. Nevertheless, even an inexpensive rain shell is adequate for mild conditions. You might indeed take a sauna, but saunas are warm, and that's what really matters. Expect to feel chilled, though, when you stop exercising and all that trapped sweat starts to cool off.

Gore-Tex and other waterproof, breathable fabrics offer a more expensive alternative based on a different principle. The fabric's weave is fine enough that liquid water can't pass through, but

water vapor will, driven by the temperature differential between the inside of the jacket and the outside.

The trouble with these fabrics is that people have heard them described as "miracle" fabrics and expect too much. Yes, they can be far more comfortable than traditional rain gear, but they're not panaceas for all conditions. They work best if you're idle: for example, a hunter waiting for ducks on a rainy day. If you're working hard, you'll overload them by generating sweat faster than it can pass through, bringing on at least a partial return of the sauna. Also, there is a new generation of fabrics, called micropore fabrics, that strike a different trade-off, sacrificing some degree of waterproofing in favor of increased breathability.

Good cycling jackets, regardless of the fabric, have side or back vents. If expensive cycling jackets are out of your price range, look for a cyclist's poncho. I once had one long enough that I could sit on its tail, while thumb loops let me pull the front out to

block wind-driven rain. It worked well in a warm rain, keeping me reasonably dry while giving a lot of ventilation. In a cold rain, however, a poncho will let in too much wind and water around the edges.

In addition to a raincoat or poncho, invest in rain pants, choosing from the same range of fabric options that you have for your raincoat. On a limited budget, get a better-grade fabric for your raincoat than your rain pants. You'll probably find that your legs don't mind overheating as much as your upper body does, and that even if they get wet, they'll warm up faster afterward.

Good rain pants have zippers near the ankle so you can take them on and off over your shoes, then zip them shut so they aren't too baggy. If there's any loose fabric around your ankles, carry something to tie the cuffs out of the way on both legs. Inexpensive elastic straps with Velcro fasteners are best. Rubber bands are cheaper but liable to break inconveniently.

Keeping your feet warm and dry is a problem. Most people just opt to get wet, but one solution is neoprene booties that pull on over your cycling shoes. Another is a set of Gore-Tex oversocks, such as those made by REI, which fit over your normal socks but inside your cycling shoes (the shoes themselves simply get wet). Since Gore-Tex is windproof, these socks may also solve the problem of cold toes in the morning if you have open-mesh cycling shoes.

For your head, consider a helmet cover or some kind of hood that runs over or under your helmet. If you wear eyeglasses, try wearing a cotton cycling cap underneath your helmet, with its brim pulled down practically on top of your glasses. A friend of mine says this is the best thing going to keep them from getting rain spattered.

Cold-Weather Clothing

Most people hang up their bicycles for the winter when the days grow short and temperatures dip. But even if you don't try to stretch the season far into the fall or early spring, you should be equipped for cold weather, especially for mountain touring in the West, where morning temperatures in the 30s or 40s can occur even in August, and long descents can expose your sweaty body to the chill of a self-generated 40-mph wind. The same clothes can also be used in camp, mornings and evenings.

Steal a trick from backpackers and dress in layers you can peel off or add, one at a time. For the upper body, carry at least three layers. The inner one should be a wicking layer, made of wool, polypropylene, or any of a number of new synthetics that pull the moisture away from the skin and keep you warm if they get wet. This is a good use for that fancy racing jersey, if you've got one, since it's probably made of an appropriate fabric.

Many people, myself included, use a T-shirt instead, assuming that eventually this is what they'll strip down to when it warms up. It works, but if the weather stays cool, you'll find sweat-soaked cotton cold and uncomfortable. To avoid the risk of getting dangerously chilled, be prepared to swap the T-shirt for a more suitable fabric.

The middle layer is your bulk or warmth layer (use multiple layers, if you prefer). You won't use it when you're pedaling hard unless it's *really* cold, but you do need it for cold downgrades or to keep rest breaks from turning into "freeze breaks." Again, get a material that will keep you warm if it gets wet. Wool is traditional, but the imitation-fleece synthetics are superb, seeming to shed moisture rather than absorb it. They're also a lot lighter weight. Their only serious disadvantage is that unlike wool, which has an amazing ability to neutralize body odor, many synthetics wick away the sweat but retain the aroma—making you wish for a laundromat, daily.

Full zippers are better than pullovers, allowing you to add or subtract a layer without removing your helmet. But if you're cutting costs, this isn't important—a well-worn wool sweater will work perfectly. You can get one inexpensively at a second-hand store or moving sale.

The third layer is a wind shell. Use the same one

you carry for light-duty use in milder conditions, but make sure it's large enough to fit comfortably over everything you want underneath. If you're really trying to save money or baggage, your rain jacket will work, but if it's not breathable you'll overheat too easily.

If you can afford expensive specialty clothes, buy a warm cycling jacket that combines the middle and outer layers by covering the front, shoulders, and arms—but not the back—in windproof nylon. This gives you wind protection where you need it while allowing the back of the jacket to breathe. Such a jacket might also have zippered pockets at the small of the back and additional pockets at the sides. Since you'll be using it as an outer layer, look for one with bright colors, especially on the back. Another specialty item is a heavyweight jersey with rear pockets, made of a wicking fabric that stands alone in cool weather or works well as the inner layer when it's really cold.

That takes care of the upper body. But it's also important to keep the legs warm, if for no other reason than to reduce the risk of straining cold, stiff muscles.

I've found two methods that won't overly restrict my freedom of motion. Most often, I combine my lightweight cycling tights with rain pants, an approach that has worked adequately for 20-mph coasts at temperatures as low as 40°F.

The other approach, which I used on my cross-country trip, when I knew I'd be spending a lot of time at high elevations, is to buy a warmer set of tights with fabric that is more breathable. Such tights are expensive, though, especially considering that you might not use them often. Some even come with a chamois, but you can save money by buying ones without, and wearing cycling shorts underneath (useful anyway, if you think the weather's going to warm up).

A budget alternative is long underwear. As with all clothing that might get wet, use fabrics that dry quickly and wick the moisture from your skin. That means no cotton long johns or cotton warm-up pants. Blue jeans are even worse. Not only will they not keep you warm when wet, but they restrict your freedom of motion, have uncomfortable seams, and are heavy to lug around.

Your biggest problem with long underwear is that it will draw stares. Of more practical concern, it isn't made to sit on and will wear out quickly from friction against the saddle, and might also chafe. Reduce the first two problems by wearing cycling shorts over the top of it, if they'll fit. Chafing, though, is a problem for which there's no solution except the cumbersome thought of wearing another pair of shorts or Lycra tights as yet another layer, underneath. If you find yourself resorting to this more than occasionally, it's time to buy those warm tights.

For your hands, wear a pair of wool or cotton gloves over or under your cycling gloves. For your ears, try a bandana or ear warmers, if they'll fit beneath your helmet.

MAKING FRIENDS WITH YOUR BIKE
—and staying that way

▼

A bicycle is like suit of fine clothes. It needs to be tailored for ideal fit. Unless you're experienced, don't try to do all of the adjusting yourself—just as you wouldn't try to tailor your own clothes.

Some choices, such as frame size, must be made before you buy. Others are a matter of fine-tuning and can be done after you've chosen the bike. Many bike shops will do this for you using a bike-fitting approach called the Fit Kit. Not a kit in any conventional sense, this approach puts your bike on a stand so you can sit on it while a mechanic tinkers with the adjustments.

Even if you've paid an expert to adjust your bike, don't feel wedded to the result. There's a lot of disagreement over adjustment rules, and people's bodies differ. What matters is what's best for you. Use the advice given by your shop and the suggestions that follow as a starting point, but don't be afraid to tinker. It can take a lot of experimentation to customize your bike to its "perfect" fit, and even then a change in shoes, saddle, or riding posture can start a whole new round of adjustments.

Before You Buy

Frame Size

Bicycle sizes are distinguished by such measurements as the distance between the top of the seat tube and the center of the bottom bracket.

To test frame size on a road bike, straddle the top tube with your feet flat on the ground, wearing shoes with approximately the same heel thickness as those you'll ride with. You should clear the tube with about an inch to spare. Mountain-bike frames are often smaller—and are a lot less standardized—so the one-inch rule won't apply; ask the dealers for the sizing rules for the brands they carry.

Such rules aren't absolute, so the straddle test won't necessarily find the perfect fit, even for a road bike. However, you shouldn't buy a bike so large you can't comfortably straddle it, since you may have to dismount in an emergency. Conversely, one that's far too short won't fit your back and might force you to put the seat and handlebars up as high as they will go, robbing you of adjustment flexibility.

Once you've found approximately the right frame size, test-ride your chosen frame and the next smaller one. Try out the next larger size, too, if you can straddle it. Do this because height isn't the only variable that changes with frame size. Make sure the bicycle isn't too long or too short, either stretching you too far forward as you reach for the handlebars or bunching you up uncomfortably. For the same reason, if you're looking at more than one brand of bicycle, don't assume that the frame size that's right for one will be right for the others.

A good bike shop is invaluable in making these decisions, especially for your first few test rides. A knowledgeable salesperson can watch you ride and help determine what's right. Later, after you've test-ridden a few models, you'll develop your own idea about what feels comfortable.

Stems and Cranks

Once you've chosen a frame size, certain other component sizes come with it, such as crank length, stem height (which controls the range of heights you can set the handlebars), and stem reach (the distance it holds the handlebars out in front of you). These are chosen by the manufacturer, based on its image of the average cyclist. That may or may not be you.

Cranks are fairly easy to swap, although the components are expensive. Consider doing this if you are particularly long -or short-legged for your height.

Stems can also be changed. This time, however, the component is relatively inexpensive but the installation more complex, especially if you're using Grab-Ons. The best time to swap stems is when you're first buying the bike; if you do it later you not only won't get to trade in the original, you'll pay a substantial labor charge.

You're more likely to want to change stems on road bikes than on mountain bikes. Road bikes are often designed to look like racing bikes, and racers, concerned about aerodynamics, set their handlebars lower than many comfort-minded touring cyclists. Racers don't need long stems, and the bike might come equipped with one that's so short you'll have to use it at maximum height, wishing you could raise it farther. If that's the case, swap it for a longer one. Similarly, if you've got a particularly long or short back, you might want to change the stem reach for greater comfort.

Unfortunately, choosing the perfect stem isn't as easy as you might wish: If you get a taller one, it could also have a longer reach—something you might not want. One way to increase your range of options is by putting a mountain-bike stem on a road bike. Whenever you change stems, make sure you know what you're getting before you buy. Undoing a goof will cost you not only another stem, but also a second labor charge.

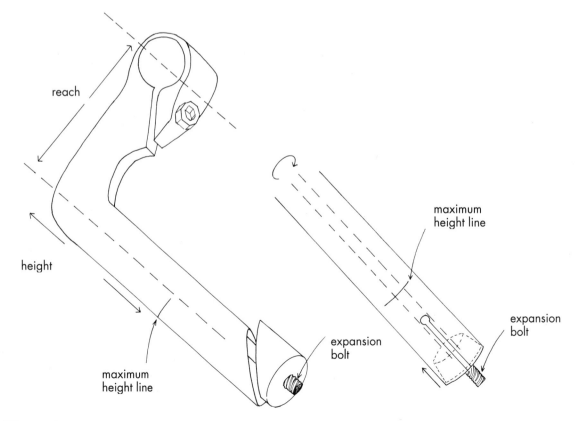

Adjustments

You can make the following adjustments after you've taken delivery of the bicycle.

Toe Clips

Begin by learning where to put your feet on the pedals. If you've never used toe clips or clip-in pedals, you've done most of your cycling inefficiently and uncomfortably, probably with the pedal under the arch of your foot. The ball of your foot should be directly over the spindle so the power of your stroke transfers to the crank smoothly and naturally.

With clip-in pedals, the adjustment is to your shoes rather than the bike. With toe clips, check if they're the right length. For comfort and to extend the life of your shoes, there should be a small gap between the clip and the toe of the shoe. If necessary, exchange the clips for ones that fit correctly. If you can't get the right size, you can make a slightly too large one fit by taping a piece of foam inside its front end.

Saddle Height

From the feet, adjustment moves to the saddle.

When you buy the bicycle, the shop should help find approximately the right saddle position, but this is an adjustment where millimeters count and it's going to take some fine-tuning to get it right.

There is no consensus on ideal seat position. The only thing that most experts seem to agree on is that a great many cyclists ride with their saddles too low. And within limits, too low is worse than too high.

If you think about the motion of your leg during each pedal stroke you'll quickly understand why saddle height is so important. At the bottom of each stroke, your knee is almost straight, but at the top it's bent fairly sharply. The higher the seat, the less bend there is in the leg, and the less knee stress there is on the downstroke. Set your seat high but not so high it hyperextends the knee at the bottom of the pedal stroke or robs you of power because your feet lose contact with the pedals.

To find this point, sit on the bicycle with someone holding it upright to help you balance. Sitting normally on the saddle, put your feet in the toe clips or clip-in pedals and pedal backward until your foot

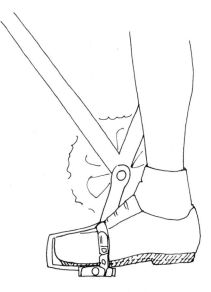

good toe-clip fit

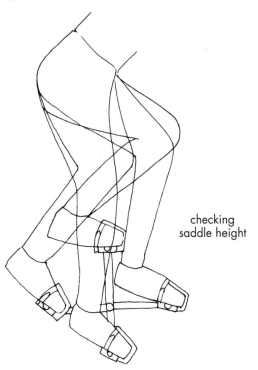

checking
saddle height

reaches the bottom. Racers, who draw power from calves and ankles as well as thighs, will tend to have their toes pointing downward at this point. Touring cyclists are more likely to have their feet closer to level, but what matters is putting the foot in the same position you'll be using on the road. If that changes as you gain experience, you can always readjust your seat height.

With your foot in this position, your knee should be slightly bent. If it's locked, you're too high. Adjust the seat accordingly.

Another approach is to take the bike out on the road or put it on an exercise stand. Pedal, while another cyclist watches you from behind. If your pelvis rocks back and forth, your seat is too high, forcing you to reach for the pedal at the bottom of each stroke. Lower it to the point slightly below the one at which you start to rock.

A third, time-tested approach is to pedal backward with your heels on the pedals, adjusting the seat until you find the maximum height at which your feet maintain easy contact with the pedals, all the way around.

These three approaches probably won't give you the same result. Try them all, and since too low is worse than too high, pick a height near the upper end of the resulting range. If you feel twinges of knee pain on your first excursions after a change in saddle height, adjust the seat by a couple of millimeters (probably upward), and see if they go away.

You might think that once you get your seat properly adjusted, you'll never need to change it. But that just isn't the case. Buying a new pair of shoes with a different sole thickness, for example, will require a change in seat height, as will the addition of a gel-filled seat cushion. And some days, the height

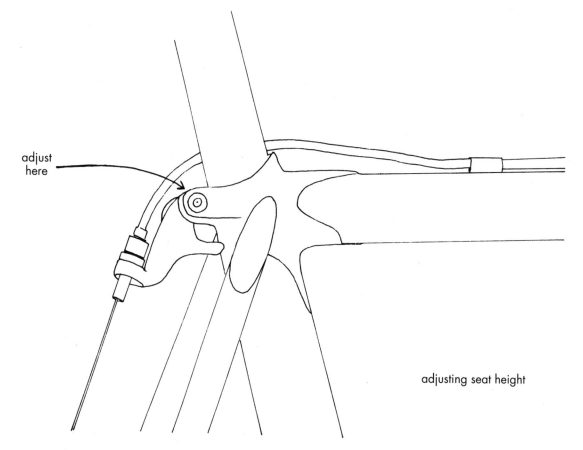

adjust here

adjusting seat height

you've always used just seems inexplicably wrong.

Remember that saddle-height recommendations aren't immutable laws. One of my cycling friends has ridden for years with her saddle so high her pelvis always rocks. It's never seemed to bother her.

Making the adjustment. Adjusting seat height is a 30-second job, faster if your bike, like some mountain bikes, has a quick-release lever on the seat post. Loosen the seat post, pull the seat up or down as needed, and tighten it again. Work in small increments; for fine-tuning, ¼ inch is a *big* change. To keep from losing track of your starting point, mark it with tape or by lightly scratching the seat post.

Whatever you do, don't exceed the maximum safe-height line inscribed on the seat post. Look for this line the first time you adjust your saddle height so you're sure you know what to look for. If you need to go higher than that, get a longer seat post.

When adjusting saddle height, wear your cycling shoes, and if you're planning on buying a gel seat cover, mount it first. Otherwise, you'll have to adjust the seat all over again.

Forward-and-Back Position of the Saddle

In addition to adjusting your saddle height, you can adjust its tilt and forward-and-back position. Begin with the latter.

This adjustment might have some impact on knee comfort, but more than anything else, it affects the power delivery of your pedal stroke. The classic rule of thumb is that when the pedal is in its extreme forward position, an imaginary plumb line dropped from the point of the bone that protrudes just below your kneecap should go through the ball of your foot, bisecting the spindle of the pedal. The best way to check this is to have a friend eyeball it as you sit stationary on the bicycle.

Making the adjustment. A saddle is clamped to the seat post by a pair of metal rails that are part of the saddle's frame. Loosen the bolt securing the clamp and slide the saddle to the desired position. Don't remove the nut completely or you might have trouble reinstalling it.

If the saddle won't go far enough forward or

back, you might need to change the seat post. Clamp position varies from brand to brand.

Saddle Tilt

Too much forward saddle tilt throws weight uncomfortably onto your hands, while too much backward tilt can cause groin discomfort. It's a trade-off you'll have to make for yourself. Men should start with the saddle level or tilted slightly upward in front. Women may want to tilt it slightly downward, though a well-designed woman's saddle will reduce the need for doing so.

Making the adjustment. This is usually controlled by the same bolt that controls forward-and-back position. Because it comes under a lot of torque as you shift your weight in the saddle, this joint often uses a notched mechanism to keep it from slipping; you'll have to adjust your saddle by full notches rather than partial steps.

To adjust tilt, you shouldn't need to loosen the nut as much as you did to slide it on the rails. Adjusting the seat forward and back might acciden-

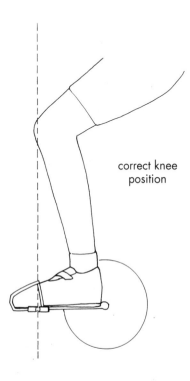

correct knee position

tally disturb your tilt adjustment, but not vice versa—convenient, since tilt is the adjustment you're more likely to tinker with.

Handlebar Height

This is largely a matter of personal choice. For racing, the issue is one of aerodynamics; for touring it's one of lower-back comfort and getting the weight off your hands. An old rule of thumb for road bikes is to start with the top of your handlebars an inch lower than the top of the saddle. I like to keep the handlebars higher, nearly even with the top of the saddle, sacrificing a little in wind resistance in exchange for comfort and an easier view down the road without craning my neck.

As with saddle height, don't exceed the maximum height line inscribed on the stem. Raising the handlebars higher than this risks breaking the stem, which could leave you cruising along with no way to steer.

Making the adjustment. The stem is held in place by a long expansion bolt inserted from the top. Tightening the bolt enlarges the diameter of the stem slightly, pressing it firmly against the inside of the head tube.

To change your handlebar height, loosen the stem bolt with an Allen wrench but don't remove the bolt completely. If it loosens ¼ inch or so but the stem won't move, bang on top of the bolt with something hard to knock the expansion nut loose. Then slide the stem to the desired position.

Retighten the bolt firmly enough that the handlebars won't twist when you hit a bump, but not so tightly that the bar ends might impale you rather than twist in a crash. To test for proper tightness, stand in front of the bike holding the front wheel between your knees. The stem should rotate—grudgingly—to a hard twist. If you don't know how tight is tight enough, ask a bike mechanic to demonstrate.

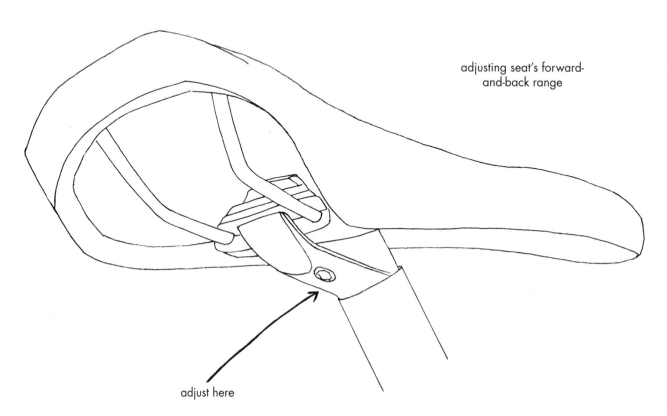

adjusting seat's forward-
and-back range

adjust here

Handlebar Tilt

The tilt of your handlebars affects how comfortable it is to reach the lower position on drop handlebars, and how much weight rests on your hands. There are enough handlebar styles that there's no simple rule of thumb for this adjustment, but most people will probably want them pointing somewhere between level and aimed at the rear hub. Tilting them dramatically upward or turning them upside down, as a few people do, is dangerous because it puts the bar ends right where your stomach might hit them in a crash.

Making the adjustment. Loosen the bolt clamping the handlebars to the stem and rotate the bars as desired. When finished, make sure this bolt is tight. If it slips, you'll be lucky not to crash. Don't tighten it absurdly; I watched a mechanic do that once, shearing it and sending the broken end shooting across the room like a bullet. Do that on the road, and you'll be stranded.

Brake Lever Position

Brake levers can be moved too, but doing so will ruin your handlebar tape and Grab-Ons if you're using them. Don't make this adjustment until you've tried the brakes for at least a couple of weeks in the position in which they were installed. The odds are you'll get used to it.

With traditional mountain-bike handlebars, you really don't have much choice about brake positions, though you can rotate the levers if you want. With drop handlebars, or multiposition upright bars, there are a lot of places to put the brakes. But think before you get too wild about it. Make sure you can reach them easily from the down position, since that's the most stable for hard braking. In addition, you want to be able to rest your hands on the brake hoods as you ride. For beginners, this feels truly weird, but with practice, it's a comfortable variation with the nice side effect of changing the pressure points in your hands. You can even reach the brake levers from there for lazy, gentle braking.

Making the adjustment. Squeeze tightly on the brakes and peer into the gap that opens up at the top of the brake lever. On most brakes, you'll see a large screw. Loosen it, slide or rotate the levers as desired, then retighten the screw. In the process, you'll almost certainly have to remove handlebar tape, Grab-Ons, or both. They're in the way, and the brake cables run underneath and need to be moved along with the levers.

BASIC
RIDING SKILLS

▼

By now, you have a bicycle, rigged it for touring, and had a shop help you fit it to your body. Now it's time to start having fun on the roads and bike paths near your home.

This book assumes you already know basic riding principles: balancing on two wheels, starting, stopping, shifting gears. While riding a bicycle is definitely something you never forget, you can spend a lifetime honing your skills.

This chapter covers basic skills—ones you'll need regardless of where you ride. Later chapters cover more-advanced skills and topics such as desert or mountain riding, useful if you live in the relevant parts of the country or visit them on a tour. A few regional topics, such as cattle guards and rumble strips, are included here because they have much in common with ubiquitous problems like railroad tracks and bumps.

Pedaling Cadence

Experienced cyclists call it "spinning." Beginners are more likely to call it impossible. But to increase your efficiency and comfort, especially on a long ride, the single most effective way is by increasing your pedaling rhythm, or "cadence."

If you've ever seen bike racers you might have noted that their feet spin at a fantastic pace—well over 100 revolutions per minute. That's because racers know something that most beginning cyclists don't: Spinning at a rapid cadence is easier—both on knees and on stamina—than grinding along in high gears.

To test your cadence, go out on a calm day to a flat, smooth road or bike path long enough to ride several minutes without slowing down. If you have a cyclometer with a cadence sensor, put it in cadence mode (sometimes called "rpm"). Otherwise use a watch or the clock mode of your cyclometer.

Your goal for the moment is not to see how fast you can spin, but rather to determine your normal cadence. After you've warmed up, settle into an easy cruising speed in a comfortable gear. Count the number of full pedal revolutions you make in a minute. Do it several times, trying not to let the test

influence your rhythm. If your cadence is 85 rpm or higher, congratulations—you can skip the rest of this section. If it's 75 or below, there's room for improvement.

Increasing your cadence takes practice. Partly it's merely the cumulative experience of thousands of miles of lifetime cycling. But you can speed up the learning curve. Riding at your normal cadence, try downshifting one gear, spinning faster to maintain speed. Your cadence should increase by 10% to 15%, e.g., from 65 to 73 rpm.

Try to maintain this faster cadence for a minute or two. It'll feel strange, impossible to maintain for long, but that's OK. This is your target; practice will make it feel natural. Check your cadence periodically to see how you're doing, especially on hills or in headwinds, when you'll be tempted to grind it out in overly high gears. Because these are the times of greatest stress, they're the most important times for rapid spinning.

You may wonder if you can spin *too* fast. The answer is yes, but it's not a problem for most

cyclists. Shift to a low gear and pedal as fast as you can. You'll probably find yourself bouncing up and down on the saddle. *That's* spinning too fast. It's uncomfortable, and you're not likely to do it unless you're sprinting and run out of gears.

What is the ideal cadence? That'll depend on your body and your bike, but the answer will be somewhere between 75 and 100 rpm. I have two bicycles: one for touring, the other a sport/racer. On the touring bike, my natural cadence is 84. On the racer it's 10 to 15 rpm higher. The difference comes in the way the two seats put me over the pedals. I would expect touring bikes and mountain bikes, designed for long-haul comfort rather than nimbleness on the sprint, to encourage lower cadences.

Riding in Traffic

Riding in traffic can be reduced to two watchwords: confidence and predictability. Being visible, discussed earlier, is also important.

Confidence and predictability are linked. Knowing what you're doing, and acting like it, earns the motorists' respect by telling them you understand the rules of the road and will follow them. Timid cyclists who wobble all over the place trying to keep away from traffic are as disturbing to drivers as maniacs who run stoplights or bring everyone else to a halt by riding the wrong way on one-way streets. The maniacs make drivers gnash their teeth, confirming beliefs that bicycles don't belong on the road. Timid cyclists bring up thoughts of children darting unpredictably in any direction.

The basic rule for cycling in traffic is simple: You are a vehicle, with all the privileges and responsibilities of an automobile. In general, you follow the same rules as a car.

Except in a traffic jam, however, you are a much more slowly moving vehicle—and one particularly vulnerable to accidents. Most of the skill of riding in traffic comes from learning to live with those two important differences. Here are a few specific pointers:

Ride on the right-hand side of the road. It's amazing how many cyclists don't understand this, apparently because their parents taught it wrong.

Pedestrians walk facing traffic; cyclists ride with the traffic. If you're not convinced, think about this: Pedestrians can always leap into the ditch to keep from being hit; cyclists can't. You need to *share* the lane, which is easier if you're moving in the same direction.

Look behind you. Keeping track of what's going on behind you is as important as knowing what's happening in front. Get a mirror and use it. Seeing if cars behind you slow down or pull to the left will let you know whether they see you (and respect you); with experience you'll soon be able to tell pretty accurately how close someone is going to pass.

Often you need to supplement your mirror by looking over your shoulder. To keep from veering in the direction you turn your head, shift your weight a bit to the opposite direction on the saddle. Practice until you can take a thorough look over either shoulder while steering a straight line.

Ride as far to the right as safety permits. You have a right—unfortunately, not always recognized by law—to avoid rocks, chuckholes, and broken pavement at the edge of the road. Furthermore, steering a straight course far enough out into the lane to automatically miss the bulk of these obstructions is usually safer—and more predictable to the traffic—than veering around them one at a time.

Some cyclists take pride in riding as close to the edge as they can, steering unerringly straight lines two inches or less from the lip of the pavement. I'm not one of them. Not only does that make it hard to watch the scenery, it's also dangerous. One gust of wind, one lapse of concentration, and you're off the road, heading for a crash. It is also gives drivers an open invitation to pass without crossing the center line.

Mark Twain once wrote story about a lady whose health was failing and who had no bad habits like drinking or smoking to give up. There she was, quipped Twain, a foundering ship with no ballast to throw overboard to lighten the load. When it comes to lane position, don't be like Mark Twain's lady. It pays to retain some "ballast" to throw overboard in times of trouble—ballast in the form of space between you and the edge of the road. Not only does this give you room to wobble, but it also

gives you somewhere safe to go if you're crowded by a passing car.

For normal cruising on a level road, I like a cushion of about 12 to 18 inches. If you find yourself in very heavy but slow-moving traffic—e.g., downtown in a big city—you may even want to "take the lane" by riding in the middle of it, making yourself more visible, and preventing cars from crowding you off the road. You also might want to take the lane if there isn't room for you and a car to safely share it. But here it may not be wise to ride in the center—that can make drivers angry. Instead, position yourself far enough out to force them to cross the center line to get around you. Watch carefully and be prepared to throw away some "ballast" if necessary.

Proper lane use can also mean waiting your turn. Trying to zip between lanes at a traffic light or other slow-down is rude, probably illegal, and unwise because drivers aren't expecting it.

Turns and stops. Always signal, to drivers and to other cyclists. The signals are standard; you were probably taught them in grade school. For a left turn extend your left arm in that direction, straight from the shoulder. For right turns the traditional signal is to use your left arm, bent 90 degrees upward at the elbow. This rule was developed for cars, however, where all hand signals must necessarily be given with the left arm. For cyclists it's starting to become acceptable to signal a right turn with the right arm, in the mirror image of the left turn signal.

To signal a stop, extend the left arm downward, slightly out from your side. It's best to hold the palm open rather than pointing with one finger, so it doesn't look like you're merely pointing to something on the ground. Some cyclists make the gesture more emphatic by waving backward with the palm.

When turning, lean into the turn and raise the pedal on the inward side (left for a left turn, right for a right turn) if there's any risk it might drag. With practice, this becomes habitual, not only on city streets, but also on steep, winding downgrades.

Get into the habit of using both brakes to stop. Many beginners are afraid of the front one because they've been told it can flip them over. This is true, but you need to know how to use it for emergen-

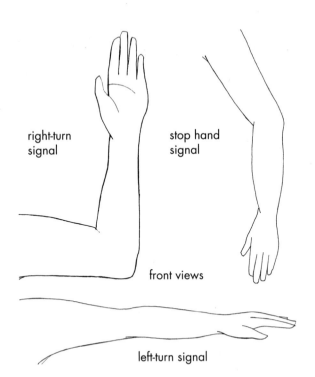

right-turn signal

stop hand signal

front views

left-turn signal

cies—or for stopping on steep downgrades with a heavy touring rig. Practice using both brakes, carefully at first then more firmly as you gain confidence. Most of your stopping power comes from the front, with the rear brake contributing to control and stability. Except at very slow speeds, it really isn't all that easy to flip. A more realistic worry is skidding the front wheel on slippery surfaces. If the road is wet or covered with sand or gravel, use the front brake gingerly; it's better to skid the rear wheel than the front.

With either brake, if the wheel thumps or grabs once per revolution, you've got a bad wobble in your rim. This can cause the wheel to lock and skid; fix it immediately.

Intersections. Even experienced cyclists can approach intersections improperly. This is one time when the stay-to-the-right rule doesn't necessarily apply, especially on multi-lane roads.

Right turns are simple. Use the right side of the right-hand lane.

To go straight, stay to the right but watch for right-turning traffic cutting in front of you. If there is a designated right-turn lane, you can prevent this (not to mention obeying the law) by moving over to the next lane. At red lights this frees the turn lane for people wanting to turn right on red and announces your intention to go straight. If heavy or fast-moving traffic makes it dangerous to leave the right lane, you can: (1) move to the sidewalk, dismount, and become a pedestrian; or (2) go straight from the right-turn lane, making *sure* the traffic understands what you're doing.

For left turns, move to the left half of the left lane (don't hang across the center line in front of the oncoming traffic!). When turning, move directly to the right side of the road, even if it's got multiple lanes. That might not be technically legal, but anything else blocks traffic and can trap you.

Changing lanes to turn left is scary the first few times you do it. Time your approach to the intersection to coincide with a gap in the traffic. Then signal a left turn, look over your shoulder to check for traffic (don't rely solely on your mirror; you have blind spots just like an automobile), and move to the center of the left lane, "taking" it so that no one tries to squeeze past. If there is traffic close behind you, try to make eye contact with the leading driver before making your move. Many will give you the right of way, but make sure of their intentions.

Sometimes traffic is just too heavy or fast for a normal, safe left turn. If this is the case when you're trying to turn from the middle of a block, pull to the side, wait for a gap in the traffic, then cross as though you were a pedestrian. Even at stoplights you'll sometimes have to do the same, crossing one way with the green light, then waiting for it to change to cross the other way. Frustrating, but at least you'll live to tell the tale.

Even more frustrating are magnetic sensors at low-traffic intersections. If you are the only traffic, you can wait forever for the light to change. One or two bicycles don't have enough metal to trip these sensors.

There are no good solutions to this problem. A few cyclists have become expert at understanding the polygonal cuts in the road marking the sensor's location. Laying the bicycle on its side in just the right manner can apparently trigger some of them.

Other cyclists become pedestrians, pushing the "walk" button—though that won't give you a left-turn arrow if that's what you need. Most cyclists simply run the light, figuring that anything else is beyond the call of duty.

If there is enough traffic, I sometimes wait until someone comes up behind me, triggering the signal for both of us. If you do this, make sure the car pulls onto the sensor, beckoning the driver forward if necessary. Otherwise you'll both wait.

Parked cars. On busy streets, parked cars are a nuisance, forcing you to swing farther out into the traffic lane than you'd prefer. Since most drivers will be oblivious to your plight, signal your intent in advance, trying to make eye contact so they'll let you in. A full-fledged left turn signal gets their attention but may be misunderstood—try signaling this minor change of lane position by holding your hand down to the side and pointing left. Most drivers will get the idea.

Another common hazard comes from parked cars that suddenly sprout open doors into your path. Always be alert to this possibility, especially if you

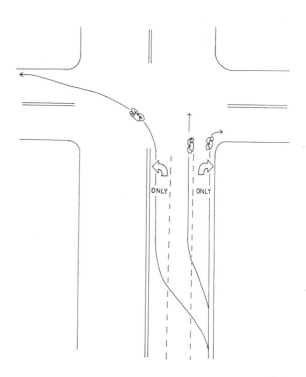

see someone in the car. If traffic conditions permit, try to stay far enough away that a door can be opened to its full extent without hitting you.

If there are a lot of parked cars, stay in the traffic lane; don't swerve into and out of it for every car. If they're spaced erratically, with occasional large gaps, courtesy—and self-preservation—dictates that you pull into the parking lane periodically to let the cars get by. Plan ahead; it's easy to get trapped. And be careful when you reenter the traffic lane; changing lanes is always dangerous.

Highways. Any road with a high speed limit requires extra caution. If it has a paved shoulder, use it. Even a two-foot shoulder can do a lot to separate you from the traffic. If there is no shoulder, watch your rear-view mirror frequently, being prepared to pull off the pavement and stop. (A mountain bike makes this a lot easier, allowing you to pull safely onto a gravel shoulder while still moving.) Also be alert to pickup trucks with odd loads, such as planks, hanging farther out to the side than the drivers realize.

Highways aren't good places to aggressively "take the lane," but it can still be useful to have a cushion of spare room. When a car passes, you can ease closer to the edge, adding a foot or so to the room the driver intended to give you. That can make a big difference.

Keep an eye on the oncoming traffic as well. If cars reach you at the same time from both directions, you might be in for a tight squeeze, especially if the road is narrow. Watch the car behind you and listen to the sound of its engine to hear if it's slowing down to wait. If it isn't, this is a good time to pull off the pavement before you have to make an emergency bailout.

Watch oncoming cars because they occasionally pass each other, scaring you badly if you've been dozing. If there's any risk at all that the passing car won't be back in its lane by the time it reaches you, pull off the pavement and stop, immediately.

Trucks can also be frightening; watch them carefully while keeping your eyes on the road. Farm trucks are rarely a threat. They're usually local, not in much hurry. Semis or logging trucks are a different matter, though. They'll seldom deliberately

crowd you but they're not all that likely to slow down and wait for a safe opportunity to pass. The deep throaty growl of a diesel engine behind you, followed by a blast on the air horn, should be interpreted as: "I'm coming through. If there's no oncoming traffic, I'll give you room. If not, you'd better get out of my way." Get angry if you want, but it's a message you'd better heed.

At highway speeds, any passing truck produces wind gusts that buffet you unpredictably. If a truck passes within half a lane-width of you, you might also feel a suction trying to pull you toward it. Or the truck may suddenly block a crosswind, causing you to swerve.

Prepare for all of these possibilities before the truck arrives. Grip the handlebars firmly, crouching low to reduce your susceptibility to wind. With drop handlebars, your hands should be spaced wide apart—ideally, in the down position—for best steering control and easy reach of the brakes. This is good riding posture any time you are facing the prospect of gusting crosswinds.

Defensive cycling. A bicycle might have the same right-of-way as a car, but defending it isn't worth a trip to the hospital. The confidence necessary to ride comfortably in traffic should be accompanied by a healthy dose of skepticism about the sanity of any given motorist.

The single most common threat comes from people making right turns in front of you, treating you like a lamppost—something that won't move after they've passed. Always be prepared for cars to make right turns immediately after they pass you, with or without signaling. When this happens (and it will), yell for attention, brake hard, and if necessary execute an "emergency right turn" in unison with the car. More rarely, left turners will also cut in front of you, forcing a similar maneuver. Be alert to traffic going in both directions.

Another danger is that a child playing in front of a parked car will run out in front of you or throw a ball into the street at just the wrong moment. Trucks and vans are tall enough to block your view of even an adult. Make a habit of looking underneath such cars when you're still at a distance, checking for feet or other signs that someone's in front. When you see feet, or a ball rolling across a lawn toward the street, expect the unexpected.

Don't pull up too close behind a stopped car at traffic lights, stop signs, or in parking lots. People have been known to back up without looking, and it doesn't take much of a bump to ruin your front wheel.

Unguarded intersections (*i.e.*, those with no stop sign or stop light either direction) are also dangerous. Theoretically, the right-of-way belongs to whoever gets there first (the vehicle on the right in the event of a tie), but only a fool races somebody to such an intersection.

Another good place to practice defensive cycling is when you see a driver poised to pull out of a driveway or side street. Don't assume you've been seen; slow down or stop until you make eye contact with the driver—and know he won't pull out even *after* he's seen you.

Riding in traffic is never as much fun as a quiet country lane, but if you're cautious and alert (but not paranoid) it can still be enjoyable and low risk.

Traffic Laws

Bicycle laws vary from state to state, as well as changing from year to year as states grant increasingly explicit recognition to the special needs of cyclists. Here is a summary of what to expect.

1 *You are a vehicle.* Bicycles have the same rights and duties as autos except for those that by their nature cannot apply. This means you don't need brake lights but you do have to stop for stop signs and stop lights—and can't go the wrong way on one-way streets.

2 *Stop signs.* I once asked a policeman, himself a cyclist, what he believed constituted a legal stop. His answer was liberal: slowing to a jogging pace and not stealing the right-of-way from someone else. But if you get a ticket, good luck defending that interpretation in court! Technically, a full, legal stop is a complete cessation of motion. If a police car is around, it's best to put one foot on the ground to prove that you have indeed stopped.

3 *Lane use.* Older laws require bicycles to stay "as far as possible" to the right of the road. Since it's *possible* to ride through chuckholes, broken glass, and gravel, that verbal formula is much resented by cyclists, and bike clubs have lobbied long and hard to substitute the more liberal phrase "as far as practicable." Whether "practicable" includes taking the lane when necessary for safety, however, isn't always clear.

4 *Corners and one-way streets.* Expect the law to allow you to move to the left for left turns or to avoid right-turn lanes when going straight. On one-way streets it will probably allow you to ride on the left, but don't make a habit of it, because the traffic doesn't expect you there.

5 *Two abreast.* Some states require you to ride single file. Others allow you to ride two abreast. Only ride two abreast, though, if it doesn't block traffic; it's common courtesy if not the law. (Three abreast is illegal in most states, if not all.)

6 *Bike lanes and bike paths.* This is a hotly controversial subject where bike law often hasn't caught up with reality. Must you use a bike path if one is provided? What if it's full of grit or stops for every driveway?

Learn the rules of your own town by asking other cyclists. Elsewhere the best rules of thumb are practicality, courtesy, and safety. If the road is a nightmare of heavy traffic, any bike path is better than none. If the road is ridable and the path unappealing, you're faced with a tradeoff that you may not be able to explain satisfactorily to a ticket-happy police officer.

7 *Sidewalks.* Bikes and pedestrians don't mix. If you must ride on a sidewalk, the law will probably require you not to go too fast or to do stupid things like suddenly popping into the street in front of a car. You may be required to give an audible warning before passing pedestrians from behind. Beware, though, that this makes many pedestrians panic. It is also my experience that more than 50% of them react to announcements such as, "Bicycle on your left," by stepping directly into your path. Give your warnings well in advance.

8   *Helmets.* There is a growing move to require helmets for children on bicycles. Helmet laws for adult cyclists may well be the wave of the future.

9   *Miscellaneous provisions.* Typically, you must have a seat on your bicycle (good idea!), and you can't cling to the back or side of a motor vehicle or carry more passengers than your bicycle is designed for. Also, you must keep at least one hand free for the handlebars. The law may also dictate how far in advance you should give turn signals, though the rules may not be practical if they're written for cars, not, cyclists.

10 *Learning the law.* To find out your state's laws ask at your local driver-testing station. If they don't know, they can almost certainly tell you who does. It's also a good idea to know the cycling laws of any states you're planning to visit on a tour. (Try asking the state police, the department of motor vehicles, or a bike shop.) In practice, though, most cyclists merely follow the rules of common sense, one of which is taking the most conservative approach whenever a police officer is in sight.

Wind

Headwinds are a cyclist's worst enemy. They're bad enough on a sleek, aerodynamic racing machine, but on a loaded touring bike or a mountain bike, they can practically stop you in your tracks.

One solution is to avoid wind. It sounds simple-minded, but there's a lot you can do. On training rides around home you'll quickly become adept at interpreting wind patterns. I once lived where the standard summer weather pattern saw a brisk west wind spring up at midday then die out a couple of hours before sunset. Riding east, I'd take advantage of that by departing when the wind was strong and returning as it was fading. Riding west I'd leave early, while the wind was light, letting it blow me home at its strongest. Usually. It's a good idea to allow some leeway in case the wind doesn't cooperate.

Another trick is to let the wind determine your route. Go upwind first, saving the easy downwind

leg for last. Better yet, do the upwind section on a road that's relatively sheltered, emerging into the open for a free ride home.

If you do get caught in a headwind, be patient. Gear down, keep up your cadence, and don't push too hard.

Drafting

Another approach to headwinds is to team up with one or more other cyclists in a drafting, or "pace," chain. Drafting, you ride in the slipstream of the cyclist in front of you, letting your friend break the wind while you rest. Taking turns so the leader never fatigues, you go faster than either of you would alone. It even works when there's no wind.

Proper drafting formation depends on the wind direction. In a straight-on headwind or one that's nearly so, the most efficient way to ride is closely spaced, single file. *How* closely spaced is a trade-off between energy savings and the risk of colliding. Drafting efficiency falls off rapidly with distance; if you're more than a bicycle length apart, you've lost much of it. Closer is scary, though, because you can't see much except the rear tire of the cyclist ahead of you, and there's not much time to react.

The trade-off between safety and efficiency is one you have to make for yourself. My own compromise is to stay well back—at least half a bicycle length—from people I haven't cycled with several times or whose skill I don't trust. I also like to move slightly off to one side. That exposes me to a bit more wind, but allows me to see what's ahead and gives me a safe direction to veer if necessary. In a larger group you can achieve the same benefits by forming a staggered line, giving each cyclist a little bit of extra time to react.

Drafting in an angling headwind is the same, except now each cyclist offsets to the same side, downwind. The ideal position depends on the precise wind direction. As a rule of thumb, imagine a line through the center of your two bicycles. That line should point directly into the perceived wind (the combination of the wind itself and your own forward velocity). Get into approximately the right position and move forward or back a few inches to see what's most comfortable. If this leaves you with part of your front wheel beside the rear wheel of the rider in front of you, think about dropping farther back or moving well off to the side. At least make sure the other rider knows where you are. You're

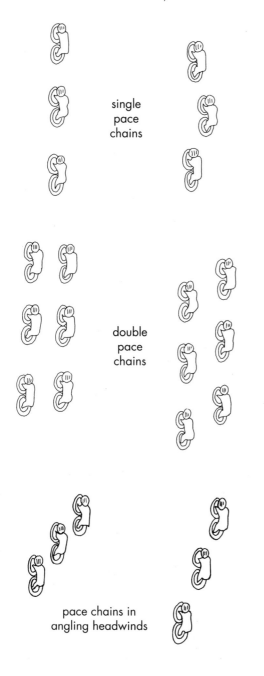

single pace chains

double pace chains

pace chains in angling headwinds

"lapping wheels," and if he swerves, you'll hit the pavement, hard.

Crosswinds are similar. Since the perceived wind still has a headwind component from your own velocity, the most efficient place to ride won't be directly beside the upwind rider, but with your front wheel somewhat behind hers.

In a straight-on headwind, there's no theoretical limit to the length of a pace chain, though chains of more than a half-dozen riders tend to stretch and contract accordion style, much to the irritation—and occasional panic—of the people in back. It's often simpler and a lot more sociable to form a double pace chain, with two lines of cyclists, side by side. But do this only if you've got a wide road shoulder; otherwise the riders nearest the traffic don't have time to get out of the way of approaching cars. If there's no shoulder, ride single file, and keep the group small enough that it's not too much of an obstacle to traffic.

In a crosswind or angling headwind, long pace chains don't work because the necessary stagger will force the trailing riders too far to the side. The leader can help by riding as far to the upwind side as safety permits, but it's best to break into pairs or trios.

Drafting Etiquette

Riding in a pace chain is a good cure for a nasty headwind but it's inherently dangerous. If you're going to do it—and at some time or another even the most cautious cyclists usually do—it requires careful attention to technique and group etiquette. It's not something to do when your primary interest is in the scenery.

Don't even consider drafting if you have trouble holding a constant pace or tend to wobble around a lot. At best, you'll drive your drafting partners batty; at worst you'll find yourself in the middle of a crash. Also beware of drafting at high speed downhill. At 30 mph, you don't need a windbreak, anyway.

Pace chains don't work well uphill either, but in this case the reason is that everyone has his own way of climbing hills, and it's hard to keep a group together.

In a drafting chain, the leader is responsible for

road hazard warnings, pointing downward on the side where an obstacle will soon appear and calling out "rock" a second or two beforehand. Cyclists in the middle of the chain often echo the warning to those behind them, but overdoing this can be irritating.

Keep the warnings simple: "rock," "gravel," "glass," "stick," "road kill," "hole," "bump," etc. If the obstacle doesn't fit any obvious category, call it a bump or a hole—the last thing you want is for other riders to be saying, "Excuse me?" when you've tried to warn them about an unidentifiable car part or a bag of litter. If there are several obstacles, wave your hand broadly on the proper side and call out "rocks," or whatever. Plan ahead, so you never have to swerve violently, and try to steer at least two feet away from the obstacle so the riders behind you don't come too close. People who can't remember to do these things consistently shouldn't be trusted in pace chains.

If the obstacle is a railroad track, stop sign, corner, or anything else that requires a major speed or course change, warn well in advance, letting the pace chain spread out as people find their own ways through. Regroup afterward.

Whether you're the leader or in the middle, don't slow down abruptly, and particularly not without warning. A hand signal and a shout of "Slowing!" or "Braking!" should *precede* the action if at all possible. If you're drafting closely (with a gap of, say, less than two feet), don't miss even a pedal stroke without announcing it.

Riders in the back of the chain are responsible for giving warnings about traffic. Since it's not safe to take your eyes off the rider in front of you long enough to look over your shoulder, a mirror is mandatory. Traditional warnings are "car back," "truck back," "RV back," or simply "another one," if you're being passed by a string of traffic. In appropriate circumstances—as when the group is about to make a left turn—you can also call out "clear back" if there's no traffic behind. Always indicate what direction is clear, since other riders may be wondering about what's going on ahead or to the side.

If this all sounds difficult and dangerous, it is. But it has its rewards—not only the tangible ones of getting there faster and easier, but also the psychological ones of facing a headwind and *doing something* about it. And drafting with a single partner or a small group of friends is a wonderful exercise in teamwork and camaraderie.

The first time you draft, the reduction in effort will feel magical. The best way to learn is by practicing with a close friend in a headwind strong enough to hold you back to a speed of less than 10 mph. That will give you plenty of time to react, and even if you do bump each other you're not likely to have a serious crash.

Dogs

Dogs may be man's best friend, but they aren't a cyclist's. There's nothing like a snarling mongrel threatening to take a chomp out of your Achilles tendon to make you wonder why you didn't take up a nice tame sport like bungee jumping.

Cycling lore is full of suggestions for defending yourself against canines. Some cyclists carry Mace, some bend pump handles over the beasts' skulls. I find dogs to be a much overrated hazard. They're usually harmless, running with you simply for the joy of the chase. Mace might discourage such a dog, but it could also turn it into a cyclist hater, creating bigger problems for the next cyclist to pass by. If you feel you really *must* squirt the dog with something, use water.

The really dangerous dogs are the ones that don't growl or bark. They're on you before you know what's happening and, in the case of the only dog that's ever bitten me, gone before I could possibly have reached my pump or a can of Mace.

So what do you do when a dog charges toward you out of a farmyard? Try not to get worried or excited, even if it's a 100-pound shepherd that looks like it could have both you and your bike for breakfast. Dogs sense fear, and it brings out something atavistic in them, greatly increasing the threat.

With most dogs, especially those that wag their tails and obviously mean no harm, it's best just to ignore them. You usually can't outrun them, and suddenly speeding up may excite them further. Consider doing the opposite, coasting if the terrain and wind direction permit. That way your heel is no longer going up and down, up and down, where even the friendliest dog may be tempted to grab it.

When all else fails, the best defense is often to dismount, use the bike as a shield and yell at the dog or scream for help. If you're lucky, the very act of dismounting will take the fury out of the attack. Sometimes it's not people a dog dislikes—it's people on bicycles.

Railroad Tracks, Cattle Guards, and Rumble Strips

Cross railroad tracks at right angles or close to it. Too shallow an angle—what that is depends on your skill, your tires, and the weather—and the track will grab your wheel and you'll crash before you know what happened.

To cross a sharply angling track, plan on using most of the lane. On a quiet farm lane or a highway with a full-width shoulder, this is no problem. If the traffic is too intense, as on a busy narrow-shoulder highway, dismount and walk. In a town or city, or on a low-speed rural road, look for a suitable gap in the traffic and give the arm signal for slowing down. If you're with other cyclists, give each other plenty of maneuvering room. Slow to a fast walking speed—less if the crossing is bumpy. Depending on which way the tracks angle, move to the right or out into the lane until you can cross comfortably while staying in your lane.

If there are multiple tracks you might not be able to cross them all at once. Use the space between them to curve back in a W-shaped course until you've gained enough room. If there's no traffic, you can also use both lanes of the road to cross the tracks in a single hitch.

If a car comes up behind you while you're zigzagging across a multiple track, let it wait. Your right to the road includes the right to cross railroad tracks safely, and it won't help anybody if you crash in front of the car because you hurried.

Even if the railroad track crosses at right angles to the road, be careful—some crossings are extremely rough. Reduce the stress on your bicycle by rising slightly out of the saddle, knees and elbows bent to absorb some of the shock. Also, watch for metal flanges that can slice big gashes in your tires. And remember that wet railroad tracks are extremely slippery.

Cattle guards. Cyclists in the West are all too familiar with these wheel-jolting contrivances. Easterners often stop in open-jawed amazement the first time they see one.

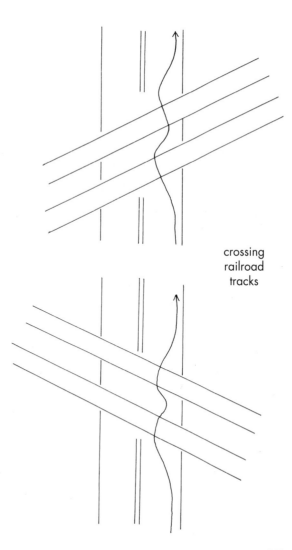

crossing railroad tracks

Cattle guards, or grates, are parallel metal bars spaced several inches apart, crossing the entire road from shoulder to shoulder. The grating is usually several feet wide, with a two-foot-deep trench beneath it. Hoofed animals such as cattle won't cross it for fear of getting their feet trapped. Wheeled animals such as cyclists are usually just as intimidated on first encounter.

Unlike railroad tracks, the trick to crossing cattle guards is keeping up your speed, especially on newer guards that use flat-topped I-beams instead of round rods. Too slowly and you'll be bounced to death as your wheels go thump-thump-thump from one bar to the next. If it's really rough, dismount and walk, but be careful not to twist an ankle.

Some cattle guards use bars that aren't as long as the road is wide, with joints in the middle of the lane. Watch for these; they often have gaps that are the perfect width to eat your wheels. Also, as

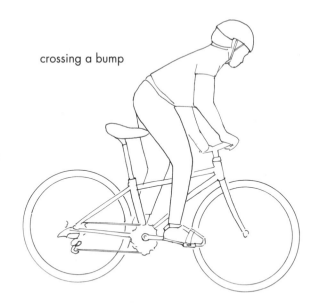

crossing a bump

with railroad tracks, rising out of the saddle, knees bent to absorb shock, reduces wear and tear on your bike. This also goes for speed bumps, chuck holes, and rumble strips, and any other potentially damaging bump.

Rumble strips. Rumble strips are the bane of Midwestern cycling, though they can be found wherever road surfaces are made of concrete rather than asphalt. A series of closely spaced seams cut crosswise into the concrete, rumble strips mark hazards such as stop signs or warn drivers that they are straying onto the shoulder. At 55 mph, they make car tires buzz loudly enough to catch the attention of dozing motorists. On a bicycle, they seem to vibrate every bolt loose from your frame.

An occasional set of rumble strips is merely a nuisance. If the road engineers were thinking of bicyclists, they may even have left a gap for you on the shoulder. Rumble strips designed to keep traffic from straying onto the shoulder, however, also force you out into the traffic lane. That can make the traffic hostile, since the drivers can't figure out why you aren't using that nice, wide shoulder. Find an alternative route.

Drain gratings and manhole covers. Most modern drain gratings are cross-hatched or turned sideways to keep your wheels from dropping in. But don't let this lull you into complacency. Not all storm sewers are so bicycle friendly, and all of them, along with manhole covers and any other metal object, can be slippery when wet. Avoid them if traffic conditions allow.

TRAINING

▼

There is no ideal, one-size-fits-all training method. What works when you're 25 might not work when you're 45, and the best training for a week of van-supported touring in the Midwest may not be ideal for a self-contained expedition through the mountains.

Training is a process of experimentation. Don't wed yourself to anyone's training schedule—including the one presented here. One of the most important components of training is learning to listen to your own body's ways of conveying such information as: *I'm feeling great, it's time to move on to the next step*, or *You've been pushing too hard for a week; if you don't take a break soon, I'll force you to*.

What follows is a basic training strategy to take you from a long winter layoff to a tour of a week or more. Set your goals according to how much previous cycling experience you've had. It's just common sense that if you're so new to the sport that you can't imagine pedaling 10 miles, let alone 50 to 100, don't target an 80-mile-a-day tour by the end of your first season. Go ahead and plan a tour, but keep the distance shorter.

Spring Training

If you're fortunate enough to live where you can ride year round, getting in shape after a winter lay-off isn't an issue. But if you live in colder, snowier northern climes, the first weeks of spring can make you feel as though you're beginning all over again from scratch. And if you've taken a long layoff for some other reason, or are just beginning the sport, begin with a spring-training regimen regardless of the season.

The basic rule of spring training is to ease back into cycling. Gentle, rapid spinning is the name of the game. Avoid the temptation to race other cyclists and, if possible, avoid big hills, especially for the first month or so. If you can't dodge the hills, go at them gently until you've toughened up not only your muscles but your tendons and ligaments as well. If something starts to hurt, back off immediately; it's too early in the season to be macho.

Some cyclists advise staying in this spinning mode until you've accumulated at least 1,000 miles, but unless you bike a lot, that could take

months. A better rule is to keep your training gentle until you've put in at least 20% to 30% of last year's mileage. (If this is your first year of serious cycling, stay in spinning mode for at least the first 500 miles.)

If you're starting up after a total layoff of more than a few weeks, your first few trips should be very short. Use the first three weeks to get reacquainted with your bicycle. When I lived in a climate where five-month winter layoffs were the norm, my spring training began as follows:

- Week 1. No more than three days of riding and no distance over 5 miles. No riding on back-to-back days.

- Week 2. No more than four days of riding, with one longer ride of 7 to 10 miles.

- Week 3. Extend the long ride to 15 miles, ride five days if desired, and bring the total weekly mileage up to about 35.

- Week 4 and beyond. Increase mileage gradually, no faster than 10% to 20% per week. Even at 10% per week, you can double your mileage in seven weeks; at 15% you can double it in five. Repeated weekly increases of more than 15% aren't recommended.

This is conservative—more conservative than some people may need. But if you "blow out a knee" in the first month of training, you'll lose not only the time it takes to recover, but all your spring training as well. Be cautious those first weeks in March, April, or May, so you can be riding full-steam in July and August.

Base Training

Your spring training goal should be to gradually build up to a weekly mileage that will allow you to take longer day rides or easy weekend tours without additional training. You could do the build-up in stages, stopping at one level for a few weeks before increasing to a higher level, again at no more than 10% to 15% per week. Once you've reached your desired weekly mileage, the process of maintaining it is what I call "base training."

What is the appropriate mileage base? There's no easy answer because factors such as age, experience, and susceptibility to overuse injuries play a major role. But if your goal is simply to *complete* a long, single-day ride or a two-day self-contained tour in reasonable comfort (as opposed to doing so quickly), you can manage quite well if your weekly mileage is at least 125% of the distance of the ride or weekend tour. In other words, 125 miles a week of training will support a single-day, 100-mile ride or a two-day self-contained tour of 100 miles—probably with a comfortable margin of error. If you're young, have a lot of cycling experience, a comfortable saddle, and never-say-die knees, you may be able to get away with a lot less.

But just racking up the mileage isn't enough. You can accumulate 105 miles a week by doing 15 miles every day, but that won't prepare you as well for a 70-mile trip as doing less total mileage but getting in an occasional ride of at least 40 miles. You need to train for endurance and long periods of time in the saddle.

Table 1 suggests schedules for weekly mileages of 50, 75, 100, 125, and 150. You could build schedules for other distances along the same pattern. There is nothing magic about the precise daily distances, but these base-training schedules do follow a few rules:

1 Use a hard/easy pattern, with hard days followed by recovery days. This is important, especially early in the season. Recovery is part of training, though a short, easy ride the day after a particularly hard one can speed recovery by working the kinks out of your legs.

2 Take at least one rest day a week. Riding every day is the road to burn-out, injury, or divorce.

3 For longer weekly distances, I've included 1 to 2 days a week of optional speed training. Do these only if you want to increase your speed. One workout is labeled "interval," the other is labeled "pace." Interval training entails repeated short sprints of up to 2 to 4 minutes. Find a way to make it fun by charging hills, dashing to stoplights, or impulsively deciding to go as hard as you can for a mile. The speed part of these workouts should total about 10 to 15 minutes.

"Pace" workouts are longer, not at a sprint but faster than your normal touring speed. The purpose is increasing the speed you can maintain over distances of 5 to 10 miles.

If you don't want speed workouts, there's no

Table 1. Base Training Schedule

Weekly Mileage	Day 1	2	3	4	5	6	7
50	10	rest	10	5	rest	25	rest
75	18	rest	10	7	rest	35	5
100	24	rest	8(I)	10	rest	50	8
125	23	10	10(I)	12	rest	60	10
150	20	10(I)	15	15(P)	rest	75	15

I = interval training (optional)   P = pace training (optional)

obligation. Take the speed days as easy ones and do the mileage at your normal pace.

A few other important tips:

1 Be flexible. If there's a gale blowing, you're hosting a dinner party, or you just plain don't feel like cycling, take a rest day and adjust your schedule accordingly.

2 If you're not a schedule person in the rest of your life, don't force yourself to become one for cycling. Just try to get in one long ride a week, with easy days after hard workouts. As long as you keep your weekly mileage reasonably close to your target, you'll do fine.

3 Keep at least a minimal training diary. A wall calendar near where you park your bike is perfect. Jot down the distance pedaled, and keep track of weekly totals to make sure you're not increasing too quickly. If you develop an ache or pain, write it on the calendar with a brief explanation. If the ailment goes away on its own, this is reassuring; if it doesn't, the training diary may provide useful clues.

4 Don't pedal if you're sick, and don't try to make up for the lost mileage later. And yes, having a cold counts as being sick, at least for the first few days.

5 Begin all workouts with 5 to 10 minutes of easy spinning as a warm up. Conventional sports-medicine wisdom recommends doing the same at the end of the ride, but unless you finish with a sprint or a big hill, this isn't necessary on the laid-back rides that provide the best training for touring.

6 If you shift training patterns even without changing your weekly mileage, do so gradually. This is particularly important if you're adding long rides, hills, or speed workouts. Don't make major changes here if you're also increasing your weekly mileage.

7 Even if training for speed is one of your goals, do most of your training at an easy pace. This reduces overuse injuries and builds up endurance. Most cyclists defeat themselves by training too fast.

8 If you're new to athletics and aren't sure you know an easy training pace from a killer one, you can find out with a pulse monitor or by counting your pulse. For touring, at least 90% of your training should be at a low level, perhaps even as low as 60% to 65% of your maximum heartbeat, determined from the following equation:

Maximum heart rate = N – (your age)

For men, N is 220. For women, it's 226. If you're a 35-year-old woman, for example, your maximum pulse rate is 226 minus 35, or 191. A training pulse rate of 60% to 70% of this would be 115 to 133 (about 19 to 22 beats per 10 seconds). A coach of elite distance runners says that the pulse rates of his athletes vary dramatically. Some people's pulses head for 180 the moment they tie their shoes. Others' stay low even on sprints. Target pulse rates are guides, not straightjackets. The ideal training pace is slower than you probably think. Realize that this measures a level of effort, not a speed in miles per hour, and that as you get in better shape, you'll go faster with the same effort.

Pulse monitors and charts of target pulse rates are racer gadgetry you don't need for touring. A cheaper and more natural approach is to develop an intuitive feel for how hard you're working. Are you gasping for breath? Slow down unless you're in the last seconds of a speed interval. Do you feel strong and able to go faster? Go for it, unless it's too early in the season. Are you chugging along at a good clip but still able to maintain a reasonably normal conversation? That's probably your ideal long-distance training pace. The charts and gadgets will tell you these same things a bit more precisely, but the purpose of touring is to relax and explore, not to shave an extra minute off your time in a 10-mile time trial.

Training for a Tour

Once you've maintained your base training for a few weeks, you're ready to start preparing for a tour longer than a weekend.

This doesn't take any special training if the average daily distance will be no more than 25% to 35% of your weekly base-training mileage (40% to 50% if you've got a van to carry your baggage), and the terrain is gentle. Your base training should be sufficient. But if the terrain is strenuous or daily distances are longer, focus your training on preparing for the tour. Increase your mileage (as before, no faster than about 10% to 15% per week) and change the hard/easy training pattern.

The key to this approach lies in phasing in a pair of long rides on consecutive days. This toughens your legs and rear end for day-after-day riding, extending your comfortable touring distance significantly. At the beginning of this training schedule, a week-long self-contained tour of more than 25 to 35 miles a day might be a strain. At the end, 60 to 85 miles a day should be achievable, depending on the terrain and how much baggage you carry.

This schedule has no speed workouts. They're not much use for self-contained touring, though you may want them for van-supported or organized tours if keeping up with faster riders is one of your goals. If so, do a speed workout on one of the short-mileage days such as Day 3 or Day 4. Or invest one of these days in a hill workout.

On your long rides, try to duplicate the conditions you expect to find on tour. If you'll be touring in heat, train at midday. If you'll be touring in mountains, do your long rides in hilly terrain. (If no hills are available, try going back and forth over freeway overpasses. Dull, but it's a good workout.) If you're not used to either heat or hills, phase them in over the course of several weeks, to let your body adjust gradually.

Training on the tour. Oddly, tours longer than one week require less training than shorter ones because you can do a substantial amount of training on the road. A transcontinental rider, for example, might start out at 25 to 30 miles a day, gradually building up to daily distances of 50, 60, 70,

Table 2. Focused Training Schedule

Week	Day 1	2	3	4	5	6	7	Total Miles
Base	18	rest	10	7	rest	35	5	75
1	rest	12	10	7	rest	40	15	84
2	rest	10	7	10	rest	45	21	93
3	rest	13	5	10	rest	45	30	103
4	rest	13	5	10	rest	50	35	113
5	rest	14	5	10	rest	55	40	124
6	rest	16	5	11	rest	60	45	137
7	rest	20	5	20	rest	60	45	150

Above is a conservative, seven-week schedule for doubling your training mileage, and more than doubling the distance you can comfortably tour. It assumes that you begin at a weekly base of 75 miles, using the training pattern in Table 1. Adjust the numbers proportionately if you start from a different base mileage, and feel free to stop before reaching Week 7 if 150-mile weeks are more than you need. Because this training pattern is more demanding—both on the body and on the social life—than the base-training pattern, I don't recommend substituting it indefinitely for base training. Save it for when you're planning a major tour.

TOSRV photo by Greg Siple

or even 80 miles. This doesn't work on short tours because it takes about a week for the training to take effect. Another way to train for a self-contained tour is to take a multi-day organized tour sometime in the month beforehand.

Training with full panniers. Some people recommend doing at least part of your training with loaded paniers. In theory this is good advice, but carrying around all that weight simply for the practice isn't my idea of fun.

Training Through the Winter

Spring training is much easier if you can do even a modicum of off-season training. That's also the only way to train for a spring tour.

If you live in California, the Pacific Northwest, or south of the Mason-Dixon line, you can maintain a mileage base of 30 to 50 miles a week through most of the winter. But if the good weather is erratic, don't overdo it. Stay in spring training mode: easy spinning, no hills, moderate distances. In three days of January thaw you can't make up for the previous month of winter.

Cross training or using an indoor trainer can also extend the cycling season.

Cross training. Cross training simply means taking up another sport. Any aerobic activity will help, but the best ones are those that use your bicycling muscles. Hiking or backpacking are superb, particularly when they involve "putting on the brakes" walking down big hills. Cross-country skiing is nearly as effective and has the advantage that the best conditions for it are precisely those under which bicycling is least practical.

Indoor trainers. Valuable as cross training is, athletes in any sport know that nothing trains you for a sport better than the sport itself. A number of companies sell devices that convert your bicycle into a stationary exercise bike. Some allow you to set the bicycle on rollers; others use the rear wheel to drive fan blades or magnets.

Rollers provide the most realistic simulation, but can be scary because it's easy to steer off them and

Commuting

Bike commuting is another superb way to extend the season, as well as painlessly accumulate training mileage during the summer. Not only is it environmentally sound and economical, but a 5-mile commute can add 50 miles a week to your training.

Most touring bikes make good commuter bikes. And by happy coincidence, most of the modifications you've made to adapt your bicycle for touring—thornproof inserts, fenders, luggage rack—are also useful for commuting.

Some hardy people manage to commute even through the winter. The biggest problems other than frostbite are snow and icy streets. You can buy (or make) studded tires or tire chains, or on the worst days, wimp out and ride a bus. If you live in a part of the country where they salt the roads, use an inexpensive junker bike until the spring rains have washed away the salt.

crash. Wear a helmet. Wind turbines and magnetic devices mount the bicycle on a much more stable stand, but some models, particularly of wind trainers, are noisy. Try muffling them with towels stuffed under the base.

Indoor trainers, sadly, aren't a panacea for the winter training doldrums. They can provide a good workout, but indoor riding is boring. Watch television, listen to music, or (except on rollers, which probably require too much concentration) read a book or magazine. Put the book on a music stand or search bike shops for a reading rack that hooks to your handlebars. Overheating is also a problem. Sit near a fan or keep a towel handy.

Even equipped with a reading stand, a TV, and a fan, you may find it hard to maintain the discipline to ride indoors through the entire winter. But you can still use an indoor trainer to get a head start on the spring or to practice increasing your cadence without the complications of terrain, wind, and traffic.

Keeping the Fun in Training

Training should be fun. Don't turn it into just another chore. Find several low-hassle, traffic-free routes near home, vary distances, and don't always ride loops in the same direction. And don't be a fanatic about getting in the "right" mileage. If Tuesday's supposed to be a 10-mile day, it really doesn't matter if it's 7 or 13.

Whether you ride solo, with a small group, or with a club is up to you, but riding with friends helps keep training rides fresh and new. It also takes some of the misery out of headwinds by giving you an opportunity to draft. If you are a loner by nature, though, don't be afraid to train solo. Just make sure you have a repair kit and telephone money in case you break down.

When picking training partners, find people of approximately your own ability. You don't want to be always struggling to keep up, but neither do you want to be stopping to wait at the top of every hill. Don't be afraid to ride occasionally with people who are slightly better than you, though. You'll learn useful skills, and if you want to increase your speed, there are few quicker ways.

Use weekends to explore the rural countryside near your home. Here's where bike clubs really come into their own. In most parts of the country, any summer weekend brings a century ride (100 miles), metric century (62 miles), half century (50 miles), or metric half century (31 miles) within easy driving distance. For a few dollars, these rides provide maps, snacks, scenic low-traffic routes, and the camaraderie of riders of a wide range of skills and speed.

Century routes are often marked with arrows spray painted on the pavement using a system known as Dan Henrys, in honor of its inventor. Usually, these use a circle with a line coming out of its top to indicate right turn, left turn, or straight ahead; occasionally the circle is replaced by some other symbol. Even if you don't ride the tour, these markers can guide you to wonderful byways that you'd never have found by yourself.

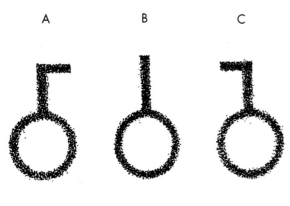

Dan Henrys

Stretching and Weight Lifting

Stretching is an important but frequently overlooked part of training. It needn't be time consuming; 10 minutes on each of your hard workout days will help prevent injuries and make riding more enjoyable.

Don't bounce when stretching. A sudden stretch makes the muscle think it's about to be hyperextended, and it protects itself by reflexively contracting. The bouncing toe-touchers and other calisthenic stretches we were taught as children merely fight that reflexive contraction. They can also pull a muscle.

Proper stretches are static. That means stretching slowly until you feel a pleasant pull to the muscle (not pain). Hold that position for 10 to 15 seconds, trying to relax the muscle, then cautiously extend the stretch farther, always being prepared to back off.

Certain once-popular stretches are major no-nos. Toe-touchers are one of these; they're hard on the back. Also taboo is the traditional "hurdler's stretch" in which you sit on your heels and lean backward to stretch the quadriceps (the big muscles in the front of the thigh). This does indeed stretch the quadriceps, but it also stresses the knee.

Stretching for cycling involves limbering up the upper body and counteracting the tendency of the leg muscles to become tighter and less flexible as they gain strength. For the upper body, use any gentle stretches that come naturally and feel good. What really matters are the legs. Some version of the following should form the core of your routine:

Calf stretch. Stand in front of a wall and lean forward, palms on the wall. Holding this position, move the left leg one to two feet behind you, foot flat on the ground. Shifting most of your weight to the other leg, dip the left knee until you feel a good stretch in the calf.

Hamstring stretch. Sit on a flat surface with one leg extended, the other comfortably out of the way (don't sit on your heel; that's hard on the knee). Without locking the knee, lean toward the extended leg, feeling the stretch in the hamstring.

Quadriceps stretch (modified hurdler). Women will find this stretch less effective than men, especially if they are already flexible. Sit on a flat surface, leaning to one side, bracing yourself with your hand. Bend one leg at a comfortable angle, out of the way. Bend the one you're going to stretch approximately 90° to the side, laying it flat on the floor, out to your side. The thigh should be more or less in line with your torso. This position should feel reasonably comfortable, if a bit odd.

To stretch the quadriceps, push forward with your hip and drag the lower leg backward, directly in the line in which it is pointing. *Don't* pull the foot toward your buttocks because that stresses the knee.

A similar stretch can be done standing on one leg. Steady yourself against a wall with one hand, grab your free leg by the ankle or shin and pull it backward, more or less horizontally, stretching the quadriceps. As with the sitting version, don't pull the foot upward toward your buttocks.

To learn more about stretching, check into the running literature (runners are far ahead of cyclists in this arena), or talk to a health club trainer.

Weight Lifting

If you've ever seen photos of bicycle racers, you may have noticed that those folks have *arms* as well as legs. That upper body strength comes from lifting weights, and it helps them control their bicycles in crosswinds and to hold themselves above the handlebars for hours on end—the same things you're going to be doing. Strong arms and shoulders are also useful for hill climbing.

Though not essential, weight lifting can be helpful. All you need is a half-hour workout three times a week. Unless you're interested in racing, you needn't work on power lifts with the legs. Concentrate on strengthening the upper body with bench presses, lat pulls, curls and triceps extensions. Also work on the abdominals, since this can prevent lower back pain. Incidentally, sit-ups are passé; "crunches" (imagine a half-hearted sit-up; see page 82) are now in vogue. You might also want to strengthen your hands for gripping the brakes on long descents.

If you have access to weight equipment, hopefully you also have access to a trainer to show you the right way to use it and recommend exercises. Remember that your goal is toning, not bulking up. That means you'll be doing larger numbers of repetitions at lighter weights—perhaps two or three sets of 15 exercises on each piece of equipment.

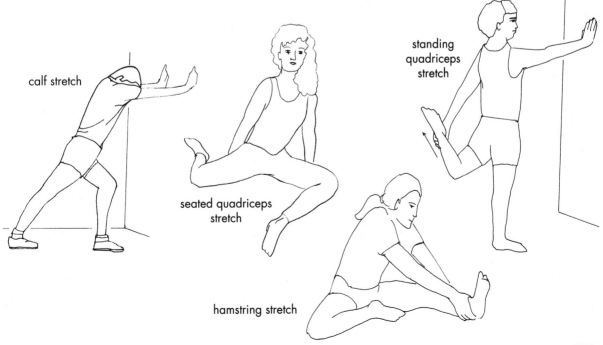

calf stretch

seated quadriceps stretch

standing quadriceps stretch

hamstring stretch

ACHES
AND PAINS

▼

Because it isn't a contact sport and doesn't involve repeated pounding of the joints like running or basketball, bicycling is relatively injury-free. The biggest risk of serous injury is from crashes or auto accidents, and that can be greatly reduced by wearing a helmet.

It's a rare cyclist, though, who never experiences discomfort from saddle sores, knee pain, a crick in the neck, bee stings, or an occasional fall. How many injuries you encounter depends on your body's biomechanics and on the style with which you approach any new endeavor. Enthusiasm is good, but temper it with common sense, especially when it comes to taking a few days' rest when needed. It will reduce the amount of time you spend on injured reserve and reduce the risk of converting a simple injury into a chronic, recurring weakness.

This chapter will examine a few of the more common problems, discuss possible treatments, and consider ways to reduce the chances of recurrence—sometimes very simply. Be aware, though, that self-diagnosis always runs the risk of error. If pain is severe, recurring, or continues despite your best efforts at treatment, consult a doctor.

Common Injuries

Sore Knee

Knee problems are one of the most common cycling injuries. Unlike the injuries that afflict football players, however, cyclists's knee pain is more likely to be an overuse injury than a cartilage or ligament tear requiring surgery. Unless you have a preexisting condition or twist your knee in a fall, the most likely diagnoses are tendonitis of the big tendons above or below the kneecap or chrondomalacia, an inflammation of the back of the kneecap.

Treatment. At the first twinge, ease off and downshift. If you're lucky, the pain was just a warning. If it continues, stop and take an anti-inflammatory such as aspirin or ibuprofen. Do not take more than the total daily recommended dose, especially for ibuprofen, without first consulting a doctor. Ibuprofen overdoses have been linked to kidney failure, and your kidneys are already being taxed by the dehydration that accompanies heavy exertion.

At the end of the day, ice the knee for 10 to 20 minutes. If it's swollen, hurts when you're off the bicycle, or hurts when you get on again the next day, you need a few days' rest or greatly reduced mileage.

Prevention. Knee pain is usually associated with five things: (1) riding in too high a gear; (2) misadjusted cleats; (3) undertraining; (4) wrong seat height; and (5) a muscle imbalance in the quadriceps. Cold weather also contributes.

If you think seat height is the problem, chances are you need to raise it, beginning with only a couple of millimeters. But don't rule out the possibility of lowering it; experimentation is the best approach.

Weight lifting is another line of defense, particularly early in the season. Strengthen the quadriceps by doing leg extensions on a weight machine, but confine the weight lifting to the top 45 degrees of the knee's range of motion. You don't need heavy weights. Pick one that allows you to do three sets of 15 repetitions three times a week without straining.

If your problem is a muscle imbalance in the quadriceps, however, leg extensions may only

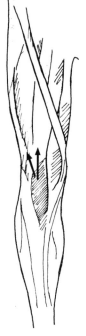

Patello-femoral malalignment.

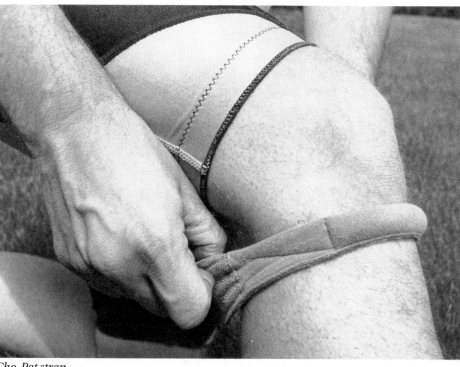

Cho-Pat strap.

make it worse. Suspect this problem if you have recurring bouts of knee pain with no other obvious explanation. It's called *patello-femoral malalignment*, and comes about because the outside portion of the quadriceps is more developed than the inside portion. This causes the kneecap to track diagonally as the strong part of the muscle pulls it sideways, creating the pain. Formal diagnosis requires an expert eye, but the solutions are simple enough to attempt on your own.

To begin with, find something to help hold the kneecap in proper position. One possibility is a neoprene brace with reinforced holes in the center (the ones without the hole, are designed for a different purpose). A simpler device, one brand of which is called Cho-Pat, is a thin padded strap that wraps around the knee just below the kneecap, fastened with Velcro. Pull it tight; its purpose is to clamp down on the tendon, preventing the kneecap from wandering. If the Velcro chafes, wear tights or put something under it.

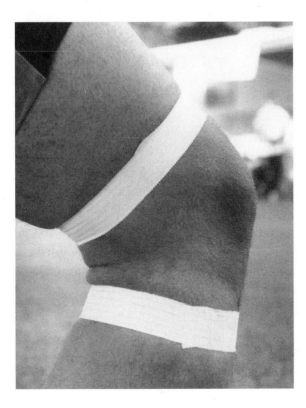

The third alternative is to wrap two bands of surgical tape around the leg, one about 4 inches above the kneecap, the other 3 to 4 inches below it. The lower band functions much like a Cho-Pat strap. The upper one should be put on with the knee bent at about 90 degrees, not so snugly that it digs into your leg when you pedal, but tightly enough that squatting is uncomfortable. To keep the tape from digging uncomfortably into your hamstring, pad it in back with a piece of gauze. You might also want to shave your legs. Because the long-term effects of this type of taping aren't well understood, it's wisest to use it only when really needed.

None of these methods will cure the underlying imbalance. That requires special exercises in your regular training routine. If you forget them, your knee pain will probably return.

Use simple straight-leg lifts, starting with no added weight and slowly building up to 10-pound ankle weights. Don't start with too much weight or the strong part of the muscle will take over from the weak part, making the imbalance worse. Once you've worked up to 10 pounds, graduate to leg extensions on weight machines or add more ankle weights. As with many leg exercises, locking the knee is unwise. Since the purpose is to exercise the quadriceps, not the hip flexor, prop your thigh up with something or sit on a table. Because boredom will be a major factor, rig a comfortable way to read or watch television.

Pain Behind the Knee

This is probably inflammation of the tendons at the base of the hamstring. This tendonitis is uncommon and much less incapacitating than front-of-the-knee problems.

Treatment. Anti-inflammatories, ice.

Prevention. Consider lowering your seat. Do hamstring stretches.

Back Pain

You may have heard that the human back wasn't made to stand erect. Neither was it made to spend all day hunched over handlebars. That said, bicycling is nevertheless a relatively gentle sport for bad backs. Unless you spend your time doing gonzo trail riding over outrageously bumpy surfaces or take a back flip onto a rock, the problems you encounter are more likely to be nuisances than long-term incapacitations.

Treatment. Take frequent rest breaks, do gentle torso rolls to stretch out the kinks, and try to eliminate the cause.

Prevention. The classic solution is to strengthen your abdominal muscles, and one way to do this is with "crunches" in which you lie on your back, knees bent, feet flat on the floor. Initially, the exercise is almost static, as you tighten your stomach muscles and flatten your spine against the floor. As you gain strength, curl your head and shoulders upward to increase the resistance.

Also check your bicycle for misadjustments. A seat that's too high, too far forward, or too far back impacts your back. So can one that tips forward, throwing your weight onto your shoulders and upper back. Handlebars that are too low have also been implicated, as have aero bars, which trap you into an even lower position.

A likely cause of early-season back pain is over-training. Ease off the mileage, keep up your cadence, and cut down on hills or speed workouts, phasing them in again *slowly* when your back recovers. Other ways to reduce back problems are:

- Change your hand position frequently.
- Buy a different stem.
- Avoid extremely bumpy surfaces.
- Get bar extenders (for straight handlebars).

If all else fails, you might need a different bike. No amount of adjustment can compensate for the wrong frame size. Or you might want to switch from a road bike to a mountain bike (or vice versa)—or even to a recumbent.

Recumbent bicycle.

Hand and Arm Problems

Tingling, burning, numbness, or a going-to-sleep sensation in the fingers or palms of the hands is caused by pressure on a nerve. It comes from extended hours of leaning on the handlebars or from road shocks transmitted through the bike into your hands. Similar problems in the elbow can produce the same sensations in the lower arm. Because these problems can become increasingly severe over the course of a season or with the accumulated wear and tear of many years on a bike, don't just ignore them and hope they'll go away.

Treatment. Shift positions frequently. To restore life to tingling fingers, periodically stretch the affected arm behind you, backward and upward as far as you can, opening and closing your fist several times. You can do this on the bike without missing a pedal stroke.

Prevention. Padding, padding, and more padding—though some people, especially those with small hands, will find that an overly bulky cushion will itself make them uncomfortable.

Start with gel-filled cycling gloves; buy the cushiest ones you can find. If that's not enough, try wearing an old, stretched-out pair over a new one. Padded handlebar covers also help. In order of increasing padding, try: (1) cork-backed winding tape, (2) padded handlebar covers such as Grab-Ons, or (3) a homemade super-cushion made from a piece cut from an old closed-cell foam sleeping pad, wrapped around the handlebars and held tightly in place with strapping tape or handlebar winding tape.

On the road, your arms should be bent, not locked at the elbows, and you shouldn't have a death grip on the handlebars. Hold on tightly enough to keep control. If you see rough pavement coming, momentarily shift some of your weight off your arms to reduce the shock.

Other solutions:

- Shift hand position frequently.
- Don't tilt your saddle too far forward.
- Raise the handlebars.
- Buy a taller stem or one with less reach.

Nerve pain in your hands is mostly a road-bike problem. Even more than with back pain, switching to straight handlebars or a recumbent bicycle should produce a near-complete cure.

Neck Pain

Neck pain is often a beginner's problem that will pass with training. It can also be a problem if you're not used to the weight of a helmet.

Treatment. Neck rubs, massages, and elimination of the cause. For short-term relief, vary the angle at which you hold your head. Also, sit back or stop occasionally to do slow, languid head rolls. Continued pain, severe pain, or pain that radiates down the arms is a sign that it's time to put your bicycle away for a while and talk to a doctor.

Prevention. Get used to wearing a helmet on all rides, not just occasionally. If your helmet is old, get a newer, lighter one.

Check your riding posture. If you tend to let your chest drop toward the handlebars with your shoulder blades pinched back, you're asking for neck problems. Even when you're tucked low over the handlebars, your shoulder blades should be flat or even dropped a bit toward your arms, not unnaturally veed out like the upswept wings of a bird.

If you're camping, vary what you use for a pillow. Your crick in the neck may have nothing to do with bicycling.

If the problem is recurring, neck-strengthening exercises may be the answer, but consult a doctor or sports trainer first.

Achilles Tendonitis

The Achilles tendon is the big tendon at the back of the ankle. Stiff, inflexible calf muscles or over-vigorous training can put too much stress on it, causing pain or inflammation. Generally, the discomfort is at its worst when you're off your bicycle, especially in the morning. As you ride, it moderates, misleading you into believing you aren't hurting the tendon.

Mild Achilles tendonitis may clear up on its own. More severe cases, which can produce a grating sensation every time you flex your foot, often get progressively worse.

Treatment. Anti-inflammatories, ice, and reduced training or complete rest. Calf stretching, described on page 76, can help prevent you from losing flexibility as the tendon heals, but keep it gentle. Foam heel lifts, available in drug stores are also useful. They won't do you much good on the bicycle, but they'll take tension off the tendon when you walk, speeding recovery. They're thin, so you might need more than one; use the same number on each leg to keep your stride balanced.

Tendons heal slowly, but mild cases can clear up in a few days. More severe ones can take weeks to months, and very severe cases (rare among cyclists) require surgery. So if you get a mild case, rest it now, before it becomes intractable.

Prevention. Religious calf stretching.

Chafing and Saddle Sores

There are three types of saddle sores: bruises (particularly where the pelvis hits the saddle), chafing, and skin infections. All can be extremely painful, rapidly turning your bicycle from friend to enemy.

Treatment. Find the source of the rubbing and eliminate it. Since sweat is often one of the culprits, a moisture-absorbant powder may help. Medicated powders for athlete's foot or jock itch can also reduce the risk of infection, as can over-the-counter antiseptic/antibacterial ointments, which may also provide a lubricating effect. Covering the sore with a bandage may also reduce further chafing—though it can be difficult to apply bandages to the places that are most prone to chafing. If your problem is bruising, there's no treatment other than a few days' rest.

Prevention. Spend some money on a comfortable saddle and good cycling shorts.

Other ways to avoid saddle sores:

- Use a nylon saddle cover to reduce friction against the saddle.
- Get a gel-filled seat cushion.
- Smear abrasion-prone areas with petroleum jelly before they start to chafe, though this is controversial. The problem is that this may increase the risk of infection by trapping bacteria.
- Ride without underwear.

Numbness or Burning in Groin or Legs

This means your saddle is putting pressure on a nerve.

Treatment. Stand occasionally on the pedals to relieve the pressure. Take more rest breaks.

Prevention. Padded cycling shorts, friendlier saddle, gel-filled seat cushion.

Gender-Specific Problems: Bruised Testicles

This isn't common, but can happen on long rides, particularly riding without underwear in hot, humid weather.

Treatment. Tilt your seat farther forward, put on tight-fitting underwear, and get off the bicycle as soon as possible. You'll probably feel fine in the morning.

Prevention. Wear bikini-style sports briefs for support without too much risk of chafing. Don't point the tip of your saddle too far upward.

Prostatitis

Male cyclists are also prone to prostate infections because, as one internist once told me, "you're sitting on the damn thing all day." Symptoms are frequent urges to urinate, itching or burning when you do so, generalized discomfort of the prostate region, and possibly blood in the urine.

Treatment. Antibiotics.

Prevention. If prostate discomfort is a problem, tilt the saddle a bit farther downward or slide it forward and sit farther back on the wider part. This position will put more weight on your pelvis where it belongs.

Female Genital Problems

According to two women cyclists I know, both with long-distance touring experience, the most likely problems are chafing and yeast infections.

Prevention. One of my friends suggested wearing panty liners, changing them once or twice a day. My other friend thought that was a terrible idea; obviously it doesn't work for everyone. Other suggestions are equipment oriented: tilt your seat slightly forward and get a women's saddle and cycling shorts. To prevent yeast infections, be scrupulous about keeping your cycling shorts clean. On tour, take at least two pairs, washing one each evening. Lash the wet one inside out on top of your baggage, where the sun's ultraviolet rays will at least partially sterilize it as it dries.

Bites and Stings

Ticks
These nasty critters hide in bushes and trees waiting for you to brush by. They can also drop on you from above, so it's possible to pick one up without ever leaving the road.

Treatment. First-aid books are full of suggestions for getting rid of ticks. Smear them with salve to block their breathing holes, burn their behinds with a recently snuffed-out match, poison them by dabbing them with petroleum products. The theory is that the tick will let go, seeking a more hospitable abode. Most would probably rather die. More likely, you'll wind up pulling the tick out, firmly but gently. If the wound becomes infected or the tick's head breaks off in it, see a doctor.

Lyme disease is a potentially crippling ailment carried by a very tiny tick, roughly the size of the head of a pin. If you get low-grade cold or flu-like symptoms and a rash, see a doctor, even if you don't remember a tick bite. Lyme disease ticks are so small they can bite you and escape unseen, but the disease is easily treatable by antibiotics if caught early.

Prevention. Ticks like to bite in tight places like the elastic band of your cycling shorts or the back of your hand, under your gloves. Check yourself over at least once a day, especially when camping in brushy areas. Ticks usually crawl over you for hours before deciding where to bite, so you're likely to catch most of them before they chomp down.

Bees
Imagine a honey bee, doing its thing on a sunny spring day. Suddenly, *wham,* it gets splattered by a spoked, two-wheeled behemoth. The bee's instinctive reaction is to apply its dying energy to stinging this strange aggressor. Your reaction is to yell and try to brush it away before it gets a chance.

Sometimes you win, sometimes the bee does.

Treatment. If the stinger's still in you, don't just grab it and pull; you may squeeze more venom into the wound. Scrape it away with a pocket knife, credit card, whatever's handy. If you're far from help, have been stung more than once, or have any concern about allergic reactions, take an antihistamine immediately, at the maximum dose recommended by the label. For topical relief, a product called StingEze is remarkable. Carry it in your first aid kit. Tingling or numbness around the mouth, sneezing, watery eyes, itching, tightness in the chest, breathing difficulty, swelling or itching in the mouth or throat, or passing out are signs of severe allergic reaction. See a doctor immediately.

Prevention. Clothing hampers the bee, increasing your chances of being able to flick it away before it stings. If there are a lot of bees around, wear tights and a long-sleeved shirt or jacket. Goggles or glasses reduce the chances of being stung around the eyes.

If you're allergic, carry your medication with you, and consider investing in a faring (a bicycle windscreen, much like the ones used on motorcycles). If you're severely allergic to anything, and don't know about bees, consult a doctor before hitting the road.

Dogs
Canines are the most feared of biting animals, but dog bite is actually rather rare.

Treatment. You may need a tetanus shot, so plan on an emergency room visit. Meanwhile, wash the wound as best you can, swab it with an antibiotic, and find out who owns the dog. It might need to be impounded even if it's had a rabies shot.

Prevention. See page 64.

Other Biting Creatures
Snakes, scorpions, and spiders are frightening but low-probability biters more strongly associated with camping than with cycling.

Treatment. Stay calm, get a good description of the creature that bit you, and hitch a ride to a doctor. Have someone call ahead so the doctor is prepared.

Prevention. Caution is the rule of thumb. Watch where you put your feet, don't reach under rocks or logs, and know the difference between poisonous and non-poisonous snakes. Likewise be careful rummaging around old buildings or wood-piles that might house spiders. Camping in the desert, be aware that scorpions look for cool shady places to spend the heat of the day. To dislodge any that might have taken refuge in your shoes (if you don't keep them in your tent), tap them on the ground before putting them on.

Heat Exhaustion and Sunstroke

These are two very different ailments brought on by overexertion and hot weather, possibly combined with dehydration.

Sunstroke can kill, though it is rare in well-trained athletes. It happens if your body's cooling mechanism overloads to the point of quitting. Sunstroke victims feel feverish to the touch and stop perspiring. They may also be disoriented, so if you ask someone if he's feeling OK, don't take an incoherent answer for "yes."

To check for the early signs of sunstroke, touch the back of the victim's neck, feeling for perspiration. Hot and dry means stop exercising *now*. Get the victim into the shade if possible, loosen his clothing, and splash him with water to cool him off (you don't need to shock him with ice water). Give him water to drink if he's still conscious, and call an ambulance.

Heat exhaustion is more common and less serious. The symptoms are almost the reverse: the victim is sweating so profusely that he may be cool or clammy to the touch. But he'll feel lightheaded, and might even faint.

Heat exhaustion happens when the body's demands for cooling dilate so many capillaries in the extremities that there's a loss of blood to the brain. Treatment is a lot like that for fainting. Get off the bicycle before you crash, and lie on your back, knees pulled up or feet elevated to get blood back to your head. Even if the symptoms pass quickly,

take it easy for a while. Anything more than a mild case should involve a visit to a doctor.

Overtraining

Even if it doesn't result in specific injuries, excessive training can produce burn-out and listlessness.

Treatment. A few days off the bike or a reduced training schedule, especially with a reduction in hard workouts.

Prevention. Have at least one rest day in your weekly training schedule. On tour, vary your daily riding distances and be prepared to take a day off as often as once a week if your body so desires. Overtraining will ultimately lead to some form of injury, so catching this problem early is a good way to prevent injuries later on. In addition to burn-out, symptoms of cumulative fatigue include:

- Unexpected weight loss
- Loss of appetite
- A series of "bad" rides
- An increase in first-thing-in-the-morning resting pulse rate
- Restlessness at night

Surviving a Crash

We all crash occasionally. Most of the time we walk away from it, scraped up, perhaps, but basically intact.

When you fall, resist the impulse to fling out an arm to catch yourself. That's a good way to break wrists, arms, and collarbones. Instead, tuck your body into a ball so you roll when you hit, distributing the impact. If you can, roll to the side, over your shoulder rather than head over heels.

Unfortunately, this is difficult to learn as an adult, and even more difficult to think of in the panic of the fall. Short of signing up for a tumbling class, visualization is the best way to acquire the right instincts. Imagine yourself doing a pain-free shoulder roll off your bicycle, tumbling once or twice and coming up on your feet unscathed. Think it through enough times and you might actually do it in a real fall.

After a fall, *think before you move.* This simple rule once saved my life when I hit a curb and went over the handlebars on a busy road. When I came to rest, unhurt, my first impulse was to roll toward what I thought was the curb. But something made me look before I moved—just in time to see car wheels speed by, right where I would have rolled.

If you're safe from the cars, take inventory of your body. That's a lot more important than jumping up to check on your bike. Can you remember precisely what happened? That's a good indicator that you probably don't have a concussion. Did you hit your head? It's possible to break your neck and not know it, so be cautious about getting back on the bike without first seeing a doctor.

As long as you're wearing a helmet, the most likely severe injury is a broken or dislocated collarbone. As broken bones go, it's not a bad one to break—it should heal completely in two or three months, but don't get back on the bike until you've seen a doctor.

Other possible injury points are wrists (especially if you're an arm-flinger in a fall), forearms, and elbows. A bad sideways fall can land you on your hip, possibly breaking it. And even if you tuck beautifully, you can crack or bruise ribs.

Road Rash

Road rash is the abrasion you get when you skid across a rough surface. The bad news is that if you ride enough miles, eventually it's going to happen. The good news is that it isn't anywhere nearly as painful as it looks.

Treatment. Flush with water and apply an antiseptic. Cover the wound with gauze or leave it open to the air. If you cover it, first apply an antibacterial cream such as Neosporin to prevent painful sticking.

Prevention. Smart, attentive riding and avoidance of closely spaced pace chains, especially at high speeds.

Cycle Touring 102

BEYOND DAY-RIDING

So far, you've learned the basics, slanted toward touring, but with lessons on skills and equipment that would be the same even if you planned to never progress beyond century rides or bike commuting.

Now it's time to specialize.

The prerequisites for the second half of this course are simple: a bicycle rigged for touring, enough training that you don't wind up deciding that your first outing is your last, and a lively sense of adventure.

The syllabus is equally straightforward. We'll begin with a primer in tent camping—with heavy applications for bicycle touring—followed by a discussion of how to carry all that equipment by bicycle. Later chapters will discuss the various types of touring, including ones on which you don't have to carry much baggage.

Life on the Road (pages 108–125) and Challenges and Adversities (pages 134–149) present useful information for all types of touring, but they are presented with the assumption that eventually you'll graduate to self-contained touring.

Self-contained touring is widely regarded as the most difficult form of touring, an impression fueled by the popular image of the touring cyclist, panniers bulging, straining to lug a 50-pound load up an endless hill.

With proper gearing, however, pedaling a loaded bicycle is only slightly more difficult than pedaling a stripped-down racer—just slower. And if you have the patience, it pays you back in freedom. No other form of touring makes it so easy to quit for the night if you get tired, or the wind shifts against you, or you simply find a pretty place—whether you've reached your destination or not. With proper equipment, you can pitch a tent on any bare spot large enough to sleep on, boil or otherwise purify water from a creek, cook dinner, and let the days unroll one by one. It's worth the extra weight.

As with Cycle Touring 101, you can mark your progress with a midterm and a final exam. For the midterm, pick a pleasant destination not too far from home and bicycle there for a weekend, camping or staying in a motel.

The final can double as a graduation exercise: Hit the road for a week. If you've taken the time to prepare properly, you'll find that there's nothing "final" about this exam after all. It's the beginning of a whole new world of two-wheeled adventure.

BICYCLE CAMPING
—what to carry and how to carry it

▼

Bicycle camping doesn't require special equipment. The first few times you attempt it, in fact, you'll probably want to make do with whatever camping gear you already have. If it's not too bulky or heavy, it will do fine for mild-weather touring.

But as you work your way further into the sport, you'll probably want better equipment, with "better" defined as lighter, more compact, more resistant to wind or rain—equipment that can turn an otherwise miserable evening into just another night on the road.

Much of the equipment is the same as is used by backpackers; except for panniers, you'll find it not in bike stores but in backpacking stores. If you're a backpacker, you've probably got most of what you'll need already.

If you've never backpacked—and don't intend to—don't let the comparison intimidate you. Bicycle touring is considerably easier than backpacking. First, the weight is on your bicycle not on your back. Equally important, cyclists can live off the land to a greater extent than backpackers, resupplying themselves with food every day or bailing out into a motel if the weather turns especially foul.

Nevertheless, particularly on longer trips, good equipment is one of the keys to an enjoyable and not overly eventful outing. Even if all of your touring will be van-supported, you'll appreciate good camping gear.

Basic Camping Equipment

Tents

The classic tent is a two-person backpacking tent, either A-frame or dome. Some models, particularly dome tents, are freestanding—meaning you don't have to stake them to hold them upright. A freestanding tent should still be staked when possible, though, so a strong wind won't blow it away like a giant beach ball: I once saw one start to roll in an Iowa thunderstorm with a 12-year-old inside it. Freestanding tents are necessary only if you expect to camp where the ground is too rocky for stakes. That's a lot more likely backpacking than cycle touring.

A good tent is rainproof and allows comfortable air flow and escape of moisture from your exhalations. Traditionally this is done by combining an interior layer of breathable fabric—sometimes nothing more than mosquito netting—with a detachable rain fly. Your exhalations still condense but they run down the inner surface of the fly to drip on the ground, outside.

Gore-Tex eliminates the need for two layers, reducing the weight slightly. But the reduction isn't as much as you might think, because Gore-Tex is heavy. Gore-Tex tents work best in warm environments, and poorest in cool, damp climates where the temperature inside the tent can be below the dew point—which causes condensation regardless of the fabric's breathability.

Two-person tents are the most versatile; larger ones obligate you to carry the weight around, even if you don't have enough people to fill them. Extremely large tents—anything designed for more than four people—aren't recommended. They are

Bivouac bag.

heavy and may not be sturdy enough in a storm. A group of my friends once took an inexpensive eight-person tent they called "the condo" on an organized tour. It stood six feet high, and the first strong wind smashed all the poles.

Too small a tent, on the other hand, isn't a good idea for rainy climates. Sitting out a long rainstorm, it's nice to have room to read comfortably or play cards.

An excellent way to shop for tents is by going on a large organized tour. Wandering around each evening's campground, you'll see almost every conceivable variety, with the owners happy to talk about them.

Sleeping under the stars. In the right climate, or at least on a good evening, where rain, dew, and mosquitoes aren't likely, sleeping under the stars is a glorious alternative to being confined in a tent. Just throw your sleeping bag and pad on a tarp, gather everything else you need nearby, where you won't lose it in the grass, and lie back, hoping for a truly spectacular celestial display. If the weather worsens you could find yourself pitching a tent by flashlight, but in more than 100 nights of sleeping on the ground I've only had to do this a handful of times.

With a big enough tarp, you can fold it back over yourself as protection against dew or light rain. If you've got the tarp to yourself, you can even roll up in it like a giant cigar, staying dry under less than ideal conditions. I once kept dry this way when an unexpected storm dropped half an inch of rain on me in the bottom of Death Valley.

Some people won't sleep without a tent because they're afraid of creatures, particularly snakes, crawling on them or joining them in the middle of the night. I won't say there's no such risk, but the only thing that's ever joined me was a friendly dog (it *was* a bit of a surprise). The much repeated stories about snakes crawling into your sleeping bag might have a foundation in fact, but if it's ever happened, it must be rare. Skunks and porcupines present more realistic concerns—and ants, mosquitoes, or biting gnats can quickly drive you into a tent. You'll find a tent to be a summer necessity in most parts of the country east of Kansas.

Bivouac bags. A tent alternative that is less chancy than sleeping under the stars is a bivouac sack or "bivvy bag." In its simplest form, it's a waterproof sleeping bag cover made of Gore-Tex or other waterproof, breathable fabric. For good weather, stuff your sleeping bag inside, and sleep under the stars. Under bad conditions, zip yourself in, away from the rain or bugs. Leaving a breathing hole is important to reduce condensation (some manufacturers also recommend it to avoid any risk of suffocation). Some models even have mosquito netting so you can leave a breathing hole without giving insects a route inside.

Bivvy bags are light, and small enough to fit in a pannier. But the simplest ones aren't perfect substitutes for a tent. In cool weather, even with a breathing hole, there's likely to be some condensation, most of which will eventually be sponged up by your sleeping bag. In warm weather, you'll overheat if you have to zip up. And whatever the temperature, waiting out rain or a prolonged bug attack is even more cramped in a bivvy bag than in the tiniest tent.

A bivvy bag is a superb lightweight, waterproof backup for trips when you expect to spend most nights under the stars. Even if occasionally you do get condensation, it's not likely to soak all the way through your sleeping bag unless you don't take time to dry it out between uses.

A basic bivvy bag is considerably less expensive than a tent. More expensive models come closer to being miniature tents—both in features and in price—with wands to keep the fabric off your face and the choice between mosquito netting or a storm flap. A lack of ventilation around your legs still makes them too warm for many climates, but for the cool evenings of mountains, deserts, or high plains, such bags are an excellent weight/comfort compromise for solo touring or for the odd person in a three-person group.

Cyclists traveling in pairs can also carry bivvies, but the advantage is considerably reduced; for their combined price you can buy a tent that won't be much heavier than two bivvies. Of course, bivvy bags *do* give you the opportunity to put some distance between yourself and a snoring buddy.

Hammocks. Another lightweight one-person alternative is a hammock. Bugs and rain may be problems with some models, but any hammock with "jungle" in its name probably has mosquito netting and a waterproof cover. The biggest drawback is that hammocks limit you to campsites with suitably spaced trees, or tree substitutes such as playground equipment.

Sleeping Bags

If it's warm enough any sleeping bag will work. Inexpensive bags are heavy and bulky, though, so if you're going to upgrade your camping equipment, start here.

The best all-purpose sleeping bags are made from synthetics. Down is lighter, but you're in trouble if it gets wet. Wet down won't keep you warm and it takes forever to dry. A damp synthetic bag, on the other hand, dries quickly in the sun; one that's been thoroughly soaked can be dried in a laundromat at low heat, perhaps with an old tennis shoe tossed in to help keep it fluffy.

A sleeping bag's quality depends as much on its design as its materials. A well-constructed system of baffles should keep the insulating material from bunching up without producing cold spots at the seams between compartments.

To stop drafts creeping down your neck or back, a drawstring and Velcro closures at the head will allow you to pull the bag tight. Conversely, a double zipper at the foot allows you to *create* drafts if it's too warm.

Sleeping bags come in a variety of thicknesses, often temperature-rated. The ratings are guides, not absolute predictors; a bag that's comfortable for one person may be too hot or cold for another.

A good sleeping bag, properly treated, will last for years. In long-term storage, it shouldn't be tightly stuffed in its sack, or eventually the fabric will compress and lose warmth. Put it in a large plastic bag or pillow case, tossing the stuff sack in with it, so you don't lose it.

Sleeping Pads

What you put beneath you is at least as important as what goes above you. I learned this on my first attempt at winter camping. Sleeping under the stars on a sub-freezing night, I fell asleep quite nicely, bundled in a warm sleeping bag and a couple of layers of clothes. Hours later, I woke up freezing, added layer after layer of clothing before I figured out that I'd rolled off my sleeping pad. Within minutes of getting back on I was peeling off the added layers as I started to overheat.

The lesson was graphic: You can sleep comfort-

Therm-A-Rest and Spider Mat.

ably on a bed of ice *if* you've got a good insulating pad beneath you. Without one, you'll get chilly, not to mention waking up stiff and sore, even at much milder temperatures.

The classic sleeping pad for most car campers is an air mattress. These work for bicycle touring, but they're not ideal. Blowing them up every evening is a nuisance, as is fighting their tendency to scoot out from under you if you roll off center. And even though air mattresses are thick, they aren't the warmest things available: Convection currents can quickly rob you of heat.

Better from an insulating perspective are closed-cell foam pads, such as the popular one made by Ridgerest. (Open-cell foams are softer, but sponge up water.) Closed-cell pads are inexpensive, lightweight, virtually indestructible, and warm enough for any conditions you're likely to encounter. They aren't very cushy, though; getting used to sleeping on one takes a few nights, especially on hard surfaces.

A more comfortable choice is a softer, nylon-covered foam pad, of the type made by Therm-A-Rest. These pads, which come in a variety of lengths and thicknesses, have an air valve that allows them to be inflated or deflated, though their spongy foam will inflate itself when you open the valve. Such pads are much thinner than air mattresses, but surprisingly comfortable. Unlike air mattresses, which are worthless if they spring a leak, the mixture of foam and air used by these pads means that even deflated, they'll keep you reasonably warm, and they're durable enough that the normal wear-and-tear of being lashed to your bicycle isn't likely to poke a hole in them.

These pads, unfortunately, are a good deal more expensive than the other options, and a lot heavier than closed-cell foam.

Ground Sheet

A ground sheet fits between your tent floor and the ground. There are durable nylon tarps made specially for the purpose, or you can buy a disposable painter's drop cloth from a hardware store.

ThermaLounger.

A ground sheet protects the tent floor from dirt or abrasion. It won't necessarily prevent leakage in a rainstorm, and might in fact do the reverse by trapping runoff between itself and the tent floor.

If rain isn't likely, I recommend a ground sheet simply to help preserve the life of your tent. In rainy weather its value is more debatable and depends on the abrasiveness of the surface on which you are camped.

Spider Mat

Spider Mat is a trade name of one of the more ingenious camping products of recent years. A narrow band of cobwebby mesh made of a no-skid material similar to carpet backing, it wraps around your sleeping pad and keeps it from sliding, even on a sloping surface.

The Spider Mat is a dream product for people who've spent too many nights shoving themselves out of the downhill corners of their tents. Weighing in at about five ounces, it rolls up to about the size of a paperback book.

For a do-it-yourself version, buy a similar material by the foot at camping stores, where it's sold for no-skid surfaces in motor homes and sailboats.

ThermaLounger

Are you the type of person who likes to get into camp early, sit back and read a book? Car camping, you can carry a folding lounge chair, but by bicycle, that's impractical. The same people who make the Therm-A-Rest pad have invented a contraption of staves and nylon into which you can insert your pad to convert it to a portable lounge chair.

A pair of straps, one on each side, pull the ThermaLounger into a V, which you adjust by loosening or tightening the straps. It's not light (about 1½ lbs), but it has the same addictive comfort as a beanbag chair and rolls up into a package not much larger than the pad, which can remain inside for sleeping or transport.

For long-distance self-contained touring, this product probably isn't worth the weight. But for van-supported touring, or organized tours, where limited baggage space still prevents you from bringing a full-sized lounge chair, it's perfect.

Pillow

If you really want a pillow, purchase an air pillow or carry a small conventional one with you. But even for van-supported touring, I merely stuff extra clothing into my sleeping bag stuff sack—perhaps the clothes I'm going to change into in the morning. Putting them in the sack isn't necessary, of course, but it reduces the risk of poking a zipper tab in your eye as you sleep.

Cooking Equipment

Cooking equipment is optional; you may prefer to eat at cafes or snack in general stores. If you decide to carry a stove, the ideal ones for bicycling are the same as for backpacking: compact, one-burner, fueled by white gas, such as the popular MSR WhisperLite.

Look for a stove with a good windscreen and compare specifications on how long it takes to boil a quart of water. The specifications will probably be based on ideal conditions—laughable in a windy camp at high elevation—but they're the best comparative guide to how long you're going to have to wait for dinner.

Some stoves have built-in flint-and-steel sparkers. Convenient, but don't rely on them; carry matches as a backup.

White-gas stoves must be primed. Consult the owner's manual for instructions, and heed warnings about not using your stove inside a tent, where a flare-up might cook you along with your dinner.

The only utensils you need are a large pot (about two quarts), a stirring spoon, pocket knife, and perhaps a pancake turner and non-stick frying pan. A second, smaller pot is useful for side dishes, particularly those that can be reconstituted from hot or cold water while your main dish simmers. Gloves or a washcloth are adequate pot holders.

You can dispense with the stove and cook over wood fires but fires aren't always possible, and it's hard to keep soot from migrating from the pot onto everything else you're carrying with it.

Bags

Bicycle bags are called "panniers" (PAN-yers or PAN-ee-ers, depending on what part of the country you're from). Occasionally, the general public refers to them as "saddlebags" because they bear some resemblance to horse-packing equipment.

Whatever you call them, panniers are the one piece of specialty bicycle camping equipment you need unless you're van-supported or on an organized tour. You could get by with a backpack, but that's brutally hard on your back, puts your center of gravity too high, and is dangerous to both you and the equipment if you fall. Even if all you can afford are cheap panniers, get the weight on the bicycle.

Panniers come in pairs carried either in front or back. The principal difference between front and rear ones is size: Front panniers are usually smaller. You can get color-coordinated sets of front-and-rear bags, with matching handlebar bags, but unless you're worried about not being able to match col-

ors later, you needn't buy all of these initially unless you're planning to start touring with a several-day self-contained trip.

If your first tours are weekend outings, a gradual way to acquire panniers is to buy rear ones first, adding front ones when you need them. Or, buy a small set of panniers first, using them as rear panniers for light touring or credit-card touring and transferring them to the front if you later buy full-fledged rear ones.

Pannier designs change from year to year as manufacturers introduce an endless succession of new features to secure the pannier ever more firmly to the rack. But the basic idea hasn't changed for years. At the bottom of the pannier is a spring-loaded hook; at the top, a pair of clips. The hook fastens to the bottom of your rack, while the clips go over the top. A nylon strap serves as a handle to ease installing and removing the bag, while some

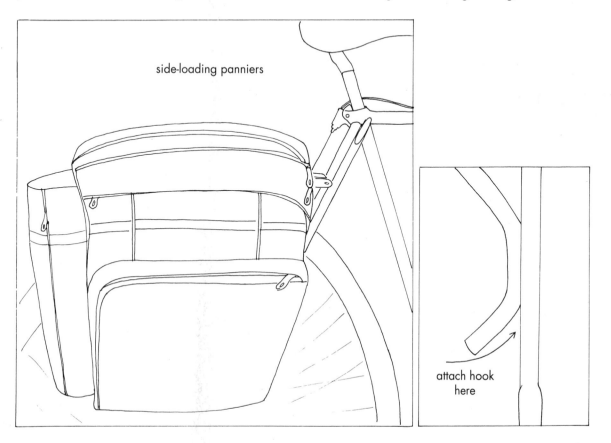

side-loading panniers

attach hook here

kind of tensioning device allows you to adjust the spring to pull the bag off easily—but not so easily that it bounces off when you hit a bump.

Front and rear panniers are either top-loading or side-loading. Side-loading are more convenient, especially for rear panniers, allowing you easy access even if your tent, sleeping bag, and pad are lashed above them. Nevertheless, top-loaders are popular, perhaps because they are more water-proof. A well-designed side-loading bag, though, should be more than adequately waterproof, espe-cially if it has good storm flaps around the zippers.

Rear panniers should be tapered on the front side so your heel will clear it at the back of the pedal stroke. Don't buy ones that won't give you enough room: There are few things more irritating than having to squash them out of the way every few minutes to keep your heels from going bump-bump-bump against them. Obviously, this will be a bigger concern if your shoes are size 13 than if they're size 7.

Side pockets are also useful. They cost more but are worth it because they make it easier to orga-nize your gear. A major plus is an external pocket big enough to hold a water bottle (upright so it can't leak). Beware of pockets on top of the main compartment; they can bulge high enough to get in

the way of your tent and sleeping bag. Also, make sure the various pockets aren't designed so they'll spill their contents when opened.

Although exterior pockets are handy, the main compartment should be a single unit to carry large or odd-shaped items such as spare spokes, cooking pots, or a backpacking stove.

You should be able to use any rear pannier in front if it's not so big it drags on the ground. Specially designed front panniers, however, are smaller and simpler, with fewer pockets because presumably you've already got plenty of pockets in back. Top-loaders aren't as much of a nuisance in front as in back.

One nice front-pannier feature is an elasticized, mesh, exterior pocket into which you can drop things such as sunscreen or sunglasses for easy access. Before buying, test the elastic to make sure it isn't so loose that things will bounce out on the road. Be leery of packs on which the elastic is replaced with a zipper—this make the pocket difficult to get into if the main compartment is full. Mesh pockets also can be used for holding wet clothing as it dries.

Bands of reflective tape on any pannier, front or rear, could literally be a lifesaver. Look for them on the back and sides of rear panniers, front and sides of any panniers you plan to put in front. Straps to

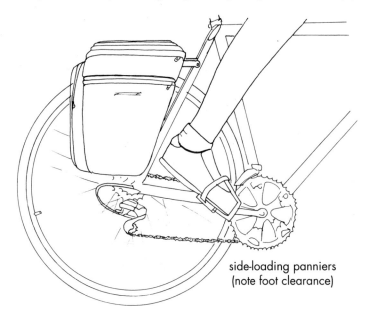

side-loading panniers
(note foot clearance)

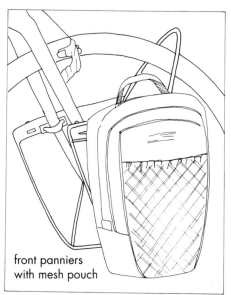

front panniers
with mesh pouch

compress the pannier to eliminate extra volume and increase stability are also useful.

Some panniers are designed more for mountain-bike touring than for road touring; the difference lies largely in the fabric's weight. Mountain-bike bags are made to be durable enough for narrow, brush-lined trails. They'll work on the road but you don't need their extra weight or expense.

Handlebar bags. Handlebar bags are controversial. They are extremely convenient places to stash everything from your camera and wallet to a snack, but they're also destabilizing, raising the center of gravity of your front wheel, and sometimes vibrating enough to make your front end shimmy at high speed. I find that the advantages outweigh the disadvantages for self-contained touring, but it's a closer call for light touring, especially on a racing bike with sensitive steering. Also, I'm short and use a small frame. Taller riders sometimes report

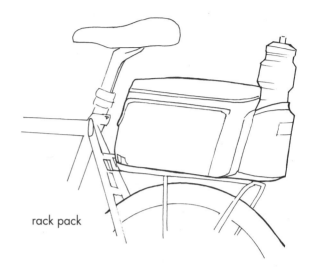

rack pack

Handlebar bag with map pouch.

that the stability problems are more significant on larger frames.

Most handlebar bags mount to a bracket that hooks over the stem and handlebars, with an elastic cord to keep the bag's bottom from bouncing. On my first bag, two such cords ran straight down to the fender eyelets on the front fork. It was stable, but incompatible with front panniers. Newer handlebar bags run a single cord around the lower end of the head tube, clipped at both ends to the bottom of the bag.

The size of a handlebar bag is up to you. I want one big enough for my camera and snacks, such as a bag of cherries from a roadside fruit stand. Extremely large bags will tempt you to load too much weight into them, at risk of destabilizing your bicycle. But it's a trade-off because they're also more likely to have one or more convenient external pockets.

Map pouches. Map pouches are clear plastic compartments that hold a map on top of your handlebar bag, folded in reading position and always dry. They are one of the principal reasons handlebar bags are worth getting; make sure yours either comes with a pouch or has a way to add one.

Map pouches have another use. If you want to lather up with sunscreen, on the move and one-handed, squirt a small puddle of it onto the top of the pouch. Now you can put the sunscreen back in your handlebar bag, freeing a hand for rubbing in the lotion. That little trick eliminates one of the great excuses for getting sunburned: *I knew I was burning, but was waiting to do something about it until the next time I stopped.*

Rack packs. There also are a variety of smaller bags that mount on your rear rack. For van-supported touring, such bags combined with a handlebar bag or small front panniers may be all you need to carry your rain gear, camera, and wind jacket.

Rack packs have lower wind resistance than panniers because they don't stick out to the side. Since they're fastened only on the bottom, though, they have a tendency to wobble when you pedal hard. Hooking bungee cords over the top solves this problem and gives you a place to lash clothing too bulky to fit in the bag. Just don't let the clothing rub on your tire.

Loading Up

A full touring rig consists of front and rear panniers, handlebar bag, and a "stack" of tent, sleeping bag, sleeping pad, and anything else that won't fit in the panniers lashed to the rear rack with bungee cords or nylon straps.

The weight should be distributed with less in front than in back. The conventional rule of thumb is a 60/40 split, but if you're carrying a lot of weight in a rear stack, you'll probably find the division comes closer to 70/30. The precise spit isn't critical; before front panniers came into widespread use, many cyclists, myself included, carried heavy loads for long distances with no weight in front except a handlebar bag. Front-heavy loads are also possible—and with Low Rider front racks a few people prefer them—but bulk problems usually make such a rig impractical.

More important is keeping each set of panniers balanced, side to side. With practice, loading this way becomes second nature, but check yourself the first few times by hefting each pair of bags, one in each hand. To keep from being fooled if your arms aren't equally strong, do it twice, reversing hands.

Similarly, the bike is easier to handle if the weight is concentrated low and close to the frame. It also helps to pack symmetrically. That means that if you depart from the heavy-items-low-and-inside rule by putting a water bottle in an accessible external pocket on one side, match it by carrying another water bottle or something equally heavy, like your tool kit, in the corresponding pocket on the other side.

There are two basic ways to stack your sleeping bag, tent, and any other large items: lashing long items either crossways or lengthwise. Lengthwise produces the least wind resistance, since the edges of the stack aren't sticking out to the side, but it's also the least stable because the lashed-on items can jiggle side to side.

More likely, you'll find that you have to lash crossways, wind resistance or not. Lashing this way, though, it's easier to add extra equipment to the stack, such as a two-liter soda bottle converted to a spare water bottle. Just slide it beneath the bungee cords, behind the sleeping bag.

A third approach, which helps if your panniers

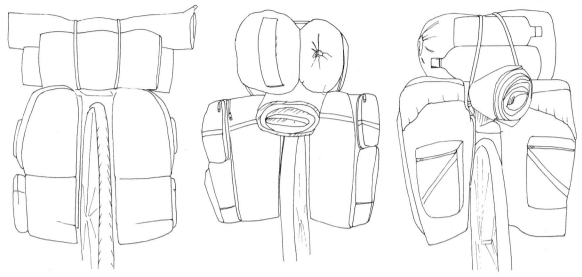

Rear-rack loading methods. Panniers on left and right are top-loading. Center drawing shows side-loading model. Note difference in accessibility to main compartment.

are so full that they bulge well above the rack, is to lash items in a T. Flat, narrow items, like your groundsheet or a fully deflated Therm-A-Rest pad can run lengthwise on top of your rack, eating up the extra space between the panniers, giving you a flatter surface on which to lash your tent and sleeping bag, crossways.

Getting Rid of the Shimmies

The first time you hop on your loaded bike, you're likely to be dismayed to find it unstable, shimmying uncontrollably even at fairly slow speeds. Because this is so common, start each tour by testing your loading job, riding around a large parking lot or a quiet side street. This helps, but don't be surprised if additional shimmy problems surface later, the first time your speed exceeds some magic number—15 mph, 20 mph, 25 mph. Don't panic; just pull to the side of the road to look for possible causes.

Shimmies can come from a variety of sources, and tracking them down is more art than science. Don't assume, for example, that a shimmy in the front wheel comes from problems in front; it may be

a manifestation of problems in the rear. Be patient; small adjustments can make the difference between a rig that shimmies unnervingly at 15 mph and one that's rock steady at 35.

Here are some of the most likely sources of instability, and their probable solutions:

- *Handlebar bag is overloaded.* The less weight in your handlebar bag, the less mass there is to vibrate. Store tire irons and a tire patch kit in it, but the bulk of your tool kit should go elsewhere. Nor should you weigh it down with water bottles.

- *Handlebar bag cord is too loose.* If the elastic cord is adjustable, tighten it. If it isn't and the bag wiggles significantly when you wobble the steering, run the cord around the head tube an extra time to take up the slack. This can take some muscle—and it might not be all that good for the cord or the points where it attaches to the bag —but it can make a tremendous difference in stability.

- *Weight distribution in panniers is uneven.* Remove them and check for balance. Shifting a couple of pounds from one side to the other may be all you need to do.

- *Stack is lashed too loosely.* Before leaving home, test your bungee cords to make sure they're the right length. If your cords are too loose, find a different place to hook them, or cross them diagonally for a tighter stretch. If this still doesn't work, carry a pair of nylon straps as a backup. Such straps are also useful insurance against destroying a bungee cord by accidentally winding it up in the freewheel.

- *Weight distribution of stack is off center.* This will cause the same type of problems as unbalanced panniers.

- *Stack isn't sitting on a firm, flat surface.* The stability of the stack is much influenced by the surface on which it's built. Strapped down, your sleeping bag and tent should make firm contact with the rack, or in the T-shaped lashing described earlier, with tightly compressed equipment sitting firmly on the rack.

- *Sleeping pad isn't completely deflated.* If a Therm-A-Rest–style sleeping pad is beneath the sleeping bag, as in the T-lashing, it's hard to make a firm base for the stack if the pad isn't fully deflated. This is a two-step process. First, open the valve and roll it up as firmly as you can, kneeling on it. Then, close the valve, unroll the pad, and roll it again, tighter, stopping to open the valve to bleed off additional air just before you finish. Lash the pad to the bike with the valve closed to keep it from self-inflating.

- *A shimmy that comes only at very high speeds,* especially in light touring, might be caused by your spoke reflectors. Since these are good protection at night, it can be hard to choose between removing them or living with the shimmy.

Other Packing Tips

Every experienced cyclist has a preferred way of packing; it won't take you long to develop your own. What matters isn't so much *where* you put things as whether you can *remember* it, not having to unload half of your equipment each evening in search of your toothbrush.

Here are a few tips, developed mostly by the grumble-and-learn approach.

- *Think in terms of accessibility.* The least accessible place is the bottom of your rear panniers, so use that for things you don't need immediately: tomorrow's clothes, dinner makings, stove, exposed film.

- *Your handlebar bag is the most accessible place,* and the only one you can reach without stopping.

- *Front panniers are highly accessible.* I use one for rain gear, wind shell, and tights, the other for lunch makings and snacks. I fill extra space with anything else I might want quickly, such as camera lenses.

- *What do you do with your bicycle when you get off it for a rest break?* Do you usually prop one side against a wall, fence, or tree? If so, the other side (for most people, the left) will be more accessible. Alternatively, do you more frequently lay it down on its side? That means you probably put the right side up to keep grit out of the chain and derailleur. That's a bit hard on handlebar-mounted mirrors, but it means the right panniers are the accessible ones. Pack accordingly.

- *With small panniers and a lot of bulky clothes,* conserve space by putting your sleeping bag in a larger stuff sack than necessary. Then stuff your warm jacket, spare T-shirts, or other clothing in with it. Stuff these clothes in ahead of the sleeping bag if you're not likely to need them on the road, afterward if you might.

- *Sharing a tent, you can split the weight* if one of you carries the poles and stakes, while the other carries the rest. Just make sure the poles and stakes are nicely bagged so you don't lose any.

- *To keep your sleeping bag dry even in a downpour,* line the inside of the stuff sack with a garbage bag. Some people put the garbage bag on the outside of the stuff sack, instead, but that means it won't be long until it's poked full of holes. You can also line your panniers with plastic, but it isn't as necessary.

Light-Touring Rig

Without much baggage, you can dispense with various parts of the full touring rig. A pair of front panniers used in the rear, for example, may be all you'll need for a weekend of credit-card touring. The same panniers combined with a rack pack and handlebar bag might keep you going inn to inn for a week. Some people do such tours with front panniers only.

For van-supported touring, you might need nothing more than a handlebar bag or rack pack for your map, rain gear, and camera. A single rear pannier, if lightly loaded, can also work without destabilizing you or damaging the rack from the unbalanced load. I carry it on the side closest to the traffic, trying to use the extra bulk to encourage drivers to pass me with adequate room.

As mentioned earlier, for weekend self-contained touring you can often get by without front panniers, using the old-fashioned touring rig of rear panniers, stack, and handlebar bag.

What to Carry

An equipment checklist for loaded touring is on pages 105–107. It is designed for a one-week trip under varied weather conditions. Abbreviate it for shorter trips or lighter styles of touring.

Don't be intimidated by the number of items. Many are accounted for by first-aid materials, tools, and spare parts. If you tour frequently, you can assemble these in advance as separate kits, storing them between uses. Just remember to replace anything you've used.

Forgetting something isn't the end of the world. Even something as vital as your sleeping bag can be replaced in a small-town discount store.

First-aid kit. Unless you're going somewhere really remote, you don't need an extensive first-aid kit; many problems, like chafing, develop slowly enough that you can buy what you need from drug stores along the way. Do carry things you'll use regularly or might need in an emergency, like water purification tablets, assorted bandages, prescription medications, bee-sting remedies, and anti-inflammatories such as aspirin or ibuprofen. If a pill bottle is too bulky, transfer the pills to small, inexpensive waterproof containers.

Tool kit and spare parts. Because bike stores are less frequent than drug stores, your repair kit will be more extensive than your first-aid kit. Not all bicycles will require everything on the list.

Some of the tools are ordinary household items; others are specialty. The most convenient Allen wrenches, for example, come linked together on a key-chain-like ring or folded up like a multi-bladed pocket knife. Similarly, a set of bike-repair socket

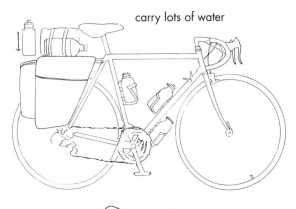

carry lots of water

coiling a tire

wrenches comes in a Y-shaped tool with a different socket on each end. Other tools and their uses are discussed beginning on page 155.

Not all of the listed tools are for bike repair; some, such as safety pins and ripstop tape, are for your tent, panniers, or other equipment.

Every rider in your group should have a minimal tool kit: Allen wrenches, tire patch kit, spare tube. But only one rider needs to have everything. The complete tool kit sounds heavy, but much of the weight is accounted for by two items: Crescent wrench and needlenose pliers. If you keep those light, you can get the weight down to two or three pounds, not counting the spare tubes or spare tire.

Spare tire. The heaviest and bulkiest spare part on the list is a tire. Your group should always have at least one of each size that might be needed. Better is for each person to have one, especially those whose wheels are of some size other than 26-inch—tires that are difficult to come by in small towns.

Van-supported, carrying spares is no problem.

But self-contained, tires can be cumbersome. The simplest way to carry one is to coil it up, being cautious not to kink it. Here's how:

1 Hold the tire horizontally in front of you, or put it on a flat surface.

2 Pull the far edge toward you, over the top of the near edge, letting the tire twist naturally into a three-looped shape like a set of eyes and nose. (If you're a history buff, you may think, "Kilroy Was Here!") The loop forming the "nose" crosses above the others.

3 Adjust the size of the loops until they're roughly equal. Then, raising the tire off the flat surface, fold both "eyes" downward, one at a time, into the "nose." Congratulations! You have reduced a large, unwieldy tire to an easily manageable triple ring.

4 Check to make sure there are no kinks, then tie the ring closed with string. You can carry it in a

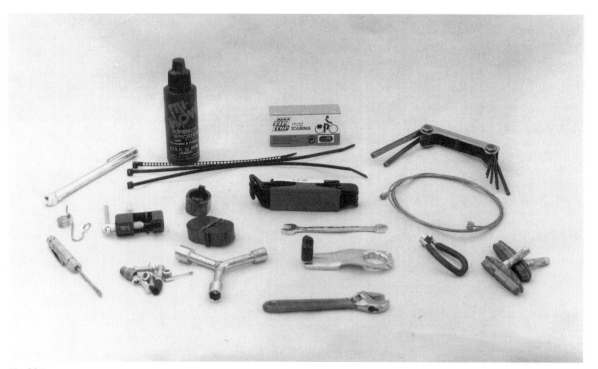

Tool kit contents.

pannier or on your rear rack as part of the stack.

Practice this at home, before you hit the road, until it feels natural enough that you can do it easily.

You could also buy folding tires that come in boxes, but they're more expensive, can't be found in every bike store, and may be harder to install than ordinary tires. They also eat a lot of space in your panniers and are most common in narrow, racing-tires widths. Once you've mastered the art of coiling a tire, there's not much reason to buy one pre-folded.

Other cyclists have carried spares by stuffing them inside the spokes of their front or rear wheels. It's ingenious, but I'd be afraid of causing a high-speed shimmy.

Water bottles. Most bikes come equipped with two water bottle cages. You can and should mount a third on the front of the down tube, behind the front wheel. Two more bottles can go in the exterior pockets on most rear panniers, one on each side, easily accessible for swapping with empties.

If you need more water than that, bury extra bottles in the main compartment of your panniers or lash a plastic two-liter soda bottle to your stack. These bottles, and the similar mineral-water bottles, make excellent water bottles because they don't leak and can be refilled time and again. Gallon jugs of distilled water can be lashed to the stack (with a bit more difficulty) but because their tops pop off easily after they've first been opened, they're good only for one-time use.

Water bottles come in 16-ounce and 24-ounce sizes. Larger is nice, but the 24-ouncers won't fit the extra cage on your down tube and may not fit your pannier pockets. Since you'll want to rotate bottles rather than pouring from one to another, think through your rotation system before buying too many 24-ouncers.

Camping and Cycling Equipment
    Tent
    Sleeping bag
    Sleeping pad
    Ground sheet

Panniers
Handlebar bag
Rear-view mirror
Water bottles
Flashlight, with spare bulb and batteries
Pocket knife
Bungee cords or nylon straps
Maps
Towel and washcloth
Nylon cord (25-50 feet)
Lock and cable
Headlight and taillight
Food (approximately 1-day supply)

Clothing
    Helmet
    Cycling gloves
    Cycling shoes
    Cycling shorts (at least 2)
    T-shirts or jerseys (at least 2)
    Underwear and socks
    Tights or leg warmers
    Wind shell
    Rain gear
    Elastic band to secure flapping pant leg
    Warm jacket or sweater

Tool Kit
    Tire patch kit (2)
    Tire levers (set)
    Pump
    Allen wrenches
    Chain lube
    Screwdrivers (Phillips head and flathead)
    Crescent wrench (6-inch)
    Socket wrenches
    Needlenose pliers/wire cutters
    Chain tool
    Spoke wrench
    Freewheel remover
    Tire gauge
    Presta-to-Schrader valve adapter
    Electrical tape
    Ripstop nylon tape
    Safety pins
    Zip ties

Spare Parts

Inner tubes (2)
Spare tire
Spokes (3 of each length needed)
Toe clip strap
Chain link
Brake and derailleur cables
Extra cyclometer battery
Miscellaneous bolts and nuts

Cooking Equipment (Optional)

Stove, fuel, and matches
1 ½–2 quart pot
Small pot
Frying pan
Pancake turner
Plate, bowl and/or cup

Eating utensils
Can opener
Stove maintenance kit
Sharp knife (pocket knife)

Personal Items

Sunglasses
Sunscreen and sun-blocking lip balm
Toothbrush, toothpaste, and dental floss
Soap and shampoo
Comb
Nail clippers
Toilet paper

First-Aid and Emergency Materials

Matches (regular and waterproof/windproof)
Telephone change

Camping gear for a single cyclist.

Insect repellent
Aspirin or ibuprofen (for inflammation)
StingEze (insect bite pain-killer)
Antihistamine
Talcum powder
Water-purification tablets
First-aid cream
Tweezers
Elastic bandage
Adhesive bandages
Butterfly bandages
Sewing kit with needle

Additional Items (as needed or desired)
Camera and film
Writing tablet and pens (2)
Playing cards
Reading material

Spider Mat
Warm gloves
Bandana or ear warmers
Waterproof helmet cover
Camp shoes
Swim suit
Water filter
Spare eyeglasses or contact lenses
Eyeglass repair kit
ThermaLounger
Day pack (for hiking)
Compass
Snakebite kit
Hand lotion
Petroleum jelly
Long pants
Wool hat
Ben-Gay

LIFE
ON THE ROAD

▼

Choosing a Destination

The best touring destinations have low traffic, plenty of places to camp, small-town hospitality, and compact topography that doesn't force you to travel interminably on straight, flat roads. Good options are:

- Islands.
- Coasts and lakeshores if there are backroads to keep you away from the heaviest traffic.
- Spectacular mountain country like Glacier National Park or the Canadian Rockies, where the scenery is worth the cost in hills and RVs.
- Gentle farm country with plentiful backroads.

Other areas such as deserts or high plains can also be rewarding but aren't good places for your first outings.

On organized tours, you have no control over the route. Pick the tour based on the entry fee, the size of the group, and your interest in the area.

Touring on your own, picking good bike routes is part planning, part luck—with an element of "winging it" with on-the-road decisions based on your developing familiarity with the region you're touring. These spontaneous decisions, in fact, are a major part of the touring experience, contributing much to the freedom of the road, especially if you're self-contained, able to camp along the way if a "short-cut" proves longer or more rugged than expected.

To preserve the spontaneity, plan your routes only in general terms and try not to schedule too tightly, especially if you have an airplane to catch at the end. Many things can slow you down, and

it's nice to have a day's grace. The best way to tour is without a fixed return date, but that's a luxury few can afford.

Point-to-point routes and loop routes each has its advantages. Point-to-point allows you to cover more terrain but complicates the transportation problem at the beginning and end. Loops allow you to leave a car at the start, but almost certainly mean that part of the route will be upwind.

A good compromise if you're touring close to home is to go to the start by train, plane, or bus and bike back home. Then, if you run out of time, you might even be able to prevail on your spouse or a friend to come get you. The disadvantage, of course, is that this limits you to places close enough to home that you can pedal all the way back.

Planning Around Wind

Most people have been taught that the average air-flow across the U.S. is from west to east. This is true enough to be important in planning cross-country trips, but local wind patterns may be considerably different. Where I live, for example, fair-weather winds are northerly and storm winds come from the south.

To get this information for a region far from home, call the National Weather Service at the nearest sizeable town. But be careful to ask for the right statistic. I once was told that the average June wind in western Nebraska was 10 mph from the northwest. Such gentle breezes weren't my image of Nebraska, and when I got there I found that the statistic I'd been given must have been a month-long average. Midafternoon winds alternated between 30 mph out of the northwest and 20 mph from the southeast.

Terrain features radically modify wind patterns. Deep valleys can trap and funnel wind into a gale that can either blow you up-slope or ruin a good downgrade. In the mountains on hot summer afternoons, the wind often blows uphill from both sides as hot air rises out of the valleys. This is so common that it's rare to get a tailwind on an afternoon downgrade, regardless of what direction you're going.

Wind is almost always stronger in the afternoon than in the morning. If a day dawns windy, hit the road early to avoid gales later.

Where to Spend the Night

If there's one question that non-cyclists most frequently ask, it's "Where do you spend the night?" Credit-card touring, the answer is obvious: motels, inns, or B&Bs. But on a self-contained camping tour, the options are wide open: state parks, national forests, church lawns, highway rest areas, or the yards or guest bedrooms of local residents—all are possibilities.

Camping

The first few times you tour self-contained, you'll want to avoid worries by heading for a state park, reserving a campsite, if possible, so you know it'll be waiting for you. But the principle advantage of self-contained touring is the freedom you have to avoid a reservation-bound schedule. As a practical matter, scheduling reservations for anything longer than a weekend trip can be difficult—especially given the vagaries of wind, weather, and the whims of your own body. After a few shakedown excursions, it's time to take the plunge and go without reservations, learning to spot the camping opportunities as they arise.

The fundamental rule in choosing campsites is safety—with comfort and cost close behind.

Established campgrounds, whether commercial or in parks or forests, rank high on the first two scales, especially since they often offer such amenities as running water, swimming, and scenery. Price-wise, public ones are the least expensive, though some private mom-and-pop operations may offer inexpensive "cyclist's specials." Large private campgrounds sometimes charge for sewer and electric hookups as though you were an RV.

Camping in such places by bicycle is different from camping in them by car. By car, if a campground says it's full, it's full, and you have to drive on in search of another place to spend the night. By bicycle that could be a catastrophe, and campground managers know it. Even when a campground is busily turning away your four-wheeled cousins, it will probably find room for you.

Even better, some campgrounds, especially in state parks along popular cycling routes, offer special bike-only sites, which you'll wind up sharing with however many other cyclists happen to be passing through. Other parks might send you to a picnic area or some other place that would be *verboten* for automobiles. These quiet areas often make ideal campsites.

In general, the quietest, most spacious tent sites are usually in the more primitive public campgrounds. But it's a trade-off; private campgrounds and developed state parks are more likely to have showers.

For another good source of campgrounds, try the national forests. Expect the camping to be primitive, with drinking water (probably) but pit toilets rather than modern bathrooms. When these campgrounds fill, though, there's not likely to be a bike-only site or a grassy picnic area for overflow; the

only level, brush-free spots are usually the designated sites. But before you give up, cruise slowly around as though you're looking for a site. If your party is small (four people is getting a bit large), there's a good chance someone will invite you to share one. It's a great way to meet some interesting people, often ones who'd love to be doing what you are—or did it when they were younger.

City Parks
In farm country, especially in the Midwest and Great Plains, small-town city parks are another good option. Generally, the smaller the town the more likely it is to permit camping, and the less likely you are to be hassled by kids. The best

choices are usually towns of 200 to 1,500 people—small enough for hospitality but large enough to have nice parks. On Friday and Saturday nights, opt for the smallest towns you can find; even there, cruising teenagers can be a nuisance. They're not likely to be dangerous, but they can ruin a night's sleep.

City-park camping is a great way to meet the local people. By the time you've pitched camp, half the town will know you're there. If the day's still young, don't be surprised if several of them come by to visit, or talk to you while you're buying groceries. Grade-school kids may also come by on their bikes. Whether their attitude is awe-struck hero worship or feigned nonchalance, being the center of all that attention will do as much as a good night's sleep to put the spring back in your legs.

Not all towns allow this type of camping. The closer you are to a big city or a major tourist area, the more suspicious the locals will be of you—and the more concern you should have about being hassled. If in doubt about safety or legality, ask someone. But expect that the answer won't vary widely from town to town; if it's legal in one, it's probably legal in neighboring ones as well.

Nontraditional Campsites

Campgrounds and city parks are the most conventional places to camp, but they aren't always available. Once you start getting creative, though, the choices are almost endless.

In ranch or farm country or a tiny crossroads too small to have a park, you can always ask to pitch a tent on someone's lawn. There aren't many rural or small-town folk who'd turn you down. The biggest obstacle is working up the nerve to ask, especially at a farmhouse surrounded by big dogs. If walking up to a door and knocking seems too brazen, try hanging out at a general store or cafe, chatting with the customers. You don't have to specifically ask to camp on their lawns. Just ask about campsites in general; if nothing else comes to mind, someone's likely to volunteer.

If the cafe or general store has a lawn (not uncommon in the tiniest towns), the same approach may get you permission to camp there. You'll proba-

bly also get access to the bathroom, at least during store hours. I've used this technique with gas stations and taverns, too, but their normal clienteles don't make quite as good company as what you'll find at cafes and general stores. Regardless of the type of store, I express my gratitude by eating there or stocking up on groceries.

Churches are another good source of accommodations. Their well-maintained lawns are ideal for camping, and the pastor may be glad to help. Ask for permission at the church office. If that's closed, one of the nearby houses is often the pastor's home. On a rainy night, you might even be invited to sleep indoors on the floor of the church's social hall.

In a slightly larger town, try asking the police. They could direct you to the nearest state park, 20 miles away, but more likely they'll give you useful suggestions, possibly including permission to camp in a park where it wouldn't otherwise be allowed. I've even had the police offer to "send by an extra patrol" to make sure nobody's bothering me.

If night catches you in the middle of a national forest or on public range land, the solution is even easier. Wheel off into the woods, out of sight of the road so that any unpleasant individuals who happen to drive by won't know you're there. To be safest, don't let anyone see you leave the road and don't light a fire. If no one knows where you are, you're unlikely to be bothered.

In sagebrush or scrub desert, look for gullies or piles of jumbled rocks to hide in or behind (don't camp in a gully, though, if there's any threat of a flash flood). Another way to get out of sight is by camping under a bridge. But don't camp in such places if they're cluttered with beer cans—they may be favorite drinking sites of local rowdies.

Abandoned buildings or houses under construction also offer tempting places to spend the night, especially if its raining, but only as a last resort. They're obvious enough camping spots that you may have unwanted company. Furthermore, abandoned-looking buildings may not actually be abandoned—and at a construction site the owner may stop by in the evening to inspect the day's progress.

Other tempting but illegal places are national parks (except in established campgrounds), Indian reservations, and private land of any kind. If you're attentive to other possibilities, there's seldom a need to trespass.

On highways, roadside parks provide camping possibilities, often with bathrooms and drinking water. These will put you on display to any passing motorist, though, so be prudent. Don't camp here if the road is heavily traveled or within an hour or so's drive of a major urban area unless you've got enough company from RVs or people napping in their cars to make you feel safe. Many roadside parks have prominent "No camping" signs or rules limiting the duration of a stay to no more than a few hours. Don't worry too much about these; the police aren't likely to chase cyclists out in the middle of the night.

Finally, if good camping spots are few and far between, talk to any cyclists you meet coming from the opposite direction. It's always fun to meet your fellow two-wheeled travelers, and each encounter is a heaven-sent opportunity to learn the lay of the land.

Hostels

Because of the prominence of the American Youth Hostels organization, and the word "youth" in its name, hosteling is most commonly associated with college students. But you'll be equally at home here even if your hair is graying. I've stayed in hostels a number of times, and the average age of my companions has usually been 30 to 45.

The difficulty with hostels is finding them. AYH can supply you with a list of member hostels, but many small-town hostels—which are the ones you're most likely to be dealing with—are unaffiliated. The best way to learn about them is by word of mouth. Ask the locals, and especially ask any other touring cyclists you meet along the way. AYH's book of hostels is available by contacting its national office (1108 K Street NW, Washington, DC 20005; 202-783-4943).

Spending the night in a hostel is relaxing. Count on running water, a stove (with or without pots and pans), and often the company of other cyclists. Some hostels have beds, some merely offer floor space. Either way, you'll need a sleeping bag. Some hostels provide gender-segregated dormitory-style accommodations; couples may have to split up for the night. Other hostels give you individual rooms or put everybody in one big (or little) one.

Inns and Motels

Credit-card touring, you'll spend all of your nights in motels and inns. Occasionally you'll stay in such places on self-contained tours—perhaps to avoid inclement weather, perhaps because you *really* want a shower.

Checking into a motel by bicycle is usually straightforward, but once in a while a clerk will object to bicycles in the room. If so, ask what the concern is. If it's a vague comment about "dripping grease on the carpets," you can offer reassurance that a well-maintained machine won't do that. If all else fails, ask point-blank if the motel will accept responsibility if your bicycle or any of your equipment is stolen. The answer will undoubtedly be "no," but that may get you access to a locked storeroom.

Even when you aren't hassled about bringing the bike indoors, don't create ill will for future cyclists by tracking mud on the carpet or leaving black tire marks on the walls.

Route Planning: You Say There's a Big Hill Ahead?

Good maps and map-reading skills are important on even the most spontaneous tours, greatly reducing the element of luck in both the planning stage and in making those mile-by-mile decisions.

There are three basic types of maps available: bicycling maps, highway maps, and topographic maps. Don't rely solely on one map or one type.

County maps are also useful, but they can be hard to find and a week tour can cross quite a few counties. You can usually manage without them.

Bicycling Maps

Bicycling maps are highway maps on which some roads have been color coded by a scheme such as green, yellow, and red, for "good," "mediocre," and "deadly." They might also show hills, campgrounds, prevailing wind directions, ferries, hostels, etc. Don't expect them to include every paved road; farm lanes are often too numerous.

The ideal map would give shoulder widths in feet, with the color codes used only for traffic volume. You can make your own trade-off between the two. A high-traffic road with a 10-foot shoulder, for example, is safe but a lot less pleasant than one that's shoulderless but with low traffic. Unfortunately, many bike maps combine such information into the color codes according to trade-offs that may not be clearly stated. Familiarity with the map will gradually give you an understanding its makers' priorities, but it's still frustrating.

Highway Maps

Cycling maps are a luxury. You can navigate almost as well from highway maps, learning to pick potential bike routes at a glance. Because these maps often show more detail than bike maps, they're useful even if you have a cycling map. Here are some route-finding tips, but don't expect them to work every time. Even the most experienced cyclists are sometimes surprised.

- Look for roads that have been bypassed by freeways or other main highways.
- Avoid roads that are the shortest routes between major cities, even if you never get close to either city.
- Look for the secondary roads, often designated as "other paved" in the map legend and identified on the map by gray or light blue lines. These are often your best choices—just make sure they're paved. In lightly populated areas, though, don't automatically rule out the main highways. I've ridden U. S. highways that carried only a few cars per hour.
- Does the road follow the pattern of the river drainages or cross from one to another? One way you're likely to be on flat bottom land; the other will be hilly.
- If the road parallels a main river, how closely does it follow the water? The farther away it is, the more likely it is to bounce along the bluff rather than stay on the floodplain.
- Curvy roads deter high-speed traffic, but when they wind all over the place, there's usually a reason, often big hills. In forested country, winding roads might also be heavily vegetated, with limited sight distance. Ride them only if you're comfortable with such conditions.
- Coast and lakeshore roads could be flat or bounce from headland to headland—it can be hard to guess from the map. On summer weekends, heavy boat-trailer traffic can make them dangerous.
- Some maps use shading to indicate topographic relief. Elevations, if given, also tell you a lot about the terrain.
- Look for national forests. These usually occupy upland terrain—or at least hilly land. If several tracts of forest lie in more-or-less parallel north/south strips, it's a good guess that each is a mountain range.
- Are the roads in an area parallel, with only a few wiggly connecting links? The parallel roads may be following valleys, while the connecting links cross the intervening ridges. For example, look at a map of eastern Tennessee.
- Know the area's overall topography. I once used such knowledge to good effect on a tour that

began by following a wickedly hilly coastline. Inland, I knew, was a range of low mountains, backed by a long, flat valley. Near the end of my trip, I crossed the mountains to use the valley for a quick, easy return to my starting point.

Topographic Maps

Topographic maps are the best way to get detail about terrain. The United States Geological Survey (USGS) maps identify the site of virtually every windmill, cemetery, church, and hamlet. They also show you every significant ditch, gully, and hill. (If you don't know how to use them, read a book on backpacking or talk to a friend who does a lot of hiking.)

The DeLorme Mapping Company of Freeport, Maine, has been publishing a beautiful series of state-by-state topographic atlases. Available in bookstores, they're too big to carry on the road, but great for planning.

Another good series of topographic maps is put out by the federal Bureau of Land Management (BLM). These maps, which also distinguish public land from private (useful for picking campsites), cover only regions with a lot of public land, generally in the rural West.

BLM or USGS topos cost several dollars apiece, and since each one covers only a small area, the price quickly adds up. Buy only the ones you need.

Asking the Locals

Don't be too proud to ask the people you meet for route advice. There's no better way to get up-to-date information.

Ironically, however, there's also no better way to be seriously misled. People usually are pretty good about knowing whether you should turn left or right at the next intersection, but don't rely too strongly on their distance estimates or descriptions of hills or road conditions. Half the time, the advice will be wrong.

The reason is simple: By car, the difference between 10 miles and 20 isn't really that much. Similarly, non-cyclists just aren't tuned in to the details (such as a 5-mile gap in the shoulder) that can make the difference between a good route and a bad one. This particularly goes for information

about road surfaces. People usually know if a road is paved or not, but "bad" gravel to a driver may be hard-packed dirt—bumpy perhaps, but passable even on a narrow-tired road bike. "Good" gravel may be so loose it's a problem even on a mountain bike.

If crude estimates are all you need (e.g., is there a town with a general store in the next 5 to 20 miles?), none of this matters. If you need better information, discreetly ask more than one person and weigh the credibility of the answers. The most reliable ones come from other cyclists; the next best from truck drivers or farmers familiar with the backroads. But even then you can get misled. I've asked farmers the distance from their farm to the nearest town—something I'd expect them to know —only to have the answers be wrong by nearly a factor of two.

Inaccurate Maps

The same caveats go for maps. Plan with a safety margin that allows for major errors. A friend and I once set out on a four-day trip we intended to be mountainous but not overly taxing. Based on three

maps and a telephone conversation with a ranger at a park along the route, we expected no more than 2,000 feet of climbing per day, probably less. Instead, we found that all of our maps lied, the park ranger had badly underestimated the elevations, and only the BLM topos (which we didn't consult until afterward) revealed the awesome truth: Our 240-mile loop had an incredible 20,000 feet of climbing—the most macho thing either of us had ever done by bicycle.

Our maps had omitted the highest pass in the region (a 3,000-foot climb) and had placed a town on the wrong side of a hill. Two other towns turned out to be ghost towns, with no sources of food or water.

Neither of us, before or since, has ever encountered such a succession of map errors. But the experience reinforced a lesson we both already knew: never trust too much to the accuracy of a map.

Farm Lanes

Farm lanes often provide the best cycling but they can be exceedingly bumpy, dead-ending or unpredictably turning to gravel. Sometimes, farm-lane navigation is best reserved for people who not only enjoy route-finding challenges, but have fat tires to see them through the occasional mistakes.

That said, there's much to recommend these quietest of backroads, which can wind so intimately through the landscape that they pass between a farmhouse and the barn that goes with it. Also, the route-finding itself carries a sense of pioneering adventure. One of the most rewarding tours I've ever taken involved navigating the backroads of central Michigan, stair-stepping southeast as I chose my route based on the quality of the pavement and the volume of traffic. Not only did I reach my destination, but much of the time I was on roads that weren't on the map.

This type of navigation is difficult to teach, but it's a skill some people find to be almost intuitive.

Begin by knowing the terrain. Don't expect farm lanes to cross major rivers—or even minor ones. In rolling terrain don't be surprised if these roads go straight over whatever's in their way, making them

considerably hillier—and steeper—than the main thoroughfares.

The quality of farm lanes varies. Some states are good about marking dead ends; others aren't. In Wisconsin, virtually all farm lanes are paved; in neighboring Iowa, most are gravel. Elsewhere, road surfaces could differ from county to county.

In some parts of the country, farm roads follow the compass lines in a nearly perfect grid, one mile apart. But in California's Central Valley, the grid is not complete and the roads aren't always spaced the traditional distance apart.

The best way to get this type of information is by asking local cyclists or stopping at a bike shop. You can also watch the farm lanes for a few miles before leaving the main roads to try them, noting how complete the grid is and what fraction of the roads are paved. Signs also help; if some roads are marked as dead ends, you can hope the others go through. A sign saying a road leads to a town is cause for hope that the pavement will continue at least that far.

Keep track of your progress on the highway map. If the road you're following isn't shown, towns, county lines, lakes, or rivers make good landmarks. Knowing where you are will help you find campsites, know which way to turn at intersections, or locate main roads when needed.

Not Getting Lost

If the roads are laid out on a geometric grid, it's easy to keep track of direction as long as you remain alert. But if they wiggle and you don't have a good sense of direction, your first realization that you're going the wrong way may be when you come to a town you weren't expecting.

Sense of direction is a skill not easily learned. But there are a few ways to keep headed the right way:

- Learn to tell directions from the sun. You can do this pretty accurately with a watch with an hour hand. Hold it flat, with the hour hand pointing toward the sun. As long as you're north of the tropics, south will be about halfway between the hour hand and the numeral 12. With a digital watch, try to imagine where the hands would point on an old-fashioned clock. Even if you don't have a watch, guessing at the time will probably aim you close enough to the right direction.

- If there's a numbering system on the farmers' mailboxes, keep track of the numbers. They presumably could go to zero in the middle of the county or at one of its corners, like house numbers in a city.
- Carry a compass.

Map Sources

Since information that shows up on more than one map is more likely to be accurate, it's a good idea to get several maps. Here are some possible sources:

- State tourism or transportation departments (best sources of bike maps)
- Gas stations
- Convenience stores
- Tourist information centers
- Bike shops
- Chambers of commerce
- Auto clubs
- Backpacking stores (for topos)
- Specialty map stores
- Adventure Cycling Association (formerly Bikecentennial)

Adventure Cycling Association, a national organization formed to promote touring during the U.S. Bicentennial, has mapped several long-haul routes across the country, dividing them into segments that many people find perfect for 7- to 10-day trips. The maps tell you precisely what to do at every corner, have contour lines, and show the locations of bike shops, campsites, hostels, and general stores. See the Appendix for additional information.

Finding Your Way Through Cities and Towns

Bicycle touring and cities don't mix. Plan your route to stick to the smallest towns possible, giving a wide berth to anything bigger than 50,000 people—preferably smaller. Sometimes cities can't be avoided, especially at the beginning and end of a trip, when you might need access to public transportation. Here's how to make those encounters brief and reasonably pleasant:

- Get a map. A bike map might have inset maps of major cities, with recommended routes. Otherwise, get a city map in advance from your travel agent or an auto club, or buy one at a convenience store on the city's outskirts. In smaller towns, look for maps posted in gas stations. A few minutes here can save a lot of wasted energy later.
- Time your trip to avoid traffic. Sunday morning is best. Avoid rush hours.
- Don't be afraid to ask directions. The biggest problem cycling through a sizeable town isn't getting into it—it's getting back out on the right road. If you're looking for a little blue line on the highway map, note the name of the first town it goes to and ask for the road by that name.
- Talk to local cyclists. They may even offer to lead you.
- Off peak, main thoroughfares are often safe, and the quickest ways through town.
- Be flexible. If one road is dangerous, a better one may be nearby. Residential streets can be a gamble, though, possibly leading to endless cul-de-sacs and stop signs.
- Marked bike routes can be both helps and hindrances. Seeing the signs might reassure you that you've picked a good route, but if the route turns a corner, you don't know whether or not to follow. Trust your own route finding.
- Parkways often provide pleasant, scenic throughways and are favorite places for bike paths. But commuters are aware of their advantages, too, so watch out for traffic.

Showers, Sanitation, and Locks

Baths and Showers

At the end of a hard day, most of us want a hot shower. On tour that can sometimes be a tall order. If you absolutely *must* shower every night, stay in motels or commercial campgrounds. Some state parks have showers, but to know which ones you'll need a statewide brochure with a facilities check list.

Nevertheless there are ways to get showers on most days, especially if you don't mind taking them midday. Most commercial campgrounds will sell you one at a reasonable price, but for an even cheaper shower, go to a municipal swimming pool. State park campground showers could also be available to cyclists, sometimes with no fee. And occasionally in a cafe or general store, one of the locals will greet you with the offer of a shower. As a last resort in a showerless wilderness, bathe in a creek, or take a minimal spit bath on the contents of a single water bottle.

Laundry

You can wash dirty clothes in laundromats, sinks, or even rinse them in creeks (but don't use soap, even if it's biodegradable, in a creek). Wet clothes can be dried in laundromats or, if you don't mind looking like a traveling clothesline, slipped under the bungee cords or straps holding your sleeping bag to air dry as you pedal. Mesh exterior compartments in your front panniers work well.

Sanitation

If you're a backpacker accustomed to urinating in the woods and digging cat holes every morning, bicycle touring is luxurious: Few areas are so desolate that you won't see bathrooms several times a day. But even in civilized country, bathrooms can be impossibly far apart by bicycle. When there's no alternative, wander off into the bushes or, in farm country, a field of tall corn.

Under these circumstances, the rules of backpacking sanitation apply. Urine is no problem, but if you take a slightly longer visit, dig a hole six inches deep—and bury the toilet paper, too. Women should bury their toilet paper when they urinate, or carry it away in a plastic bag.

Locks

Many touring cyclists rarely lock their bikes, even if they leave them unattended for an hour or longer. Similarly, on large organized tours, thousands of cyclists leave their machines unlocked overnight.

I like to be a little more cautious than that. Bike theft and equipment pilfering are rarely problems in rural areas or small towns, but they can be if your route carries you through a major tourist area. Bike shops along the popular Pacific Coast route, for example, all seem to have tales of cyclists who've lost everything and had to replace it. And bicycles are stolen occasionally on organized tours, perhaps by professional thieves from nearby cities.

For a lock, I prefer a lightweight cable, padlocked behind the saddle, accessible but out of the way. The U-shaped locks popular in cities are overkill for touring, and too heavy. If you lose the key, lighter locks have the advantage that even a small-town police station will have bolt cutters sufficient to get you back on the road.

If there's nothing to lock your bike to, make it more difficult to steal by passing the cable through the wheels or locking several bicycles together.

Even the best lock guards only your bicycle. The best defense against losing equipment from your panniers is never to let your bike out of sight. Eating in a cafe, choose a table near a window, where you can keep an eye on it. At night lock your bike, and sleep close to it. You might be such a heavy sleeper that someone could carry you away with everything else, but a thief won't know that.

If you do leave your bike unattended for long, try to find someone to keep an eye on it. Or park it in a well-traveled place where a potential thief won't know you're not nearby, watching. If you go hiking, though, there's seldom any alternative to leaving your bike at the trailhead. Lock it securely, cross your fingers, and enjoy your hike—but don't leave your camera or wallet behind.

Food

The first time I toured, I was amazed by how much I ate. By the end of the trip, I'd lost four pounds, was wolfing large pizzas without assistance, and was eating every high-calorie snack I could get my hands on.

Cycling all day burns calories—lots of them—though how many is an open question. Such things as equipment efficiency, wind direction, tire inflation, and whether or not you're drafting, make good estimates hard to come by. For level-terrain riding without panniers, I've seen numbers ranging from 30 to 50 calories per mile. For mountain terrain, one organized tour, the Cycle Oregon, plans an 8,000-calorie-a-day diet for a 450-mile week. That's about 85 calories a mile, not counting normal base metabolism. And that's without panniers.

If you're bicycling to burn off calories as part of a diet regimen, the vagueness of these numbers is frustrating. But the bottom line is that on tour you'll be using 5,000 to 10,000 calories a day, maybe more. It's possible to gain weight, but difficult.

The ideal source of those calories is the subject of jibes between health-food addicts and the junk-food contingent. If you're looking for a diet to give you maximum athletic performance, consult one of the many detailed books on this subject. But the basic rules for eating on a tour are simple:

- The best energy foods are high in carbohydrates. Pancakes and spaghetti are classic ways to begin and end the day.
- Don't radically change your food choices simply because you're on tour. Eat foods that you know you like—ones that like you, as well.
- Remember that you're not trying to set speed or endurance records. So what if your lunch isn't ideal?

When you get home, though, beware—it's easy to gain a lot of weight before your appetite readjusts.

When to Eat

Another thing that changes is your eating schedule. Not only will you be eating a lot, you'll be eating frequently. Otherwise you may encounter "the bonk," a mild version of what marathoners call "hitting the wall."

Bonking comes on suddenly. One mile you're feeling fine; the next you can't concentrate and feel as though you're pedaling through molasses. If you're a racer who has to keep going no matter what, bonking is bad news. Touring, it's merely unpleasant.

Since bonking occurs because you've run out of energy, the solution is simple. Stop and eat something, particularly something high in carbohydrates. In a few minutes you'll probably feel almost as good as new.

With practice, you'll learn your limits and how to avoid bonking. Regardless of how many pancakes I have for breakfast, I know I'll bonk after 40 miles—less with panniers, considerably less in hilly terrain. I carry a snack and eat it or stop at a general store *before* I hit those limits.

Beyond that, your eating pattern is up to you. Some cyclists snack all day long and never eat a real meal; others want to sit down and relax three times a day. Here's my usual meal plan; yours will undoubtedly be different:

- Dawn. Eat a cold breakfast, so I don't spend the cool morning hours in a cafe or waiting for water to boil. Pita bread, bagels, or granola are excellent starters. Toaster pastries such as Pop Tarts carry well, can be eaten cold, and are high in carbohydrates.
- Midmorning. A second, "real" breakfast at a cafe, usually a stack of pancakes.
- Late lunch, 2:00 p.m. This can be anything from a sandwich to a milk shake to the lunch special in a cafe. Sometimes I graze on snacks from a string of general stores and convenience stores.
- Afternoon snack.
- Dinner. Sometimes cooked in camp, sometimes another cafe meal.

Whether you eat in cafes or cook your own meals, there's no need to carry a lot of food—seldom more than a 24-hour supply. If there's any kind of civilization around, you can resupply at least daily.

Camp Cookery

Cooking is optional. You can travel all the way across the country living off general stores and cafes. But a stove substantially increases your range of menu choices.

Buying stove fuel in quantities smaller than a gallon can be a problem—one you'll encounter even on short trips if they begin with an airplane flight, where carrying fuel is illegal. But the problem is easily solved once you're on the road. You can buy fuel by the pint from a camping store, and many gas stations, particularly in camping country, have white-gas pumps. You can also beg or buy fuel from fellow campers.

A gourmet backcountry chef can do wonders with a single-burner stove or a wood fire. Most people, though, are at a loss dealing with anything more complex than spaghetti or pancakes. Freeze-dried backpacking dinners offer easy options (just add boiling water to a foil pouch and wait a few minutes), but they're expensive, difficult to obtain on the road, and even the best are pretty poor fare. You'll eat better at a fraction of the cost by buying food in supermarkets. Here are some suggestions:

- *Packaged rice or noodle dishes.* Designed as side dishes for use at home, these make good main courses on the road. Check the cooking time before purchasing (some take 20 minutes), don't believe the stated number of servings, and add cheese to make them heartier.

- *Ramen stew.* Start with one or more packets of ramen noodles; add dehydrated soup mix, vegetables, and cheese. Quick and tasty.

- *Pseudo-falafel.* Start with bulk falafel powder from a supermarket. Mix to a paste, form into thin patties, and fry in vegetable oil at low heat. Serve with pita bread. It's not deep fried, but this falafel bears a reasonable resemblance. Carry the oil in a small plastic bottle, sealed in a plastic bag to guard against leaking.

- *Burritos.* Warm them in your skillet or fry lightly in oil. Use cheese, a tomato (you can carry one if you're careful), and any other vegetables you want. Packaged meat will travel safely for a few miles. Or use refried beans, either from a can or as a powder obtained in health food stores, reconstituted with boiling water.

An excellent reference for preparing tasty dishes with a minimum of equipment is Don Jacobson's *One Pan Gourmet* (Ragged Mountain Press, 1993).

Guarding Against Things That Go Munch in the Night

Bicycle touring, you can't store your food in the safety of your car. Like a backpacker, you're open to the possibility of having it eaten by anything from a mouse to a bear.

The traditional backpacking solution is putting your food in a spare stuff sack and hanging it in a tree, high enough and far enough from the trunk that even a bear couldn't reach it. Most cyclists are much more cavalier. You won't encounter bears in a city park; there the problem is more likely to be rodents. I carry a length of nylon cord to hang my food in a tree, but rarely use it. More often, I put my leftovers in my panniers, operating under the assumption that mice can't climb spokes. So far, it's worked.

To be safe, I never keep food in my tent, nor do I eat there. It's one thing to have food stolen from my panniers; it's another to have a raccoon gnaw through the wall of my tent. If you *are* camping in bear country, hang your food in a tree, and don't sleep too close to it.

Water

Water, at two pounds per quart, is the heaviest and most important thing you'll carry. Count on going though upwards of a gallon a day —twice that in hot weather.

How much you'll need to carry at any given time depends on the distance between water sources, but at a minimum you should have three bottles (five if you're carrying heavy baggage), refilling them at every opportunity. If water sources are more than three hours apart (or temperatures are over 80°F), you could need even more than that.

Dehydration is insidious. Drink *before* you feel thirsty. The sensation of thirst develops slowly: By the time you feel it, it's well past the time you should have been drinking. The tepid liquid in your water bottles may be unappetizing, but if you're working hard, drink at least one or two bottles per hour even in cool weather.

If your water supply is limited, drink it, don't pour it over your head. Ounce-for-ounce it will do you more good inside you.

To tell if you're drinking enough, pay attention to your bladder. Drink a lot in the morning, even if it means visiting the bushes several times in the first few miles. On the road, start drinking when you realize it's been a while since you felt any bladder pressure.

If you never need to urinate as the day progresses, you're dehydrating. Similarly, urine color in the morning is a valuable indicator of whether you've recovered from the day before. If it's dark, you probably haven't.

More urgently, a sensation of chills on a hot day is a not-to-be-overlooked warning sign of dehydration. Rest and drink, immediately.

Sampling Local Life

Touring is more than pedaling from place to place. It is a process of learning about the land and its people. After a few days on the road, it can also become a new, relaxing way of viewing life.

Part of that lifestyle is pausing—not just for the grand attractions that would catch the attention of any tourist, but at small, intimate places passed up by motorized tourists: mountain streams, small-town museums, off-the-beaten-path wildlife refuges. Sometimes you may find yourself chatting with a general-store proprietor who's lived in the same small town all her life, or taking a siesta at a tiny roadside park—that in itself an experiment in a lifestyle quite different from both normal work and the average vacation. Learning to mix these with your pedaling is a formula for cycle touring at its finest.

Group Size

The cycling experience varies dramatically with group size. Large groups give you a wider variety of companions and ease van-supported tours by providing a larger pool of drivers. Decision-making, however, can become cumbersome. Large groups also have fewer choices of campsites and more chance of friction between people with different riding styles or preferred times of day for pedaling. Someone is bound to be dissatisfied with the daily mileage.

For self-contained touring, groups of two or four can be ideal. That gives you companionship and the ability to draft in a headwind without making your group so large that finding campsites is difficult. And because less of your energy is devoted to group dynamics, you'll have more opportunity to talk with the locals and get a feel for the culture you're visiting. A group of four is usually better than three because a foursome can split into pairs if people's riding paces vary. Threesomes can be awkward if you're not good friends, since it's easy for one person to feel left out.

Going Solo

The ultimate form of self-contained touring is going solo. It's not for everyone, but if you like your own company, it's one of the most rewarding ways of travel. Since there's no group, there are no group dynamics to worry about, and solo touring puts you in the closest possible touch with the landscape and the people who inhabit it. You can stop when you want, ride when you want, and do however many miles a day you want.

It's also not as lonely as it sounds. Riding solo, you personify a deep American wanderlust, a dream shared by many people in the towns you pass through; you'll find that many will want to talk to you. You may also meet other cyclists along the way, solo or in small groups, joining them for anything from a few miles to several days, perhaps even making lifetime friends with people you'd barely have spoken to riding in a group.

Riding solo, expect to cover more terrain than in a group, even though you don't have a drafting partner. In a small group, when one of you has a flat, everyone stops. When one of you is tired, you all take a rest. Traveling solo you avoid that, as well as being more likely to ride at odd hours or late into the evening.

The downside is that your pack is slightly heavier, since there's no one with whom to share community gear such as stove, pots, tool kit, and tent.

The risk factor is real but greatly exaggerated. If you crash or get sick, you won't have a companion to render first aid, but in rural country, people are usually extremely helpful. If you do get hurt, the chances are that the first person to come along will help you out.

When it comes to traffic, you might actually be safer than in a group. To begin with, you won't be tempted to ride two abreast. However companionable, it's more dangerous than single file. Secondly, when drivers encounter a group of bicycles, they often pass all of them at once, even if they shouldn't. Solo you're less of an obstacle, and therefore may be less likely to be crowded.

The precautions to reduce the risk of being mugged or harassed are similar to those that apply to women, discussed on the next page.

Special Concerns for Women

by Vera Jagendorf

As a woman with thousands of miles of touring alone, with other women, or with men, I find that two concerns are greater for women than for men: safety and bathrooms.

Safety is what everybody first thinks of. When I spent a 2,500-mile summer traveling through the West, mostly solo, one question people constantly asked was, "Aren't you afraid?" My response was always the same: "There's no reason to be. Everyone has been friendly and helpful."

The potential dangers aren't all that different from everyday life. Obviously, if you find yourself being threatened in the middle of nowhere, you're at a loss. But that can happen in everyday city life, too, and is probably more likely there than in the rural areas or small towns you'll be visiting.

As anywhere, the most important deterrents to hassles are awareness, avoidance, and confidence. It's when you show fear that you open the door to more than a verbal taunt. And somehow, after climbing a big pass or traveling hundreds of miles, it's hard not to do anything but exude an aura of *I can take care of myself just fine!*

Even verbal taunts are rare. When I traveled alone, women tended to react to me with mild bewilderment; men usually gave me instant respect. Even the "Hey, baby" macho types were no problem. What I was doing seemed to strip them of that *I'm-better-than-this-this-female* attitude. Awed out of their pretense, they became ordinary people, more likely to offer a beer than a catcall.

Being on a bicycle piled with gear itself arouses people's curiosity, encouraging them to talk to you when they'd never do so otherwise. Being a woman makes you even more of an oddity. You're also more obviously nonthreatening than a man. That brings out the best in people, making them want to show off the friendliness of their towns, while they live vicariously through your story.

People will want to help you, inviting you in for showers and meals. Once, when I was traveling with another woman, a rancher let us sleep in an empty house. Other people invited us to camp on their lawns. Men get such offers, too, but as a woman you'll get them more frequently—probably daily, or close to it.

If you're traveling alone and are at all friendly, many people will want to buy you lunch or an ice cream cone or give you some other such invitation. Don't let city-bred sensibilities scare you away. There's nothing wrong with going into a restaurant with a stranger, especially if afterwards you're going to be camped in a campground with dozens other people. You'll find out a lot about the town and the people.

Bathrooms. Men can relieve themselves on the side of the road and not look like they're doing much but staring at the scenery. Women are likely to want more privacy. But if the biggest plant around is a sagebush and the nearest town is 10 miles away, you have to learn to be quick or not to care. If you need more decorum than that, you should avoid touring in remote desert areas.

VANS
AND CREDIT CARDS
—you don't have
to camp or carry
a lot of weight

▼

Types of Tours

If seeing the world at a bicycle's leisurely pace is appealing but you can't imagine carrying 30 to 60 pounds of camping gear—or sleeping in a tent—credit-card touring could be the perfect solution. If it's only the weight that bothers you, traveling with a support vehicle might be an answer. A vehicle allows you to rest and grab a ride if you get tired or simply don't feel like pedaling as many miles as your friends.

Even people whose primary interest is self-contained touring may occasionally want to shift to these lighter styles. Early in the season they offer ways to tour before you're well enough trained for heavy loads; in the fall they offer alternatives to long nights cooped up in a tent, and they're good ways to begin the sport with a minimum of specialized equipment.

Credit-Card

Credit-card touring draws its name from the assertion that you need only a credit card. That's an overstatement. You also need rain gear, a change of clothes, jacket and tights, tools, and street clothes for dining out or exploring your destination by foot. What you don't need is camping gear, cooking equipment, or (frequently) lots of water bottles. All told, you'll carry no more than half as much as you'd carry self-contained.

For an extended credit-card tour—anything more than one or two nights—the best destinations are conventional tourist areas, where you have enough lodging choices to plan your accommodations around your desired route, rather than the reverse. Such areas also give you more day-to-day flexibility, allowing you to set out for a week without a complete set of reservations, confident that you can find *something* on relatively short notice. But don't make the notice *too* short unless you're traveling well off-season. That can leave you searching desperately for a church couch, or sitting up all night in a 24-hour restaurant or gas station.

Although areas with a lot of overnight accommodations are easiest for credit-card touring, more remote areas aren't out of the question—many small towns have motels. You won't find luxury, but you *will* stay warm and dry. Start by looking in travel guidebooks, but don't quit there. Some of these motels are too tiny to be listed—perhaps having only a half-dozen units. A better source of information is local chambers of commerce. When you find a motel, make sure there's a restaurant nearby; that isn't always the case.

If you stay at expensive inns or B&Bs, credit-card touring is by no means a budget vacation. But the price can be kept lower. Some of my friends often do spring and fall weekend tours on which they've crammed as many as nine people into one large room. There's a charge for the extra bodies, but it's usually reasonable.

Another trick for a weekend touring loop where motels are far apart is to drive out the night before, staying in a motel and reserving your room for a second night. In the morning, drive to a point halfway around your intended loop from the motel, bringing nothing with you but day-trip necessities. Park, and ride back to the motel for the night. In the

morning, check your baggage at the front desk, pedal back to your car, and pick up your checked baggage on the way home. A similar approach would be to check into a centrally located motel and explore the neighboring terrain by a series of day rides.

Catered

If you really want to indulge yourself, sign up for a catered tour. Many organizations, large and small, offer such tours. Destinations can be as exotic and challenging as Vietnam or Baja, or as safe and familiar as New England or the antebellum South. None will be cheap, but you'll stay in better inns,

and dine with some degree of style, and have your baggage carried by van.

Choosing such a tour is like choosing any other vacation package. The larger and more established organizations are more likely to offer a consistent package, but that doesn't mean the smaller outfitters can't do an excellent job.

Look for ads in outdoor or bicycling magazines. You may also find fliers in bike shops, especially those that cater to touring.

Van-Supported

With credit-card touring your route and daily distances are dictated by the need to reach a motel

before dark. Van-supported touring gives you the option of camping without carrying heavy weight.

Your packs for van-supported touring will actually be lighter than for most forms of credit-card touring. You don't need to carry the next day's clothes, and if the van meets you occasionally during the day, you can also let it carry much of your tool kit.

"Van-supported" touring is another misnomer: The support vehicle doesn't have to be a van. All you need is something large enough to carry everyone's baggage, with a bike rack capable of holding at least two bicycles.

There are two basic van-supported tours. In one, the van serves as a baggage truck, meeting you at each night's destination and giving tired or aching riders a chance to hitch a ride. This approach is easy on the driver, who is free to spend the day sightseeing. The cyclists need to be prepared to fend for themselves.

The other approach is to have the van meet you every 10 to 20 miles to dispense water and snacks and give you a place to shed or retrieve clothing. Ideally, the driver plays leapfrog with the cyclists, giving them a head start between rest breaks then checking up on them en route to the next stop. The biggest problem is finding a driver who's willing to spend a weekend, let alone a week, at this rather tedious pursuit. People who are willing to do it should be cherished as the golden resources they are.

If you can't find a full-time driver, rotate the job among yourselves. Obviously, the more of you to share the burden, the easier it will be. The first day will be the most difficult since no one is likely to *want* to drive. One approach is to divide the day's mileage among all the cyclists, with everyone taking one or more shifts. I've done this with groups as small as three, rotating drivers every 10 to 12 miles.

Finding volunteers isn't as difficult after the first few hours; by then, somebody's usually happy for the rest break—except perhaps on long downhill runs.

In many ways, van-supported touring sounds idyllic. You can stay in motels and dine in fine restaurants, but after a while being tied to the apron strings of the van may feel confining, continuously reminding you of your dependence on the internal

combustion engine and all it symbolizes. Don't be surprised if the time comes when you wish to cast loose and strike out on your own, regardless of the weight.

Light

"Light touring" is often used as a catch-all term for any touring other than self-contained. But a better use of the term is for touring that avoids motel- or van-dependency without a lot of extra weight. On a light tour, you're prepared to camp but carry only the bare minimum of equipment, remaining fairly close to civilization.

Plan the excursion either as a camping trip with motels as a foul-weather bail out, or as an inn-to-inn trip with camping as an option for greater route-planning flexibility. The difference is in intent, not equipment.

In both cases all you'll need in addition to your credit-card touring gear is a lightweight sleeping bag, sleeping pad, and a minimal tent, tarp, hammock, or bivvy bag. You won't carry cooking gear and you'll stick to warm enough climates that you won't need heavy clothes. By avoiding bulky clothing, you also avoid the need for both front and rear panniers, saving weight. To balance the load front to back, use front panniers, with your sleeping bag, pad, and tent lashed on a rear stack.

All told, if you're careful about keeping down weight, you can do a light camping trip with only 6 to 8 pounds more equipment than for credit-card touring—even less if you can get away with a nylon tarp instead of a bivvy bag.

ORGANIZED TOURS

▼

Summer Camp on Wheels

Traditionally, cycle touring is enjoyed in small groups or even solo. Whether you go self-contained, inn-to-inn, or van-supported, you'll spend much of the time alone or with one or two close companions. For those who are more gregarious—or who want to try something different—there's another option. Each year, tens of thousands of cyclists hit the road on inexpensive, week-long tours sponsored by clubs, newspapers, state tourist departments, or a growing assortment of budget-minded tour companies. Groups range from fewer than 50 to several thousand, with an atmosphere like an adult summer camp on wheels. Best of all, there are trucks to carry your baggage.

The typical tour package includes sag wagons (to carry riders or bicycles if either "sags"), route maps, water stops, group camping, and baggage transport. Many offer indoor accommodations (seldom more than a gymnasium for "floor floppers"), and some provide meals. If a food package isn't part of the tour, churches or service clubs usually offer reasonably priced meals. On point-to-point routes there is often a modestly priced shuttle bus back to the start or to the nearest airport.

Usually, overnight stops are in very small towns whose populations are doubled or tripled by the influx of cyclists. For the locals it's frequently the most exciting thing since the last near-miss by a tornado. For the cyclists it's an introduction to small-town hospitality.

These tours aren't races. There's no finish line, no time clock, no prize for being first except the dubious honor of being asked to help unload baggage.

A typical day begins before dawn with a "zipper serenade," as one by one, cyclists peek outside to see what the weather is likely to bring. After breakfast, riders flow from camp in small groups, often riding with different people each day, or even from one hour to the next. On the smaller rides they quickly disperse, but on large ones the pack never thins out, producing what one observer described as an army to please the likes of Attila the Hun.

On the Tour

Except for the fact that you'll be cycling every day for a week, life on one of these tours is similar to a long training ride. In some ways it's easier because you'll have sag support and several water and snack stops. On the larger tours there are even roving repair vans combing the course for cyclists who need assistance. All you'll need to carry is the minimum gear to get to camp: full water bottles, a tire patch kit, sunscreen, a spare tube, lunch money, and rain gear. You also need room for unwanted clothing, since you're likely to start early and shed layers as the day warms up. Fast riders and those who like to be first out of camp may want to carry a book as well, in case they beat the baggage truck to the next night's stop.

Know group riding etiquette, even on the smaller rides. Announcing, "On your left," or "Braking!" all week will get tiresome, but it's better than crashing. Think twice before getting into tight, fast-moving drafting chains with strangers. Pace chains are probably the leading cause of serious accidents on this type of ride.

When hundreds or thousands of cyclists descend on a small town, the result has to be seen to be believed. Fairgrounds, high school football fields, and lawns of willing residents turn into mammoth tent cities that spring up overnight only to melt away with the dawn. On smaller rides, finding a good camping spot is seldom a problem, but on the large ones, it pays to be portable. If your baggage is light enough to carry a few hundred yards from the truck, you'll have fewer neighbors and a better chance of a quiet night's sleep.

Showers are generally available in school locker rooms, and that's where many cyclists go the moment they reach camp. If the hot water's gone, be patient. Water heaters recharge and there's usually little demand for showers after dinner. Some rides—at least in the West—charter portable shower units designed for forest fire crews, making good on promises of hot water and short lines for as many as 2,000 cyclists. It adds a bit to the price, but for most people it's worth it.

Packing is different from packing for a self-contained trip. Because most of these tours have a one-

or two-bag limit, a touring rig—which disassembles into too many pieces—is a disadvantage. Buy the largest duffel bag you can find. A heavy-duty nylon or canvas bag is adequate; make sure it has a sturdy shoulder strap. Waterproof material is also a plus. Some tours automatically move baggage indoors or under an awning if it rains, but don't count on it.

Think about trying to find your bag in a giant pile. Buy something distinctive. A green canvas duffel isn't a wise idea—too many other riders will have something similar.

Realize that the bag is going to be thrown around, stepped on, and buried under hundreds of pounds of other baggage. Don't put anything fragile in it. If you wouldn't trust it to an airline, don't trust it to the baggage truck.

On tours with a one-bag limit, practice stuffing everything into your bag beforehand. If it's a tight fit, leave something behind. There may be no scientific explanation, but baggage seems to expand as the week progresses. If the fit is still tight or the bag heavy enough to be unwieldy, add an empty gym bag to your luggage. Many tours enforce the bag limit only on the first day, not objecting if, having proved that you can compress your gear to a single bag, you later distribute it into two.

Your baggage will be similar to what you'd take on a self-contained trip, except you'll probably want more shirts and a couple of sets of street pants. For a fresh shirt each day in camp, put on the next day's cycling shirt after you shower. You'll have a clean shirt each evening, and one that's still reasonably fresh the following morning.

Don't count on visiting a laundromat midway through the trip unless you *really* enjoy waiting in lines. The same applies to pay phones. Don't rashly promise to call home every night, or you'll spend a significant portion of each evening waiting for a phone. If you must call, do it before you reach camp, even if you have to pay a higher midday rate.

The biggest problem living out of a duffel bag for a week is keeping things organized. If you're one of those people who throws everything around haphazardly anyway, you'll be right at home. Otherwise, invest in a collection of gadget bags so you can at least separate your toothbrush from your socks. Something larger, such as an extra sleeping bag stuff sack, will help keep dirty clothes from contaminating clean ones.

Choosing a Tour

New tours start every year, while old ones change format periodically. Some run the same route year after year; others try to avoid ever doing the same route twice. Also, mailing addresses and phone numbers often change yearly, particularly for tours organized by bike clubs rotating leadership duties among their members.

Good sources of information are the ride listings in the backs of cycling magazines. Don't just check the current issues; go to a library and scan the previous year's listings as well. Even if they're out of date, important factors such as group size, mileage, registration fee, and time of year aren't likely to change dramatically from one year to the next. And the addresses should be current enough to at least forward to the proper place.

The tours you're looking for will show up as multi-day events, ranging from two days to a week. A few will even be multi-week. Sometimes, though, it's difficult to distinguish camping tours from races with names designed to evoke images of the Tour

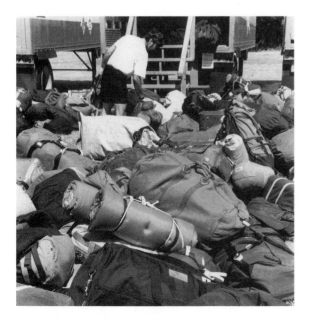

de France. Ironically, the use of the word "tour" in a ride's name makes it more likely to be a race.

Another way to find tours is to contact bike clubs, bike shops, or the American Youth Hostels in the area you'd like to visit. If a full week is too much of a commitment, many clubs sponsor two- or three-day weekend rides. There are also a multitude of well-organized pledge rides run by such charities as the MS Society or the Lung Association. If all else fails, go on a popular tour in your home state, reading T-shirts and asking other riders what tours they'd recommend; I've learned about many good rides that way.

Well-established tours, mostly week-long, are listed in the Appendix, along with their addresses, approximate dates, usual routes, and group sizes

Preparation

Once you've chosen a ride, send a self-addressed stamped envelope (SASE) to the tour director for registration materials. The SASE is common courtesy and can save a lot of time. Some rides may not answer you without one. Don't wait until the last minute; many tours fill months in advance.

If a ride is full, don't give up. There might be a waiting list, or registrations might be traded through classified ads or notices in bike shops. It's often possible to get on rides through late cancellations.

Once you get an application, feel free to contact the tour director to ask questions not covered by the brochure. What's the traffic like? How hilly is the course? Will it be hot, cold, or some of each? Are there guaranteed hot showers? What kind of repair facilities are available?

Don't expect to be pampered. Most of these tours are organized by cyclists for cyclists. They aren't run by posh catering companies, and the workers—who may be unpaid volunteers—don't like to be treated like servants. A good ride should be well organized and prepared to help you in an emergency—but not to wait on you hand and foot.

Train adequately, and train early. If the course is hilly, train on hills. If it's going to be hot, get used to heat. And expect to have one of the great adventures of your life and to make friends you'll keep in touch with for years to come.

CHALLENGES AND ADVERSITIES:
with proper preparation, both can be fun (almost)

▼

Hills and Mountains

Bicyclists use "hill" indiscriminately to describe terrain ranging from freeway overpasses to full-fledged mountains. Often, they reverse the meaning of the word "good." If someone tells you that the Continental Divide in Colorado is a "good hill," it's likely to mean it took her all day and she thought she was going to die before reaching the top. With practice, though, even "good" hills aren't so bad. Climbs test your stamina; descents are exhilarating but require more skill.

When approaching a daunting climb, resign yourself to taking however long is necessary to reach the top. If it's a mountain, it might be hours, so pace yourself accordingly.

Before the going gets steep, downshift to a gear close to the one you think will be appropriate. You can shift one or two gears easily enough on the hill, but it's hard to make big jumps when you're grinding to a halt.

Try standing up occasionally to vary the rhythm. Because your optimum cadence standing is lower than sitting, *upshift* one gear before you stand. But be cautious about charging up long hills this way; it's easy to injure a knee, and some touring bikes—especially when loaded—are unstable when ridden this way.

Sitting, choose a gear that lets you keep up nearly the same cadence you'd maintain on the level. This takes practice; even experienced cyclists often climb hills in gears that are too high. Sliding backward a bit on the saddle also helps, particularly on steeper stretches. You'll find yourself doing this automatically; it changes the leverage of your pedal stroke and gives you more hill-climbing strength.

If the hill is too steep to climb any other way, flatten it out by "tacking" up it in a series of broad, sweeping S-curves. It takes forever, and you have to be particularly alert for traffic, but sometimes it's the only way other than walking.

On long hills, playing mind games can help get you to the top. "I'm going to take a break at the

next milepost," or "in 20 telephone poles," or "when the sun comes out from behind that cloud"— any of these converts the climb into a series of smaller, less daunting goals.

Rest breaks. When you take a break—and only macho racer-types feel they've been defeated by a hill if they do—shift into your lowest gear before you halt. Stopping somewhere other than in the middle of the steepest pitch in sight also helps make it easier to start back up.

Rest before you get seriously tired; numerous short breaks are preferable to one long one—if you stop for more than 5 or 10 minutes, your legs will start to stiffen up, especially if it's cool.

I ride frequently with a friend who is a master of the short rest break, stopping as often as twice a mile for 30 to 60 seconds. Riding with her, I reach the top feeling fresh and energetic, and not spending a great deal more time than I would have if I'd been more macho.

Machismo is your worst enemy. It can hurt your knees or increase the chance of painfully sore muscles. If you have trouble forcing yourself to stop until you're about to collapse, remind yourself that you'll be pedaling again tomorrow. Frequent rest breaks allow you to cover more distance per day with greater comfort.

Descents

The fun part starts when you finally reach the top.

If the descent is "slow" and you want to go faster, hunch forward, bending low over the handlebars in a "tuck." Pull in your knees and elbows to reduce air resistance further, but keep your head up to see what's happening far in front of you.

Loose flapping clothing or equipment will slow you down. Zip up, tuck in, and button down for maximum speed. You might want to do this anyway since the downgrade will be chilly. Also, check your equipment to make sure nothing is in danger of getting into the spokes. If that happens at 40 mph, you'll regret it.

And 40 mph is the operative phrase. Depending on aerodynamics, your terminal velocity on a long, steep hill will be somewhere between 30 and 55 mph. What speed is safe depends on your confidence, your bicycle, and the wind direction. If your wheels aren't perfectly round, they could shimmy at high speeds. Spoke reflectors may also be destabilizing, and some bicycles respond differently to headwinds than to tailwinds.

Most people find that 40 to 45 mph is the maximum speed at which they feel safe. Cyclists have been known to tuck in behind trucks and ride the draft at 65 mph, but this is insane—think about

tucked

most wind resistance

what would happen if you blew out a tire.

If your natural coasting speed is too fast, do the reverse of a tuck, holding your shoulders high and wide apart, leaving your jacket partially unzipped. This can knock several miles an hour from your speed. And the wind drag of your panniers will slow you down more than their weight is likely to speed you up.

You'll also need your brakes. Because your weight shifts forward on the downgrade, you won't get much stopping power from the rear brake without locking the wheel. You might not even be able to come to a full stop with the rear brake alone, so you *have* to be confident about using both brakes.

If all you're trying to do is hold down your speed, either brake will suffice; the best approach is to alternate between them, letting one cool while you use the other.

If you must brake a lot, stop occasionally to let your rims cool, especially if you're carrying heavy baggage. It's rare, but enough of a temperature change can pop a tire when the air expands inside it. Radical climate changes can have the same effect; I once met a California cyclist who blew a tire after dropping 6,000 feet from the Sierra Nevada into the blistering heat of the Sacramento Valley. Such events could be due more to improper tire installation than to temperature change, but I wouldn't run down big hills on overinflated tires, regardless.

Blowouts are more likely from running over something sharp or letting a piece of baggage get in your spokes, skidding the wheel. If it happens, don't panic. It's usually the rear wheel, which is easier to control. Brake to a halt, using the unaffected wheel as much as possible. Try to go straight, especially for those first important seconds that you're shedding most of your speed.

Sudden blowouts are uncommon, so don't let the fear of one intimidate you. One of the great joys of a downgrade is speed—as long as you're not going so fast that you're on the verge of losing control.

Technical Descents

If a downgrade is smooth, broad, and reasonably straight, just put down your head and "let 'er rip."

But if it's winding, rutted, or full of gravel, it's much more "technical," requiring skill and judgment mixed with caution. Ruts, even ones that are hard to see, can grab your front wheel and wrench it sideways; gravel can appear suddenly as you round a bend and cause a skidding crash.

Avoid gravel patches if you can. If you must cross one, do so by going straight, without braking hard when you're on it. On curves, don't go so fast that you couldn't stop if you found the lane to be unexpectedly blocked.

You can negotiate technical descents even if you're not used to them by inching your way down. With practice, descending even a series of full-fledged switchbacks is a wonderful exercise, with mind and body working in perfect harmony as you lean right, then left, then right again, easing your way down the mountainside. You might be surprised to find that your hands become so tired from braking that you have to stop to rest them. It's a good opportunity to enjoy the view.

If there isn't a good shoulder, don't get too close to the edge of the road. Crosswind gusts are common on hills and can knock you two or three feet sideways before you have time to react. Rounding right-hand bends with limited sight distance, ride well out into the lane to increase the distance you can see, as well as the distance from which others can see you. On left-hand bends, riding well out in the lane allows you to ride faster by reducing the tendency of a crowned road surface to throw you in the wrong direction. Just don't ride so close to the center that you lean into the path of an oncoming car.

Traffic

On an upgrade, cars usually present no problem. Drivers sympathize with your sweaty efforts, and you're going slowly enough that it's easy to maneuver out of the way.

On downgrades cars are more dangerous. You're going faster, so you won't meet as many of them, but that same speed makes it harder to get out of the way. Take enough of the lane to discourage cars from passing you on blind corners.

If someone does pass you with insufficient sight distance, slow down immediately to let him get by quickly. If a car pops into sight coming from the opposite direction, the driver passing you will have to choose between hitting it head on or hitting you.

Even on straight roads, slowing down when a car passes is a good idea. Many drivers just don't understand how fast you're going, and it's not uncommon for them to start pulling back in the moment their front bumpers reach you. Trucks and long RVs are particularly dangerous. After hearing of a cyclist killed this way by the rear wheels of a logging truck on a 40-mph downgrade, I decided that the moment a long vehicle starts to pass me, the safest thing to do is to brake hard—until I'm going as slowly as the driver probably thinks I am. Being able to shy away from a long rig that cuts in too soon is yet another reason for keeping a safety cushion of ridable pavement between you and the edge of the road.

In some parts of the country, cars are almost uniformly courteous, even if they have to follow you downhill for miles. Reward that courtesy by looking for the first good opportunity to pull over.

Roller-Coaster Hills

In many states, mountains are conspicuously absent but hills are plentiful, forming rolling terrain in which you climb the same 50 to 100 feet several times a mile—an endless roller-coaster that's every bit as exhausting as the Continental Divide.

If you've got good knees, stand up on the pedals at the base of the hill, upshift, and "pop" the hill in a few swift, sweaty pedal strokes (this works best if you're not carrying heavy panniers). When you reach the top sit back down, shifting to a gear where you can find a proper, fast cadence. Then use the downgrade to build up momentum for the next hill, repeating the process again and again and again. It's great fun—unless you run out of energy before you run out of hills.

Poor Visibility: Forest and Fog

Wooded areas are cool, shaded, and often threaded by scenic, little-used roads; in short they can be perfect for cycling. Take care, though, to make sure you're visible despite sharp corners or dense vegetation.

As with blind curves anywhere, keep your ears open to what's going on behind you, and ride well out into the lane to be visible from a greater distance. If a car comes up behind, move over to be safe, but try to encourage the driver not to pass unless there's enough visibility.

Logging trucks. In most places, weekends present the most dangerous traffic conditions as thousands of urbanites flood to the hinterland. In logging or mining country, the usual cautions can be reversed: the greatest threats are on weekdays. Pedaling through such a region on a work day, keep your ears open and give the trucks the road if necessary.

Warning pennants. Carrying a slow-moving vehicle symbol is one way to make yourself more visible under poor conditions. Another is to use a different kind of high-visibility symbol such as a warning pennant on a tall fiberglass wand. These orange flags are eye-catching and may give motorists advance warning of your presence over the top of hillcrests or around curves obscured by dense vegetation. They're useful even in the open, and in a crosswind from the right they bend sideways into the traffic lane, encouraging cars to give you a wider berth as they dodge the flag.

These pennants aren't stylish, and they increase your wind resistance. But their biggest drawback is that the pole, mounted by a bracket to your rear frame, may droop backward—right at eye level for any cyclist close behind. If you use one, angle the bracket so this doesn't happen, or tape the wand to your rack to give it a second support point.

Fog. Fog is extremely dangerous; wait it out if you can. If you absolutely must ride in it, use lights and reflectors but assume you're invisible. Yield to everything that moves—or looks like it might.

Deserts

Deserts and semiarid country present unique challenges, along with some of the most beautiful scenery in the nation, but they're not good choices for your first tour. The heat, big hills, and long distances between outposts of civilization make them places to graduate to after you've developed your skills under more forgiving conditions.

The biggest of these difficulties are the sheer, raw distances. You can avoid heat by cycling at dawn or dusk or picking a season when the temperature is moderate. Hills can be inched up in low gear; dry air can be overcome by drinking plenty of water. But scenery unfolds slowly over the distances, in rare cases (such as parts of the Great Basin) so slowly that you might spend 24 hours or longer between resupply points.

Van-supported touring eliminates most of these problems by giving you a mobile snack shop and water-supply point. Self-contained, though, you need to be comfortable with heavy loads. Part of

the weight will be clothing; even if it's hot at midday, a desert can be cold at night. But most of the excess will be water, especially if towns are far enough apart that you might need to camp on the open range.

Precisely how much water you'll need depends on the temperature and your body's water efficiency. The latter can vary widely. On one recent journey through 24 hours of hilly, semidesert mountains, I carried more than two gallons of water, and used it all. My companion drank only two-thirds as much.

Don't ration your water—it's a myth that doling it out in tiny sips will make it go further. All it will do is make you miserable earlier. A better way to reduce your water use is to dress sensibly. Wear a white helmet and a loose, light-colored shirt. White would be ideal for the shirt, too, but high visibility is also important, especially if you're in an area where long, straight roads and dancing mirages can

hypnotize drivers into reacting slowly. Going without a shirt not only risks sunburn, but dehydrates you faster as the wind sucks moisture from your body.

If you'll be riding in midday heat, some of your training should be in hot weather. Some people, stupidly, try to train their bodies to use less water by not drinking on training rides. It doesn't work, *does* run the risk of serious medical complications, and teaches you nothing about how much water you actually need. Drink what you need, and keep track of the amount so you have a good idea of how much to carry on tour. Also, do your first desert touring in areas where the towns are close enough that you'll never have to carry more than a few hours' supply.

At each town, ask if the next one shown on your map really exists, and find out if it has a store. Highway maps are littered with tiny hamlets where nothing remains but the name and one or two buildings.

Not all arid areas are stark rock and cactus. The high desert of eastern Oregon, for example, is a land of sagebrush, ponderosa pine uplands, and frequent snow-fed rivers. But it is still desert cycling, with blazing midsummer sun, challenging hills, and long, unpopulated distances.

Thorn Country

Thorns, commonly associated with deserts, are even more of a problem in semiarid regions that don't quite qualify as desert. A simple warning: there are things out there than can eat your tires. The two I'm most familiar with are sand burrs and goatheads. Both will puncture tires even if you've got thorn-resistant inserts. In dry country, never ride through grass, even in a well-watered city park. In extreme situations you can pick up a dozen or more burrs all at once. Some types are even reputed to grow in tar strips, so steer clear of anything green and carry more than one spare tube.

Living—Or at Least Drinking—Off the Land

In some areas, much like a backpacker, you can reduce the amount of water you carry by drinking from streams. This is particularly appealing in the mountains, where creeks run clear and cold, but it can also work in semidesert country if it is well laced by creeks fed by distant mountains.

Anywhere, though, you must first purify the water by one of three basic methods. The most surefire is to boil it for five minutes, a nuke-em-dead approach to bacteria, viruses, and giardia (a nasty, single-celled parasite that has become the bane of backpackers). But even boiling won't do any good if you suspect chemical contamination.

A second approach is to use water-purification tablets. Lightweight and portable, these are perfect for emergencies and should be a normal part of your first-aid kit. The label will tell you how many to use, depending on water temperature and clarity. Make sure you also treat the lip of your water bottle

by splashing a little of the water onto it after the tablets have dissolved. Don't forget the drinking nipple. Then let it stand for the length of time recommended by the label—about 20 minutes.

If boiling or pills is too time-consuming, or you don't want to drink chemical-tasting water, backpacking water filters offer a high-tech solution that gives you a quick drink with all the flavor of a mountain creek. These filters use a hand-operated pump to force the water though a very fine filter, sometimes combined with activated carbon. They're expensive, so take time to check out the various designs before you buy. Don't get one that requires three hands, and look for a pump handle that's easy to use, quart after quart.

Touring in the mountains, I prefer water filters because they allow me to camp on the spur of the moment beside a creek or in a remote, primitive campground. They aren't light, weighing about as much as a full water bottle, but a party of three or four people needs only one. And the filter can save you far more than its own weight by reducing your load of water.

Be aware, though, that filters clog easily. Avoid muddy water, or strain it with cheesecloth before filtering it. Also read the manufacturer's description to see precisely *what* the filter removes. Most filters are rated to remove giardia and bacteria, but they won't remove viruses, such as the one that causes hepatitis. It's important, therefore, to choose the water sources that are the least likely to be contaminated.

"Need water." If you're brave and outgoing, there's another way to avoid carrying large amounts of water. I once met a cyclist who went all the way across Nevada with only a couple of water bottles—and a cardboard sign reading "NEED WATER." When he ran low, he hung the sign on the back of his equipment rack. The first RV, he said, always stopped.

If you don't have a sign, you can also flag down an RV by holding out a water bottle and waving it. Of course, if you're in an area so far off the beaten path that there are no RVs . . . .

Bridges, Tunnels, and Freeways

Bridges

Most bridges are no obstacle, but occasionally a wide, comfortable shoulder vanishes at the start of the bridge, forcing you to share a lane with the traffic, even on a busy road.

As with any narrow road, the best defense is usually to be assertive. Or take a sidewalk if one is available.

Where to ride in the lane depends on its width. If it's roomy enough for both you and the traffic, stay well to the right. If not, wait for a gap, then enter the bridge far enough out into the lane to force cars coming up from behind to either follow you or cross the center line to pass. Most drivers will understand. If they don't, let them get angry; don't invite someone to sideswipe you by moving to the side if there isn't room.

Gusting crosswinds with weird eddies or backdrafts around pillars or railings can also be a problem. Be alert, ready to steer whichever way is necessary. Be assertive in your choice of lane position: If you need to steer sharply to the right to keep your balance, it's nice to have room.

Some bridges have odd road surfaces such as an open steel mesh that gives you a disconcerting view of the water below—sometimes *far* below. Unless you're acrophobic, the worst problem with these meshes is that they're slippery when wet. But small objects can also drop through, so make sure your bags are tightly closed.

Tunnels

Tunnels, even short ones, are dangerous. Inside, it can be dark enough that you're riding blind, and usually there's no way to get out of the traffic lane if you need to. A tunnel presents all the hazards of a narrow bridge—in the dark. If you've got a support van, you can let it follow you, emergency lights flashing, or even carry you through.

That's the bad news. The good news is that as long as the tunnel doesn't bend, you're probably more visible than you think, beautifully silhouetted against the exit. Furthermore, drivers are likely to be as uncomfortable about finding you inside as you are about being there. Most will react with exaggerated caution.

To ride through anything but a short tunnel, begin by putting on your night-riding equipment: a reflective jacket, headlight, and taillight, if you have them. You're mostly worried about cars behind you, but remember that you're in big trouble if an oncoming driver doesn't see you and decides to pass someone else.

Treat the tunnel as you would a narrow bridge, waiting for a gap in the traffic, then pedaling through as briskly as safety allows. Some tunnels have sidewalks, but they're usually narrow, slanting, and dangerously close to the wall. Use the traffic lane instead, far enough out from the edge to be clear of rocks and debris. You'll be more visible here than if you hug the wall. The worst mistake you can make is to crash—that *would* make you difficult to see.

Some tunnels have warning lights and signs proclaiming "Bicycle in Tunnel," which you can activate by pushing a button. These are reassuring, but don't rely on them too strongly; never underestimate the ability of spaced-out drivers to cruise ahead, uncomprehending.

Freeways

It might surprise you, but bicycles are sometimes permitted on freeways, particularly in the rural West, where they can be the only paved roads. In

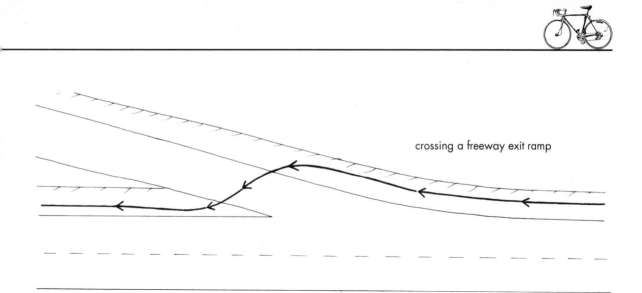

crossing a freeway exit ramp

some states, all but the most urban freeways are open to cyclists, but even if a state isn't that liberal, you may be allowed to use freeways to cross major rivers, or for other short distances where there are no reasonable alternatives.

To find out if you're legal on a particular section of freeway, check the "prohibited" sign at the entrance ramp. If bicycles aren't mentioned, they're probably allowed. If you're using the freeway to cross a river, you'll sometimes get after-the-fact reassurance from a sign telling you where cyclists must exit.

Although freeways have wide shoulders that safely separate you from the traffic, riding them is no fun. They're noisy and smelly, and occasionally some driver who doesn't know you're legal feels honor bound to yell at you. There is also an endless succession of tire retreads, broken fan belts, hub caps, and other debris, forcing you to keep alert.

The biggest problems on freeways are interchanges. The difficulty doesn't come when you're getting on and off; then, the nice, wide shoulder allows you to do your own thing unimpeded by the traffic. Instead, the problem arises when you're already on the freeway and want to go straight, through an exit. To do that, you've got to cross the exit ramp without knowing which of the cars coming up from behind might suddenly veer into the exit lane without signaling.

Unless there's a big gap in the traffic, reduce the time spent inside the exit lane by crossing it at right angles, much as you would a railroad track. Follow the exit ramp until you have some room to maneuver. Then turn sharply left, aiming for where the shoulder resumes on the other side of the exit. Signal your intention as a left turn, don't veer into

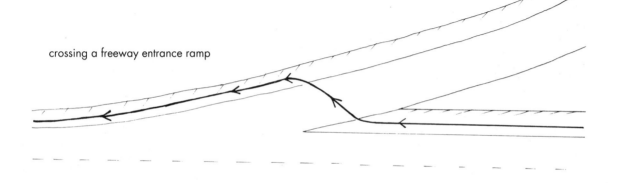

crossing a freeway entrance ramp

the traffic lane until you're sure you can get across safely, and don't loiter. Crossing an entrance ramp is similar, but here you can breathe easier because at least you don't have to guess which cars are coming your way.

Another problem with freeways are narrow bridge shoulders covered by pebbles and litter that force you out into the traffic lane. Although the traffic lanes are usually wide enough to share with cars, drivers don't expect you and can't be trusted to be alert. Wait for a big gap in the traffic, especially one that's clear of trucks, and don't loiter. Luckily, narrow stretches of shoulder like this don't occur on all bridges, especially ones that are specifically intended as bike routes.

Gravel

Most cyclists who don't have mountain bikes won't venture onto gravel. But many gravel roads can be handled perfectly well on a loaded touring bike with 700 x 32c or 1.4-inch tires. The biggest problems are washboard surfaces, loose stones, and sand, where your tires can bog down all the way to the rims. Nevertheless, on a good gravel road you can still cover 6 to 10 miles in an hour. On hard-packed dirt you can make even better time.

The trick to riding gravel is to take it easy, seeking out the smoothest, most rock-free path you can find, often following the tracks where repeated traffic has knocked most of the loose stones out of the way. Sometimes, you'll need to cut back and forth from one track to another, passing though loose gravel in between. Do so gently to avoid skidding the front wheel, but not so slowly that you run out of momentum in the middle. Similarly, avoid sharp turns. If you have no choice but to make one or feel unstable for any other reason, pull one foot out of

the toe clip and hold it to the side, ready to brace yourself if you slip. Meanwhile, coast or brake lightly for a controlled speed reduction.

Downhills are more difficult because you need the brakes, increasing the chances of skidding. Don't be surprised if a speed that felt safe on the level is too fast downhill.

As on the level, find a smooth surface, watching well ahead for patches of loose rock. Use both brakes for maximum control, with your hands in the down position if you have drop handlebars. Since going downhill shifts your weight forward, your back wheel will skid more easily than on the flat. Nevertheless, do part of your braking in the rear because a rear-wheel skid is easier to control than a front-wheel skid. To reduce the chances of a rear-wheel skid, transfer weight by sliding as far back on the saddle as is practical (this probably won't be necessary with full panniers). With practice, you'll learn to tell by the feel of the brakes if you're getting close to skidding.

Going up a steep hill, stay in the saddle to keep from losing rear-wheel traction, and don't accelerate hard in a low gear. That can spit gravel backward—"cool" if you're a kid, not much use otherwise.

Gravel roads usually have little traffic, which you can hear or see coming from a long way off. That helps because it allows you to find the best place to ride, even if it's on the wrong side of the road. Gravel also provides a good opportunity to ride side by side, one in each wheel track. Just don't get too close, and beware of traffic on blind summits.

If the road is crowned, keep close enough to the center that the crown doesn't make you veer gradually but inexorably toward the ditch. Expect slow going in rolling terrain. Gravel roads often climb steeply over every little hill in their path.

Construction Zones

Construction zones are an irritant. Sometimes you get through easily enough, but often you wind up riding on gravel or very bumpy surfaces, dodging construction equipment or sharing a narrow lane with one-way traffic.

The worst construction zones are those where a flagger stops traffic as a pilot car shuttles it through one direction at a time. When you encounter one of these, ask the flagger if a bicycle really needs to wait. You may not have to.

Shuttling though with the traffic is easier on a downgrade because you can come closer to keeping pace with the cars. Some cyclists like to follow at the back of the line to avoid blocking traffic, but I prefer starting in front because it gives me a head start.

On rare occasions you won't be allowed to pedal through at all. If so, you'll probably be shuttled through in the back of a pickup. Even in situations where you are permitted to pedal through, the construction crew will often be happy to offer you a lift.

Bridge out. Closed bridges can force you to detour miles out of the way. More often than not, though, the bridge will be passable, especially if you're willing to dismount and carry your bicycle. The real question is how paranoid the construction crew will be about breaking their liability insurance rules by letting you pass.

Much more rarely, you might encounter bridges on which bicycles are prohibited. Usually this means there's a safer alternative nearby, but on one memorable occasion, I was denied passage of a toll bridge because the insurance carrier was concerned about the risk of ice prior to some arbitrary date in the late spring. The fact that it was 60°F didn't matter; I had to find another bridge.

If you're self-contained, such setbacks are a nuisance, but on day rides or credit-card tours, they can be catastrophes. In unfamiliar terrain, plan your route with an eye to what would happen if a critical bridge were closed, trying not to schedule such crossings too late in the day.

Hitching a Ride

Sometimes you encounter situations where you either can't ride, or really don't want to. Perhaps it's because of mechanical breakdown, or truly abominable weather, or being caught by night without adequate lights. Maybe you're just tired. The only solution is to stick out your thumb.

It's amazing how easy it is to catch a ride. I've only had to hitch twice, but both times, the first van or pickup truck stopped immediately. Other cyclists report similar success. Sitting by the roadside with a bicycle, you are obviously non-threatening—and obviously in need of assistance. The bike, even though it is bulky, is an asset: It proves your *bona fides*, and it's best to stay with it, rather than chaining it to a tree and trying to walk.

Similarly, it helps to be wearing your helmet as you hold out your thumb. It's one of the signs of a serious cyclist, subtly helping to prove that you aren't a bum. You might still wait a long time for a ride, but it's more likely to be because you're on a back road where there are no cars than because no one will stop.

Avoiding Confrontations

A loaded touring bike weighs 80 pounds, has a comfortable cruising speed rarely more than 15 to 20 mph, and is powered by frail muscle, bone, and sinew. Automobiles weigh a ton or more, can accelerate from zero to 60 in seconds, and are driven by people who sometimes carry guns and have been known to use them on each other. With those odds, why pick a fight?

Many rude motorists are ordinary people who aren't used to dealing with bicycles. A shouted "Hey" to get their attention if they're about to cut you off is reasonable, but other than that your best reaction is to get out of the way, congratulating yourself on your defensive cycling skills and forgetting about it.

People who harass you by shouting obscenities, telling you to get off the road, deliberately cutting closer to you than necessary, or—as was popular in one place I once lived—leaning out the passenger window and barking like an angry dog are harder to be so philosophical about. Keep a cool head, even if they throw things or deliberately run you off the road. Ignore them if possible, pull off the road if not. Get the license number if the behavior warrants it, and get a description of the driver or the number is useless.

Part of keeping a cool head is not letting the driver know how much he shook you up—that just adds to the sport. And don't wave your fist, curse, or flip the finger. You don't want a driver to stop and get out of the car, waving his fist in return.

These confrontations—rare unless you provoke them—seldom escalate to violence. If an angry driver does stop, keep your distance so he isn't tempted to throw a punch. Calm yourself *now*, prepare to apologize even if you weren't wrong, and think about escape routes. At the same time, a no-nonsense, I-can-take-care-of-myself attitude can do a lot to keep the situation from escalating further, even if you know nothing about fighting.

If instead of stopping, a motorist comes back at you for a second pass, let him have the road. Don't wait for the third pass. Look for people—a gas station, general store, occupied farm house, whatever—and head for help.

In camp, avoid harassment by staying in estab-lished campgrounds or somewhere so secluded that nobody can possibly find you. If you choose the latter approach, avoid fires and make sure your bike reflectors aren't visible from the road.

Once in a great while, camping in a city park, you could be hassled by kids. This isn't likely to be more than an annoyance, though—cruising teen-agers honking at you every time they pass by, or pre-teens dashing through camp, displaying their courage by thumping on your tent. The best solution is to let them have their fun.

Rain

Rain is seldom welcome. Perhaps in August, if it's a light drizzle holding down the temperature when it would otherwise be unbearable. But riding in rain is usually miserable.

A good rain suit helps, as do fenders, and it helps to have clothing that will keep you warm when wet. Being wet is uncomfortable; being cold and wet will quickly rob you of energy and trap you into a cycle of alternately freezing and wearing yourself out pedaling hard enough to keep warm.

Even if the temperature isn't all that cold, getting over-chilled can be dangerous, impairing both your coordination and judgment. Hypothermia isn't usually as serious for cyclists as for hikers and back-packers, simply because you're close to civilization. But don't venture out onto long, lonely stretches without clothing to keep you warm enough even if it gets wet.

Camping in Rain

Camping in the rain, your comfort depends on the quality of your equipment. A good tent won't leak except under extreme conditions. To avoid camping in a puddle, stay out of low spots that might flood. If you're using a ground sheet, tuck it completely underneath the tent so it won't trap rain running off the fly. Digging trenches around the uphill side of your tent to "ditch" it is an environmental no-no, unnecessary with modern waterproof floor materials.

You can buy waterproof covers for your panniers and handlebar bag, or toss a tarp over your bicycle in camp, but with high-quality panniers this isn't necessary. Just make sure they're properly closed, with the storm seals folded down over the zippers. Bicycles are made under the assumption they'll occasionally get wet. Check the lubrication of your chain in the morning, but otherwise, your machine should weather a storm more easily than you do.

Thunderstorms

Take thunderstorms seriously. Not only do they entail strong winds and rain so hard that neither you nor the drivers can see the next bend in the road, they also involve lightning.

Start thinking about your options from the moment you see the storm. On the High Plains, it could be hours away, but so could the next town. In other parts of the country, towns may be closer, but haze can cut visibility, reducing your warning to less than an hour.

The best places to wait out thunderstorms are cafes or general stores. In farm country the farmers will almost certainly be happy to let you seek refuge in a barn. I've done this more than once, always having an interesting conversation with the farmer in the process.

When the storm gets close enough to hear the thunder, count the number of seconds between the flash and the boom. Sound travels at five seconds a mile, so you can determine how far away that particular flash is. The leading edge of the storm, of course, may be closer.

Thunderstorms can travel at up to 30 mph, so if the flash is only five seconds behind you, the storm can be on top of you in as little as two minutes. It's long past time to take shelter.

Caught in the open, you're in a potentially life-threatening situation. Find a place where you're not the tallest thing around—a road cut, a string of telephone poles, anything that's more likely to draw fire than you. But don't stand too close to an isolated pole or tree—if it gets struck, the electricity will fan out into the ground.

If you're caught totally in the open, conventional wisdom says to lie down in a ditch, getting as low as possible. But recently, a group of Nebraska

cyclists—who should know a lot about thunderstorms—told me that this isn't ideal. Instead, they said, squat as low as possible, touching the ground with only your shoes. The sole material will serve as insulation, apparently protecting you better than lying flat. It's not wise to stay too close to your bicycle, though, since it's metal.

Thunderstorms usually don't last long. Most of the lightning and the greatest wind fury come in the first few minutes, with the danger declining after that. Growing up in the Midwest, I've known thunderstorms to last as long as 24 hours, dumping 10 inches of rain in the process, but such monsters are rare. More likely, the storm will be gone within an hour, followed by sun, a rainbow, cooler air, and gentle breezes.

Showers

Scattered showers are another story altogether. They don't move as quickly as thundershowers, aren't as violent if they catch you, and are often small and slow enough to dodge by adjusting your pace or zigzagging though the backroads.

The art to dodging showers is keeping track of which way the clouds are moving and how fast. With long experience, this becomes nearly subconscious—you simply *know* it, without knowing how you know.

Night Riding

Riding after dark is best avoided, but if you're forced into it, you have two concerns: to see and to be seen.

The latter is the most immediately important. Your helmet, wind shell, panniers, and bicycle should have reflectors or reflective tape back, front, and sides. For a rear light, a flashing red strobe like that made by VistaLite is highly visible, relatively inexpensive, and runs for a long time on a pair of AA

Courtesy TurboCat Lighting Systems

batteries. The light is designed to replace your rear reflector, but touring you'll have to mount it to the back of your rack where it won't be blocked by your sleeping bag. Finding the proper bracket may take some effort.

Ankle-mounted strap-on lights are attention getting, but again aren't useful with panniers, which block them from sight. You could put the light on your elbow, but then it doesn't move up and down with each pedal stroke, robbing it of much of its effectiveness.

Most states require a headlight, but one isn't as critical for safety as a taillight because oncoming traffic is less likely to pass close to you.

Tiny reflectors and lights won't do much to help you see. On a dark country lane, you can manage with a battery-powered headlight strapped to your handlebars, or even with a flashlight taped to them as a rough-and-ready substitute. But in traffic, oncoming headlights will periodically ruin your night vision, and most lightweight lights don't give enough illumination to compensate.

Generator-powered lights, run by a small dynamo that rolls against your tire, are brighter but sap enough energy to slow you down appreciably.

Their brightness depends on speed, with the light shutting off completely if you stop.

The best headlights, favored by bike commuters, use large rechargeable batteries to produce a dramatically bright beam. Unfortunately, battery life and weight are problems. One manufacturer rates a 40-ounce battery pack at 5.3 hours; a 27-ounce at 3.3 hours. Rechargeable batteries must be recharged, preferably after each use. On camping tours, that can be impossible, though on a credit-card tour, plugging a battery pack in at night is easy.

Ironically, that makes such lights easiest to use for credit-card touring, when you're supposedly traveling light. And that's also when good lights can be the most important because being caught by darkness is a worse problem then than if you're self-contained.

Most self-contained cyclists don't carry much in the way of a headlight. On the rare occasions when I've had to do more than bicycle to or from a restaurant after dark, I've been content to inch along by the weak glow of a handlebar strap-on, knowing that if conditions get really bad, I can give up and walk.

GETTING THERE:
planes, trains, automobiles, buses, —and ferries

▼

Making a Choice

Unless a tour begins and ends at your front door, you'll need to get your bicycle to or from your destination.

By Car

Sometimes you'll want to avoid the hassles and expense of public transportation by driving. A single bike, sufficiently disassembled, fits the trunks of many sedans; two, separated by a blanket to reduce scratching, fit in the back of a hatchback or station wagon. Pickup trucks and vans can carry even more. But most people will need bike racks, of which there are two traditional designs: roof racks and racks that mount to a trunk or back of a hatchback.

Roof racks allow access to the trunk and let bicycles be taken on or off in a matter of seconds. Some can carry up to four bicycles on a passenger car, more on a van. Roof racks, though, can be expensive and awkward to store when not in use. They also have to be left on the roof of the car when you're cycling, though the best models have locks that greatly reduce the risk of theft.

Rear-end racks are lighter and often fold compactly enough to fit in a closet—or a car trunk. The traditional design holds two bicycles, with the rack attached by hooks that fit into the crack formed by the trunk or hatchback door. Rubber feet help keep the rack from scratching your car but may leave black marks that are difficult to wash off.

Loading one of these racks, especially with two heavily customized touring bikes, is more time consuming than loading a roof rack. Mount the bikes head to tail and don't be surprised if pedals clash with spokes or derailleurs, handlebars with rear racks. Take heart; patience triumphs. To keep the rack from bouncing, fasten its lower end to the bumper or undercarriage with bungee cords or straps, being careful that hot exhaust can't damage the cords or your tires. Tie both bicycles securely to the rack, and use rags or old socks to prevent scratching.

When traveling with your bike on either kind of rack, remove anything that might fall off or be damaged by wind or rain. Pumps, cyclometers, and strap-on mirrors are obvious items. Also, make sure your handlebar bag is zipped shut; remove it if you don't want it bug spattered. Top-of-the-line roof racks have a cable to lock the bikes when they're unattended. A budget alternative is to pass a cable around both bicycles plus part of the rack.

Leaving a car. At your starting point, you need a safe and legal place to park. Many towns tow cars after a few days, so inquire at the city hall or police station. Probably you'll be given permission to park somewhere nearby. The smaller the town— so long as it's not too small for a police station—the more cooperative the officials are likely to be. Other good places to ask are at parks or ranger stations.

By Plane

If you're flying, you can carry your bike with you as baggage. Many airlines supply boxes, obtainable at check in. The boxes are free, but a sizable shipping fee more than makes up for it.

Boxing a bike takes only a few minutes; you'll need an Allen wrench and a thin Crescent wrench for the pedals. When you're done, store them in the handlebar bag. Loosen the handlebars and turn them sideways, remove the pedals, then wheel the bike into the box. Put the pedals in your handlebar bag, if they fit, so you don't have to carry them as hand luggage. Don't leave the pump on the frame, or it'll fall off and rattle around. Similarly, remove your cyclometer head in case the bicycle winds up resting on its handlebars.

Tape the box liberally with nylon strapping tape or stout plastic tape supplied by the airline, running the tape completely around it in at least four places, two in each direction. This should hold it together even if it gets badly sliced up. Write your name and address on the box in at least two places, and you're ready to go.

At your destination you'll need a pocket knife to cut the tape. Be careful not to strip the threads on the pedals when putting them back on.

If you're met by car you can carry the bike away, still boxed. If the box is damaged, open it immediately to check your bike; it's a lot easier to make a claim right away.

Not all that many years ago, airlines wouldn't insure a bicycle for anything but loss. But today, many accept responsibility for damage. When making reservations, have your travel agent inquire about this, and avoid carriers that aren't sure enough of their baggage handling skills to take responsibility for them. Reduce handling by planning a minimum of connecting flights. In particular, try not to mix carriers; not only does that increase handling, but you may have to pay fees to both airlines.

While making inquiries, check also on the availability of boxes. The airline almost certainly won't let you ship your bike without one, and lack of a box is a horrible way to get stuck an hour before a flight.

If you're planning on bicycling into or out of the airport, ask your travel agent for a map. In small-town airports, the way out by bicycle is often obvious, but in bigger cities, you'll need a map to locate a backdoor that isn't a freeway.

Bulletproofing your bike. Airline boxes are flimsy, protecting your bike only if it's reasonably well handled. As long as the airline takes responsibility, I accept the convenience of the box provided. If something goes wrong, I draw reassurance from the fact that any city large enough to have an airport will almost certainly have a bike shop. But if you want extra protection there are sturdier ways to box your bike.

The simplest is by using your sleeping bag, tent, and sleeping pad as padding. Make sure your name is on everything in case the box bursts. Wadded-up newspaper also helps.

If you want a stronger box, ask a bike shop for one used for shipping new bikes. If there's a charge, it won't be much. These boxes are still cardboard, but they're sturdier, partly because they're smaller. Unlike the airline boxes, these come

in a number of sizes, so get one that's big enough. For touring bikes, remember that the long wheelbase means you'll need a bigger box than was used to ship a similar-sized racing bike; if in doubt get the biggest box you can find.

Packing one of these boxes requires partially disassembling the bike. Doing this for the first time on the evening before a flight is a good way wreck a night's sleep; if you've heavily customized your bike, everything from the water bottle cages to the front and rear racks may get in the way, and much of it will have to be removed. Consider saving yourself a lot of grief by paying a shop to do the work.

For even greater protection you can buy a hard-sided bicycle suitcase, but these aren't recommended for touring. They're extremely expensive and more likely to be designed for racing bikes than touring bikes, making fit a potential problem. It's also hard to figure out what to do with them when you're on the road.

By Train

Trains are a good way to carry bicycles, especially because they stop in smaller towns than airplanes, with the stations readily accessible by bicycle. Trains give you more schedule flexibility, since the reservation requirements aren't as restrictive as for airplanes. A good way to plan a bicycle trip is by starting at one train station and ending up at another, which also gives you bail-outs at intermediate stations along the way.

As with a plane, you need a box but can hope to get it at the station. Trains are more likely to charge for the box, but the shipping fee will almost certainly be lower. Unfortunately, you can't ship your bicycle to or from every train station; some have no baggage facilities. Check this out in advance, along with the availability of boxes.

By Bus

Buses have many of the advantages of trains, plus a much wider route network. It might take a while, but you can get bus connections to or from almost anywhere. Like trains, buses carry bicycles at much more reasonable fees than airplanes. They too

require boxes, though, and probably won't supply them, especially in small towns.

Finding a box on a tour. If you need a box at the end of a tour, start by looking for a bike shop. If none is around, fabricate a box from large pieces of cardboard scavenged elsewhere—a furniture or appliance store, for example. The result will be non-standard, but I've used such boxes by bus and even by plane. Check ahead to find out what's acceptable, and get to the station or airport far enough in advance that if the ticket agent has a different interpretation of the rules you're not stranded.

The carrier's interest in requiring a box is primarily to protect other people's luggage, so any contrivance that completely covers your machine will probably suffice. To increase the chances of its being accepted, remove the pedals and put extra padding at the ends of the axles. Don't expect an airplane to insure such a jury-rigged box, but going uninsured is better than leaving your bike behind.

By Ferry

Ferries and bicycles go together. Not only do they take you to pleasant, low-traffic destinations, but carrying a bike by ferry is ridiculously easy: You simply walk up the ramp, pay a fee, and enjoy the ride. Reservations shouldn't be necessary; there's always room for a bike. Would that other forms of public transportation were so bike friendly.

ON-THE-ROAD
REPAIR PRIMER

▼

Some cyclists are tinkerers whose first question about any gadget is "How does it work?" They don't seem happy unless they've got grease up to their elbows. Other perfectly intelligent people fall at the opposite extreme, feeling like fumble-fingered idiots at the very thought of fixing anything. Such people can and do bicycle long distances, but they're confined to sag-supported tours or staying close to friends. And it's a rare friend who won't eventually object to fixing your flats.

You don't need to be a master mechanic to cope with most on-the-road problems, especially if a good bike shop inspects your machine periodically. Major problems, such as worn-out bearings, develop slowly enough that if you pay attention to the early symptoms, you have time to limp to a bike shop before they become incapacitating.

This chapter will introduce you to the most frequent repairs—things you can take in stride if they need to be done on the road. They are also skills that may save you money at home by making you less dependent on bike shops for minor repairs.

I've included a few slick tricks to overcome seemingly impossible obstacles—such as tying a knot in a tube to fix a flat after you discover you left the tire patch kit at home.

Since you're not likely to have this book with you when you're broken down on the roadside, have your bicycle nearby as you read this chapter. If you take the time now to figure out how the bicycle is assembled, repair procedures are straightforward.

One important caveat: Equipment varies from brand to brand, and changes with time. Know your bicycle's idiosyncrasies before venturing into the hinterland.

To learn more, take a repair course at a local bike shop, or buy a book dedicated purely to bicycle repair.

Basic Maintenance and Adjustments

Other than flat tires, the most frequent on-the-road repairs are maintenance and adjustment problems you can fix in less than five minutes.

Lubrication and Cleaning

On-the-road maintenance consists of lubricating and cleaning your chain, checking for loose nuts and bolts, and checking tire pressure. On tour, do each of these at least once a day. On training rides, do them at home.

To clean the chain, wrap a paper towel or rag around it, gripping firmly as you rotate the pedals backward to slide the chain through the cloth. This will remove the worst of the built-up grit. You can also scrape dirt out of the cogs of the freewheel with a screwdriver blade or a pocketknife. When you're finished, lubricate the chain with a high-quality chain lube.

Chain lubes come either in plastic squeeze bottles or in spray cans with long plastic nozzle inserts for a finely directed spray. Both work equally well, but the squeeze-bottle is lighter, more compact, and more environmentally friendly. Hold the bottle upside down, touching the top of the chain. Allow a small amount of lubricant to flow as you rotate the pedals backward until the chain has made one complete revolution. The lube will distribute uniformly over the chain as you ride. It doesn't take much; a few drops covers the entire chain with a thin layer—which is all you want.

If during the day your chain starts to squeak or dries out (most likely after a rainstorm) stop and lubricate it. Those squeaks are wearing out your chain.

With the exception of squeaky derailleur wheels (discussed below), don't oil anything other than the chain, especially not bearings. Oil dissolves bearing grease.

Brake Adjustments

Tools: none for simple adjustment; otherwise, wrench, needlenose pliers

Parts: none

Time: 1 to 5 minutes

Brakes must be adjusted as cables stretch, brake blocks wear, or both. New cables are particularly prone to stretching, especially in the first 100 miles or so; if you've recently installed one or the bike is new, expect to make this adjustment at least once. Tighten your cables if the brakes feel soft or "spongy" when you use them, or the brake lever bottoms out before you've applied maximum pressure.

On rare occasions you may need to *loosen* your brakes slightly if the wheel has a big enough wobble that the rim can't pass through the blocks without rubbing. Do this only if you can't get the wheel fixed right away, and make sure your brakes will still stop you.

Brakes are most easily adjusted by a "barrel adjuster" at either the brake or brake lever end of the cable. The adjuster is a small hollow cylinder through which the cable passes, threaded into a socket. Twisting it one way lengthens the adjuster, removing slack from the cable and tightening the brakes. Twisting it the other way adds slack to the cable, loosening the brakes. A retaining nut prevents the adjuster from slipping. When tightening the cable, always leave enough of the barrel adjuster screwed into its socket that the threads won't strip under stress.

The barrel adjuster can accommodate up to about ¼ inch of cable slack before it runs out of room—something that will eventually happen. Then, you'll have to loosen the bolt that clamps the cable to the brake, pull about ¼ inch of cable through it (no more than the length of the barrel adjuster), and retighten the bolt. Before doing so, screw the barrel adjuster about ⅔ to ¾ of the way into its mount. That way you can use it to fine-tune your cable adjustment, with room left over for later.

All of this can be done in 5 minutes, but it requires a few tools. The hardest part is that before loosening the brake cable you must release the brake tension so the cable won't slip.

To start, know which of the two main styles of brakes your bike has: side-pull or cantilever. (A less common third type is the center-pull system, which adjusts much like a cantilever but is a bit harder to work with.)

Side-pulls have a single cable, bolted to one of the brake arms; usually the bolt loosens with an Allen wrench.

The distinguishing feature of the two types of cantilever brakes is that the overall cable structure has a Y shape that attaches to both sides of the brake. On one, the brake cable attaches to a small metal hook attached to a second, short cable called the "straddle cable," which connects the left and right sides of the brake. On the other type, the main brake cable runs all the way to one arm of the brake, with the second cable connecting to it a few inches from the end with a circular fastener.

Cantilevers are the simplest to adjust on the road. One of the cables attaching to the brake arms should have a metal knob protruding below the brake arm. Using one hand to press the brake block firmly against the rim to get some slack, use this knob to release the cable from the brake arm. Presto! You've taken the tension out of the brake cable, and the adjustment is now simple. Make sure you have the proper tools; you'll need two wrenches for the hook style of cantilever.

When you're done, tighten the bolt enough that the cable won't slip. Then reconnect the brakes by again pressing the brake block against the rim to get the necessary slack. Because you've tightened the cable, this will take a bit more effort than removal did, but if it's not fairly easy, you've probably overtightened the cable. Loosen it a bit and try again. If you've got a circular connector, move the connector to distribute tension evenly to the two brake arms. On some models the connector slides along the cable at slack tension, making this easy. On others you have to loosen a nut. Don't make any radical changes—just re-center the connector above the brake.

Side-pull brakes look simpler than cantilevers, but releasing the tension is more difficult because you can't simply unhook the cable.

Begin by looking on the brake assembly for a

"quick-release lever," which allows the brakes to open more widely than usual. It's also useful for removing the wheel without banging the brake blocks. Flip it open, then squeeze the blocks tightly together. This should take enough tension out of the cable to allow you to work with it.

Holding the brakes shut while simultaneously working on the cable takes three hands. Ask a friend to help, or carry a tool appropriately called a Third Hand, which holds the brake blocks for you. If you're alone and don't have this handy tool, try a toe-clip strap.

Working on the brake cable, needlenose pliers give you a nice, secure grip. Even better is a tool called a Fourth Hand, which simultaneously grabs the cable and pulls on it. This tool is heavy for touring, though, and not as all-round useful as needlenose pliers.

Other brake problems. Brake blocks occasionally get knocked askew, often as you remove a wheel or put it on. Simply twist them back into proper alignment. If this happens frequently, tighten the bolts that hold the blocks in place.

Never let brake blocks rub the tire when you squeeze the lever. If they do, the first time you use them you'll have a spectacular blowout.

Chain Chatters on Gears

Tools: none for simple adjustment; otherwise, wrench, needlenose pliers
Parts: none
Time: 1 to 5 minutes

The chain will chatter if it's slightly out of gear. On older bikes, it means you didn't shift properly; on newer ones it means your index shifting is misadjusted.

To adjust an index-shifting system, look for a barrel adjuster on your derailleur. Use it to fine-tune your index shifting as you ride. Otherwise, you'll have to dismount. Since you likely only have index shifting on the rear derailleur, that's where you'll be working. Put the derailleur in one of the middle gears. Twist the barrel adjuster to see how the

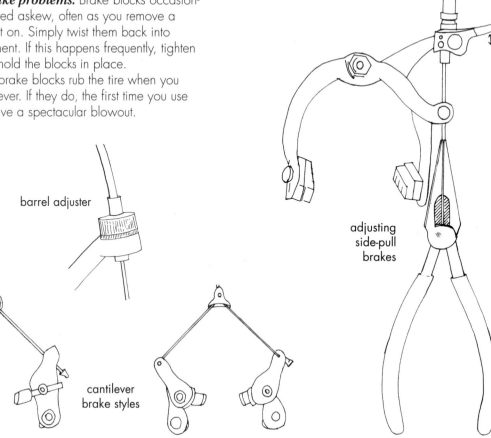

barrel adjuster

cantilever
brake styles

adjusting
side-pull
brakes

derailleur cage moves, then line it up directly beneath the gear. That should be all it takes. Or you can probably disconnect the index mechanism by rotating a small D-ring on the shift lever.

Like brake cables, derailleur cables stretch, particularly when they're new. Eventually, you may find that you've adjusted the barrel adjuster so many times—always in the same direction—that you've exhausted its range (about ¼ inch).

Proper adjustment is similar to what you would do for a brake cable. Tighten the barrel adjuster most of the way, so it's available for future adjustments. If you also have one of those adjustment levers on the down tube, flip it to the slack position also. Then, for maximum slack in the cable, shift the derailleur to the smallest gear. Loosen the bolt that attaches the cable to the derailleur, and use needlenose pliers or strong hands to pull up to one barrel-length of cable through it. Don't take up too much slack, or the derailleur won't be able to reach the small sprockets. Retighten the bolt and fine tune your adjustment with the barrel adjuster.

Derailleur Throws Chain or Won't Hit All Gears

Tools: screwdriver
Parts: none
Time: 5 minutes

When this happens your derailleur is bent or out of adjustment. Start by looking for bends. The derailleur should hang straight down, with its flat surfaces parallel to the plane of the freewheel or

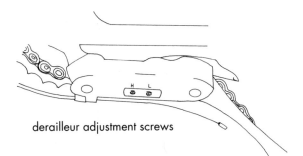

derailleur adjustment screws

chainring. If something is twisted, gently bend it back into shape and see if this solves your problem. If the twisting is severe or happens repeatedly, replace the derailleur before it snaps from metal fatigue.

The next most probable cause of thrown chains or inability to get into certain gears is an improper setting on one of a pair of adjustment screws controlling the derailleur's motion. If you're in a hurry, you can live with the problem for a while, but if the rear derailleur is throwing the chain into the spokes, adjust it now, before you start breaking spokes.

First, look for the adjustment screws. They'll be close together, in the main body of the derailleur, obviously not holding the derailleur together. If you're lucky, they'll be labeled "H" and "L" for high and low.

Get a friend to hold the back wheel off the ground as you spin the crank forward. Watch the misbehaving derailleur move side to side as you run it through its paces. The adjustment screws stop it at each end of its range. On older models you can actually see how they work, but on new ones everything's likely to be hidden by plastic moldings.

Figure out which screw is out of adjustment. If you're throwing the chain over the top of the biggest gear on your freewheel, for example, your problem is with the low gears, and if there's any logic to the derailleur's labeling system, you'll want the one labeled "L."

If the screws aren't labeled, shift the derailleur as far as it will go toward the problem end of its range. Pick a screw at random and loosen it slightly. Does the derailleur move? If so, that's the right screw. Otherwise return it to its original position (no sense messing up both ends of the derailleur's range) and try the other. When you find the right one, the effect is obvious.

Once you've located the correct screw, loosen or tighten it to extend or limit the range of motion. Again, you'll probably have to experiment, running the derailleur through its paces, shifting quickly back and forth between high and low gears. Fine tune the adjustment screws until the derailleur comfortably hits all gears—and all gear combinations—without throwing the chain. Then test the bike on the road;

sometimes what works with the wheel off the ground doesn't work in real life.

Cyclometers

Tools: screwdriver
Parts: none
Time: 1 minute

Cyclometers—which use a pair of magnetic sensors to count wheel revolutions and, in some cases, pedal strokes—are notorious for getting out of adjustment. One sensor is in the spokes or on the crank; the other mounts to the frame.

Problems occur if either sensor slips. Tighten them periodically with a screwdriver. The frame-mounted sensor is often attached so it twists when bumped, either moving so close to the wheel that the spoke sensor bangs it at every revolution, or so far away that it doesn't sense the passage of the spoke-mounted magnet. Learn its proper position and twist it back into place when necessary.

Do the same for the spoke-mounted sensor. It's also sensitive to spoke tension; if one of the spokes it's mounted to becomes loose, it may give erratic readings. Tighten the offending spoke, but only if you're confident you can "true" a wheel (discussed below, under wheel wobbles). If you don't know what you're doing, adjusting spokes is playing with fire—you're likely to wind up with an unridable wheel.

Fixing a Flat Tire

Tools: tire levers, tire pump
Parts: tire patch kit, tube (possibly)
Time: 10 to 20 minutes

Every experienced cyclist has a method for fixing flats. Here's mine for conventional tubed tires. It's not as complex as the number of steps makes it look:

1 Move safely off the road, avoiding grass or weeds where you might lose tools or a valve cap. Lay down the bicycle, chain and derailleur side up.

2 Remove the wheel. If you have quick-release levers on your brakes, flip them open—it's easier for the tire to pass between the brake blocks. With cantilever brakes, release the cable as dis-

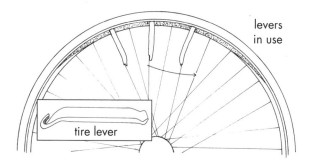

levers in use

tire lever

cussed earlier, under Brake Adjustments.

To remove the rear wheel, use one hand to swing the derailleur back and up, out of the way. Lift the frame and let the wheel drop straight down until it comes free of the chain. Look for a handy knob on the inside of the seat stay, just above the freewheel, where you can park your chain out of the way, and out of the dirt.

Remember what gear you were in. Putting the wheel back on is easiest if you shifted to the smallest cog before stopping—but that means a tough start when you're ready to go, especially with a full touring rig. An intermediate gear is probably the best choice.

3 Sit down, with all of the necessary tools within easy reach. Hold the wheel off the ground to reduce the chances of getting grit inside it.

4 Deflate the tire as far as possible, then use tire levers to remove the tube. These are metal or plastic levers that help you pry the tire over the rim. Plastic ones are better because they're less likely to poke holes in the tube.

   Tire levers come in sets of three, but you usually don't need all of them. Each has a smooth tip on one end, bent upward at about 30°. The other end is slotted and serves as a handle. Starting on the part of the rim farthest from the valve stem, carefully insert the non-slotted end of the lever between the tire's sidewall and the rim, with the bend turned so the handle slants away from the wheel. Push the tip of the lever beneath the lip, or "bead," of the tire, then pry toward the wheel until the handle almost touches the spokes. This should cause a short segment of the tire to pop over the rim. Gently run the tire lever around the rim, holding the handle near the spokes so the tip won't gouge holes in the tube. Most likely, a single pass will free the entire side of the tire.

   If that doesn't work, start over, but this time hook the slotted end of the tire lever beneath a spoke. This will hold the gap between rim and

tire open while you repeat the procedure with a second tire lever, a few inches away. Try the run-it-around-the-rim trick with the second lever—or hook it under a spoke and use a third. If that still isn't enough (and if it isn't, you've got one tough tire!), the lever in the middle is no longer needed; use it to extend the gap, leapfrogging around the rim as far as necessary. It sounds complex, but the entire procedure only takes a few seconds once you get used to it.

5 Starting at the side opposite the valve step, pull out the tube. It's not necessary to remove the other side of the tire.

6 If you're in a hurry and have a spare tube, you may not want to bother with a patch. Get your spare tube and skip to step 9. And if the tube has already been patched several times, you might wish to discard it; multiply patched tubes are prone to slow leaks.

7 If you decide to patch, pump air into the tube and try to locate the hiss that marks the hole. If you're not sure if you've found it, spit on it and look for bubbles. If you still can't locate the leak, immerse the tube in water and look for the trail

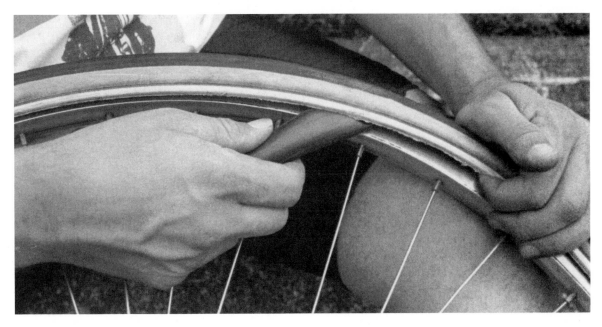

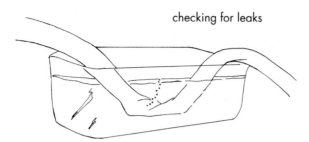

checking for leaks

of escaping bubbles. At home, you have a sink. On the road, you'll need a river or lake. Be patient; a slow leak may produce only one bubble every few seconds.

8 Patch the hole. Your patch kit should contain patches, glue, and a small piece of sandpaper. First, sand the surface of the tube near the hole. This helps the patch stick.

Make sure the tube is dry, then spread glue over it on an area slightly bigger than the patch. Don't worry if you cover too large an area; it won't stick to the inside of the tire or rim.

Let the glue dry a few seconds, until it loses its glossy sheen. The patch probably has a flat side and a rounded side. Pull the backing paper off the flat side and press it onto the tube. Most people also peel the backing paper off of the rounded side, but that's not necessary. If you do so after applying the patch, make sure you don't pull it loose.

9 Now check the tire, trying to find the cause of the flat. There may be a thorn or piece of glass still poking through, waiting to cause another flat. Being careful not to cut your finger, run your hand around the inside of the tire, feeling for it. Some people turn the tire inside out to help find small pieces of glass, but don't be too concerned if you find nothing. It may already be gone. And many flats, especially those with small side-by-side punctures (often called "snake bites") are caused by pinches, particularly when you hit a big bump with underinflated tires.

10 While inspecting the tire, also inspect the inside of the rim. Flick out any grit, and make sure that the plastic or cloth "rim strip" that covers the heads of the spokes is in place. The

strip keeps the spoke heads from poking holes in the tube, and it's important.

11 Insert the tube inside the tire and smooth it into place around the rim, beginning with the valve stem—easier if you first pump a little air into the tube. Try to avoid pinches or wrinkles, and work symmetrically from the valve stem to keep the stem from being pulled to one side or the other. I divide the tube into quarters, beginning with the valve stem, then moving to the side directly opposite it, followed by the points in between. This allows me to distribute the tube evenly.

12 Snap the tire back over the rim, again beginning at the valve stem and working symmetrically away from it. Do it with your fingers if they're strong enough; poking a hole with a tire lever would be a lot more irritating now than

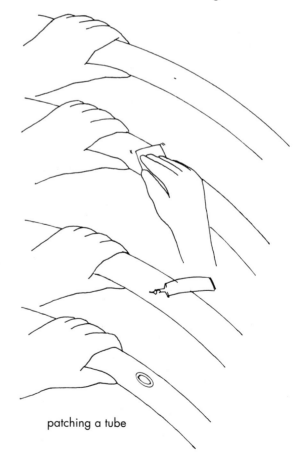

patching a tube

inserting tube

earlier. If you can't do the job by hand, insert a tire lever under the wall of the tire, this time with the curved side facing inward, and lever the tire into place one section at a time. You may need to use two tire levers, one on each end of the obstinate section of sidewall. Be very careful not to pinch the tube.

A more surefire way to avoid poking holes in the tube is using a specialty tool that grabs the tire on both sides like oversized tweezers, allowing you to pinch it over the rim without poking anything beneath the bead. The Var "Wishbone" and the Kool-Stop "Tire Jack" are two such tools.

13 Look the tire over before inflating it. Most tires have a thin line showing just above the rim; it should be a uniform distance from the rim, without suspicious bulges. Check both sides, beginning at the valve stem. If the stem doesn't look right, push it firmly into the tire, then pull it back again, wiggling it as you do so to help settle it in place. Elsewhere along the rim, pinch the tire away from the rim at any suspicious spots, looking for flaps of tube caught under the bead. If you find one, try to push it gently back where it belongs by squeezing the tire sidewall. Try to avoid using a tire lever.

14 Inflate the tire part way, and examine it again. If it looks OK, deflate it then pump it back up again; this gives unwanted wrinkles in the tube a chance to smooth out. If you have quick-release brakes or released the straddle cable on your cantilevers, reinflate the tire completely; if not, it's easier to get the wheel on if the tire's not yet fully inflated.

When pumping be careful not to break the valve stem by letting it wiggle too much. One way to immobilize it (not the only one) is by putting your thumb on the outside of the tire and your index and middle fingers across the end of the pump head, braced against a spoke. The other fingers circle the pump near its head. Squeeze tightly to hold the tire, valve stem, and head of the pump as a single, solid unit. With each pump stroke push against your hand, not the valve stem. This is particularly important for Presta tubes, which have metal valve stems.

15 Remount the tire, making sure it lines up straight in the brake blocks. This is usually no problem in the front, but the rear wheel may rub the chain-

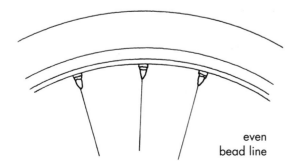

even
bead line

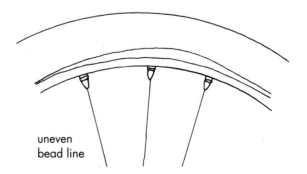

uneven
bead line

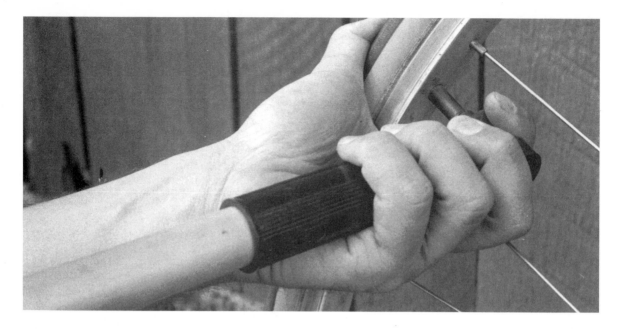

stays. Some bikes have a pair of set screws in the rear drop outs (the slots from which the wheel "drops out"), automatically lining up the tire. Other bikes aren't so nicely equipped.

Mounting a rear wheel is confusing the first few times you do it—but it merely takes a bit of thought. First, insert the end of the axle into the chain loop. Pull the derailleur up and back, so it's out of the way, and as you slide the wheel into the drop outs, let the chain settle into the gear it was on when you removed the wheel.

16 If you released your brakes, reconnect them!

Cut Tires and Blowouts

Tools: tire levers
Parts: spare tube, spare tire
Time: 20 minutes

Not all flats can be patched. Sometimes both the tire and the tube have long gashes, or the tube has a ragged hole where it went flat with a noise like a gunshot. Both can mean serious trouble.

The tube is unsalvageable if it has a cut more than about ¼ inch long or if it suffered a blowout. Any hole bigger than a pinhead can be a source of slow leaks even if you get it patched. It's best just to

use a new tube—if you've got one.

The tire may also be severely damaged. Serious blowouts often mean that the tube poked under a weak spot in the bead, much like an aneurysm finding a weak spot in an artery. Your replacement tube is likely to suffer the same fate. If you're carrying a spare tire, use it now; if not, be very careful when you pump up the tire after replacing the tube, checking regularly for bulges. Don't put in any more air than you have to—it's better to ride a low tire than blow out your last tube.

Similarly, if a cut longer than about ⅜ inch penetrates the tire, the tube may bulge out the hole and explode. Before replacing it, insert a dollar bill inside the tire, covering the hole—a trick successful often enough that it's known as "dollar billing" the flat. Ripstop Tape also works.

Recently, cyclists have discovered that the plastic wrappers on Power Bars (a high-energy snack) are even better—after all, they're so strong it's hard to open them to eat the bar. Another alternative is one of the nylon labels used in clothing. You're almost certain to have at least one of these in your possession all the time.

Whatever you use, don't push your luck by over-inflating the tire.

Other Tire Problems

Tools: ingenuity
Parts: whatever's available

What do you do if you have a flat only to discover that the glue in your patch kit has dried to a useless crust?

I carry two tire patch kits. But I've met a cyclist who says he solved that problem with ingenuity rather than redundant patch kits, looping the inner tube into an overhand knot, then working the knot into the proper position to pinch off only a small section of tube at the precise location of the hole. He then pulled it as tight as he could, reinserted the tube, pumped it up—and rode it more than 100 miles. It was a bit bumpy, he reported, but it held.

What if the rim strip breaks? You could proceed without it, but you risk an irritating succession of flats. Try taping the broken ends together, or to the rim. Electrical tape, is ideal, but even Scotch tape or masking tape are strong enough. Or, replace the rim strip with electrical tape or the cloth tape used to wrap handlebars, using a pocket knife, spare spoke, screwdriver—whatever's handy—to punch a hole for the valve stem. If you don't have anything sharp enough, leave a gap for the stem; 99% of a rim strip is better than none.

Broken Cable

Tools: Allen wrench (possibly two Crescent wrenches), needlenose pliers/wire cutters
Parts: replacement cable
Time: 10 to 30 minutes

The best cure for broken cables is good maintenance. Inspect them periodically and replace any that are frayed—before they snap. Even so, a brake or derailleur cable can break unexpectedly.

A broken brake cable is instantly incapacitating. Stop immediately and fix it. Yes, you have a second brake, but what would happen if its cable snapped, too?

Broken derailleur cables, on the other hand, don't pose safety concerns so long as the broken ends don't get into your spokes. When a derailleur cable snaps, the derailleur's spring automatically shifts the chain to the smallest sprocket—high gear

in the back, low in the front—and depending on the terrain, you could still ride. But you'll save time and energy by fixing the cable on the spot.

Before doing anything else, note how the old cable was attached. Brake cables have a metal plug on one end that fits a socket in the brake lever. Flex the brake lever to see how the cable threads through it. If you're confused, compare the broken one with the unbroken one.

From the brake lever, the cable runs through a housing and barrel adjuster to the brake, where a bolt clamps it in place. Often the bolt has a hole drilled in it, through which the cable passes. At the cable's tip there should be a crimped-on metal cap to prevent fraying. Save it.

Derailleur cables are similar; the plug end fits into the shift lever and the free end attaches to the derailleur. On old-style shifters, it's easy to find the socket for the metal plug. But on some of the newer mountain bike shifters—especially ones with hand-grip shifters—it's anything but obvious. Figure it out before you hit the road, asking a bike mechanic for advice if necessary.

Whether brake or derailleur, remove both pieces of the broken cable and examine the replacement cable. One end has a plug that fits most road bikes; the other end fits most mountain bikes. Carry separate spares for brakes and derailleurs; they aren't interchangeable.

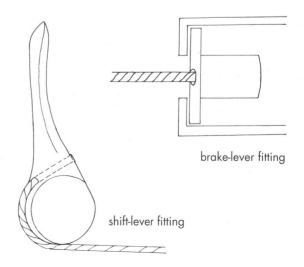

brake-lever fitting

shift-lever fitting

Use wire cutters (the ideal repair-kit tool combines these with needlenose pliers) to cut off the unwanted end, making sure the "good" section is more than long enough for the job.

To attach the new cable, start at the brake or shift lever end and thread it through the attachments and housings in proper order, trying not to fray it. If the cable frays anyway, cut off a short piece so you've got a fresh end to work with.

On most brakes sold since the late 1980s, the cable housing passes beneath the handlebar winding tape for part of its length. If your winding tape is tight, the housing should stay in place, permitting you to thread the new cable through it without unwrapping the tape.

Finally, adjust the tension as discussed under brake adjustments on pages 157-158. When the cable is adjusted, cut off all but about two inches and use the needlenose pliers to crimp on the fray-resistant cap you saved from the old cable.

You can save time on the road and free yourself from the need to carry wire cutters by preparing spare cables in advance, cutting them to length at home and soldering the cut ends to prevent fraying. Make spares for both front and rear, and don't cut the cable too short. Too long isn't a serious problem; after installation, you can bend the end out of the way or tape it to something, trimming the excess later.

Unless you bought an expensive prestretched cable, expect stretch during the first 100 miles. You may need to adjust it several times.

Broken straddle cable on cantilever brakes.

This is a rare event, but it can happen. The simplest solution is to carry a spare. If you don't have one, you may be able to jury rig something by wiring a piece of brake cable to the brake arms. Test it thoroughly before you trust it, and get a real straddle cable at the first opportunity.

If your cantilevers have a side cable attached to the main one in a Y-shaped joint, carry a spare side cable appropriate for your model of brake. If you don't have a spare, jury rigging something that will withstand the stress may be difficult. With the right spare parts, it's possible to convert it to a straddle-cable brake.

Broken Chain

Tools: chain tool
Parts: spare link (useful but not necessary)
Time: 15 to 30 minutes

Bicycle chains seldom break; in tens of thousands of miles of pedaling, I've broken only one. But I didn't have a chain tool with me and was forced to phone for a 30-mile drive back home. I vowed then that this simple breakdown would never incapacitate me again.

If you look closely at a bike chain, you'll see that it consists of a series of metal plates held together by small pins. A metal spacer fits over each pin, separating the plates and sized to fit the sprockets of the freewheel and chainwheel. The metal plates overlap in an alternating pattern that repeats every two pins. This double unit is what you should think of as a single "link."

To fix a chain, you need a chain tool, a small but ungainly contraption consisting of a toothed channel to hold the chain while you use a screw-threaded punch to drive one of the connecting pins into or out of it. A handle helps you get a firm grip on the chain/chain-tool combination when the tool is in use. Make sure your chain tool fits your chain.

Fixing a broken chain is simple but dirty. Resign yourself to getting chain lube all over your hands. You'll be lucky not to get it on your arms and legs as well.

First, prop the bicycle against a wall, fence post, or other stable support, or lay it on the ground, derailleur side up.

Remove the broken link. Remember to take a whole link, not just half of one—otherwise the plates won't overlap properly when you connect them. To remove all the broken pieces you might have to take half a link from each side of the break. With the chain tool, drive the connecting pin through the chain, just barely far enough out that the

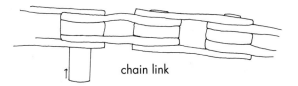

chain link

Proper threading of chain through derailleur.

Chain tool in use.

broken link comes free. Don't push it all the way though the outside plate or you may not be able to reinsert it. If you lose the pin, simply remove another link—properly this time.

If you have a spare link that fits your brand of chain (obtainable from a bike shop at a nominal price), connect one end of it to the broken chain, using the chain tool to drive the connecting pin into position (its ends should protrude the same amount on each side). If you don't have a spare link ignore this step; your chain will be about an inch shorter than it was, and may no longer fit all of your gears, but you'll still be able to ride.

Now reconnect the broken ends. First make sure the chain properly threads around the freewheel and through the derailleurs. Pay particular attention to the jockey wheels (the tiny wheels that guide the chain through the rear derailleur); it's easy to get that part wrong. Then reconnect the chain. Wiggle the new connection a few times to loosen it, wipe the chain with a rag (by this time you've probably gotten dirt all over it), lubricate the new link, and you're ready to return to the road. Buy a new chain at the first opportunity.

Broken Spoke

Tools: spoke wrench, freewheel tools
Parts: replacement spoke
Time: 30 to 60 minutes, or more

Spokes are another of those inexpensive parts whose sudden demise can strand you. But given the stresses they have to endure whenever a heavily loaded bike hits a bump, it's surprising they don't break more often.

Any rider can break a spoke, but some are particularly prone—a 200-pounder, for example, as opposed to someone who weighs in at 130. It's just an unfortunate fact of life. Likewise, you'll break more spokes touring, when you're loaded down.

Riding style is also a factor. If you like to stand up on the pedals to "pop" hills with a few strong strokes, you're more likely to break spokes than someone who approaches hills more sedately, downshifting. The same goes for people who take bumps, railroad tracks, and cattle grates at high speed.

Broken spokes on the front wheel, or on the non-freewheel side of the rear wheel, are easy to fix. But if you break one on the freewheel side of the rear wheel (the most likely ones to break since they're the ones under greatest stress), it's a major job.

Location aside, all spokes are similar. One end is threaded to fit a retaining nut called a "spoke nipple" protruding from the rim. The other end fits through a hole in the wheel hub and is flanged to keep it from pulling free. On the freewheel side of the rear wheel, the freewheel is in the way and must be removed first.

Your tool kit should contain at least 3 spare spokes. Consult with a bike mechanic to make sure they're the right length.

Replacing a spoke is a 6-step process.

1 Remove the wheel.

2 Remove the freewheel, if necessary. On older bikes, this requires a "freewheel puller," a sturdy metal cylinder with prongs that mate to the freewheel on one end. The other end is square to fit a large wrench.

   This freewheel type threads tightly onto the hub. Using the freewheel puller, you can loosen it with a large wrench, but a better way is by clamping the freewheeler puller to a vise. Put the wheel/freewheel assembly on top of it, fitting the prongs of the puller into the freewheel, then carefully rotate the wheel.

   Without a vise or a pipe wrench—not

exactly on-the-road tools—the job is virtually impossible. You'll have to find a gas station or a farmhouse, though desperate cyclists have reported success by such approaches as wedging the freewheeler puller into a fence gate.

On newer bikes, the freewheel is a cartridge assembly that slides onto a spindle protruding from the hub. In some models, it is held in place by a threaded lock ring. In others, the smallest cog of the gear cluster serves the same purpose.

Neither of these is so tight that it's particularly difficult to remove, but you do need specialty tools. One is a "chain whip"—basically a short length of chain attached to a long handle, used to immobilize the the freewheel or unscrew the small, locking cog, as needed. The other is a lock-ring tool, essentially a wrench that fits a set of holes in the lock ring.

These tools are a bit heavy to be happily carried in your repair kit. If you shop around, you can find on-the-road models of each—chain whips or lock-ring tools that clamp onto the chainstay near the freewheel, allowing you to loosen the freewheel by rotating the wheel itself. "Cassette Cracker" and "Hyper Cracker" are two brand names. Ask your bike shop which one you need, and make sure it fits. Also, consult a bike shop before trying this tool on a bike whose frame is made of some exotic material—the chainstay may not be designed for this kind of stress.

3 Remove the broken spoke and snake the new one into place, starting at the hub. Note how the existing spokes cross each other in a complex over-and-under pattern. Wheel builders cheerfully debate the merits of various crossing patterns, but your task is to duplicate the pattern of the other spokes.

4 Screw the spoke nipple onto the spoke using a spoke wrench, a specialty tool which provides the only way to get a good grip on the nipple. Pretend you're trying to drive a screw into the rim. Clockwise tightens. Make sure your spoke wrench fits your spoke nipples; they're not all the same.

If you don't have a spoke wrench, all may not be lost. Remove the tire and tube. Many spoke nipples are slotted on the inside to fit a screwdriver.

5 Replace the freewheel, being careful not to strip the threads, particularly easy to do on the old style that threads directly onto the hub.

On new freewheels, make sure the locking mechanism is properly tightened. The old style doesn't need to be tightened all the way; it self-tightens as you pedal (that's why it's so hard to remove).

6 "True" the wheel, as described in the next section, about removing wobbles.

Note: If you've only broken a single spoke and don't want to replace it immediately—or can't because you can't remove the freewheel, you can true the wheel temporarily so it works with one spoke missing. If an end of the broken spoke is in the way and can't be removed, twist it around another spoke or tape it out of the way. Fix the wheel as soon as possible.

spoke wrench in use

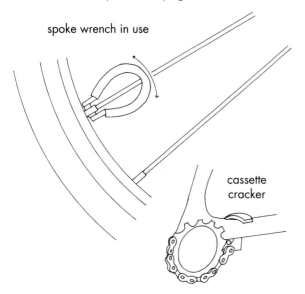

cassette cracker

REPAIR PRIMER

Fixing a Wobbly Wheel

Tools: spoke wrench
Parts: none
Time: 20 to 60 minutes.

Hitting bumps, and in extreme cases, breaking spokes, bring on wheel wobbles. If a broken spoke is the cause, replace it if you can, then true the wheel, as discussed in the last section.

Leave minor wobbles alone unless you are an experienced bike mechanic; it's all too easy to make them worse. The only wobbles you should fix on the road, where you can't go to a bike shop if you botch the job, are those big enough to make the tire rub the brakes or cause the bike to "shimmy" unnervingly. Then you don't have much to lose.

Lay your bicycle on its side with the wheel free to spin. Resist the temptation to set your bike upside down on its handlebars and seat—that's hard on brake levers and cables. Spin the wheel, locating the wobble by watching the rim as it passes the brake blocks. If you have chalk or a felt-tip pen you can hold these near the tire to mark the wobble. Brace your hand on the frame to steady it.

Once you've located the wobble your goal is to tighten and loosen spokes to pull the rim into a straighter line. It's easiest to work with a small cluster of spokes, usually three, rather than one at a time.

Look closely at the wheel. Some spokes mount to the right side of the hub, some to the left. If you want to move the rim to the right, tighten the spokes drawing it that way and loosen the ones on the other side. With a spoke wrench, rotate the nipples as though you were driving a screw into the rim.

Be patient and work incrementally. Adjust all the spokes in your chosen cluster, making the biggest adjustment to the one in the center. A quarter turn of the spoke nipple is a big change—don't adjust any spoke by more than that without spinning the wheel to observe the effect.

Wheel truing is an art. It is frustratingly easy to turn one big wobble into several little ones, then, just when you think you're making progress, to convert the little wobbles back into a big one worse than what you started with. Don't try for showroom perfection; your goal is to get back on the road

with a comfortably handling machine. A good way to learn is to beg, borrow, or buy a "junker" wheel from a bike shop and practice.

Squeaky Rear Derailleur

Tools: chain lube
Parts: none
Time: 1 minute

A squeaky derailleur can drive you crazy, especially because there is no sure fix. Start by spinning the pedals backward, listening for the source of the problem. Most likely, the culprit will be the small wheels the chain wraps around between freewheel and derailleur. Called various names—I prefer "jockey wheels"—they rotate on a small, fat spindle. Work some chain lube into the gap between the wheel and the spindle and cross your fingers. Sometimes that's all you need. If not, live with the squeak until you can get to a bike shop.

Signs of Serious Problems

Even the best bike mechanics prefer not to attempt some types of repairs on the road. Keep alert for warning signs indicating that it's time to find the nearest bike shop.

One of the most important of these problems is a worn out bearing. Your bike has bearings in the bottom bracket, wheel hubs, and headset—and possibly in the pedals and jockey wheels of the derailleur. If any of these starts to squeak, grind, wobble, or feels loose when you ride the bike or test the bearing by hand, get it overhauled—and probably replaced. If you pay attention to the early warning signs, you've probably got at least 100 miles notice before the bike becomes unridable.

Another common problem is a worn-out chain. The simplest way to check for wear is to push sideways on the top loop of the chain with moderate pressure, midway between the crank and freewheel. A new chain deflects not much more than an inch to the side. As the chain wears, the links loosen and the sideways deflection becomes greater.

A worn-out chain isn't serious, but replace it at the next opportunity. It stretches slightly with each pedal stroke, robbing you of energy, and it may also cause freewheel or derailleur problems.

Freewheels also wear out, usually indicated by difficulty in shifting or a chain that won't "settle down" in certain gears—generally those you use most frequently. Don't be surprised if your old chain won't work well on a new freewheel. As a freewheel wears, the chain often wears to fit it; replacing the freewheel often means replacing the chain.

Chains and freewheels have short enough lives that you could easily be replacing them every year or two. On older bikes, chains were good for 2,000 to 5,000 miles, while freewheels lasted 3,000 to 10,000. Index shifting, however, eats drive-train components quicker. Count on a new chain every 600 to 2,000 miles, and a new freewheel every 1,000 to 5,000.

Touring wears out tires at a prodigious rate. Replace tires that have lost their tread or show numerous cuts or nicks, and count yourself lucky to get more than 1,000 miles out of a rear tire. Front tires, which carry less weight, last a lot longer. Not carrying baggage also extends tire life by reducing weight.

Improvisation

If you carry a tool kit and know bike repair basics, most repair problems are routine. Irritating perhaps, but nothing more than a delay.

But like the cyclist who found himself tying a knot in his tube, occasionally you'll find yourself in situations where—because of bad planning or unusual events—conventional repair techniques don't work.

When that happens, think before despairing—improvisation can work wonders. I once heard of a Minnesota cyclist who collided so hard with a dog that he bent the rim of his front wheel beyond the realm of what can be fixed by conventional wheel truing. The dog walked away but the bicycle looked unridable.

The cyclist, however, wasn't ready to accept the condolences of the people who'd gathered at the scene. Laying the wheel on the ground in front of him, he did what he called a "rain dance" on the rim. To the amazement of all who watched, the wheel was ridable when he finished.

This isn't to say there's a solution to every on-the-road mishap—or even that you'll always think of it if there is one. But it's an excellent lesson in using unconventional approaches when you've got nothing to lose. And there are few pleasures to rival that which comes from ingeniously fixing something that looked impossible.

APPENDIX

Touring Information

Here's a list of organized tours in 29 states. Every week, there's at least one ride somewhere in the country from early June to mid-October. There's something for everybody, ranging from the mammoth, rolling party of Iowa's RAGBRAI (7,500 riders) to tours limited to fewer than 50 people, from the laid-back 30-mile-a-day pace of Cycling Jersey to mountain challenges in Arizona and Oregon. It's a great way to see the country—and where else can you get a week-long vacation for as little as $200?

Most of these tours have run for several years, many for more than a decade. But the usual caveats apply: Routes, dates, distances, group sizes, and mailing addresses are all subject to change. Even well-established tours have been known to go out of business.

East

Maryland
Cycle Across Maryland—Late July; about 300 miles. Group size: 1,500. Contact: P.O. Box 21572, Baltimore, MD 21208.

Massachusetts
BAM (Bicycle Across Massachusetts)—Early July (2-5); 240 miles. Group size: 100–200. Dormitory accommodations. Contact: Joe Nai, 3900 Simms Ave., SE, Albuquerque, NM 87108.

New Jersey
Cycling Jersey—Mid-August; about 200 miles. Group size: 100. This is a relaxed tour modeled on Michigan's PALM. Contact: The Wayfarers, P.O. Box 73408, Washington, DC 20056.

New York
NYRATS (New York Ride Across the State)—Late July; 650 miles between Buffalo and New York City. Group size: 75. Dormitory accommodations. Contact: Niagara Frontier Council AYH, P.O. Box 1110, Ellicott Station, Buffalo, NY 14203.

Pennsylvania
Penn Central—June; about 300 miles. Group

size: 50 but expect it to grow. Route includes 25 miles of abandoned railroads. Contact: The Wayfarers, P.O. Box 73408, Washington, DC 20056.

Virginia
Bike Virginia—June; 250 miles with optional side trips for those desiring higher mileage. Group size: 1,000. Contact: P.O. Box 203, Williamsburg, VA 23187-0203.

Midwest

Illinois
BAMMI (Bicycle Across the Magnificent Miles of Illinois)—Early August; 500 miles, point-to-point, starting in Chicago area. Group size: 400. Contact: Chicago Lung Assoc., 1440 W. Washington Blvd., Chicago, IL 60607.

Indiana
TRIRI (The Ride in Rural Indiana)—Late June; 450-mile tour of Hoosier country; spends each night in a state park. Group size: 500. Contact: Bloomington Bicycle Club, P.O. Box 463, Bloomington, IN 47402.

Iowa
RAGBRAI—Late July. This is the ride that started it all more than 20 years ago. Crosses state west to east; about 450–500 miles. Group size: 7,500. Fills by lottery in early spring. Contact: P.O. Box 622, Des Moines, IA 50303-0622.

Kansas
Biking Across Kansas—Early June; west-to-east tour by several different routes, all about 500 miles. Group size: 300 per route. Tour is extremely popular and fills early. Contact: Norma Christie, P.O. Box 8684, Wichita, KS 67208.

Michigan
PALM (Pedal Across Lower Michigan)—Late June; west-to-east across southern Michigan by two routes, about 250 miles each. Because of its low mileage, this ride caters to beginners and families.

Group size: 500 per route. Contact: P.O. Box 7161, Ann Arbor, MI 48107.

SummerTour—Mid-July; 500-mile loop tour through north-central Michigan. Sponsored by the same organization that runs the highly successful DALMAC. Group size: 150. Contact: P.O. Box 17088, Lansing, MI 48901.

Shoreline Bicycle Tour—Early August; follows Michigan shoreline by two 350-mile routes. Group size: 500 (west), 275 (east). Contact: P.O. Box 16201, Lansing, MI 48901.

DALMAC (Dick Allen Lansing to Mackinac Bicycle Tour)—Early September; 4- or 5-day event, with options to suit almost every level of ability. DALMAC offers several route variations—including a 4-day, 400-mile version—running most of the length of Michigan, culminating in a mass crossing of the Mackinac Bridge. Group size: 1,700. Contact: P.O. Box 17088, Lansing, MI 48901.

Nebraska

BRAN (Bicycle Ride Across Nebraska)—Early June. Route varies each year, generally crossing state from west to east, ending near Omaha. Distance: 450–500 miles. Group size: 600. Send SASE before January 1, and when the registration form comes, send it back by return mail. Ride generally fills within one week. Contact: Northwest Rotary, Attn. BRAN, 10730 Pacific St., Suite 218, Omaha, NB 68114.

Ohio

GOBA (The Great Ohio Bicycle Adventure)—Late June; about 350 miles. Group size: 3,000. Nightly entertainment. Contact: P.O. Box 14384, Columbus, OH 43214.

Wisconsin

TOBRAW—A collection of tours run by a single company, following various routes, most of them in Wisconsin. Distances are about 300 miles; group sizes are about 50–100. Choice of tent or gymnasium accommodations on most routes. In 1994 TOBRAW expanded to include a cross-country course as well. It isn't clear if this will be repeated.

Contact: Mel Welch, 3632 W. Maple St., Milwaukee, WI 53215.

GRABAAWR (Great Annual Bicycle Adventure Along the Wisconsin River)—Late June; 500 miles. Group size: 500–1,000. Riders can sign up for individual days or the entire ride. Gymnasium option on most nights. Contact: P.O. Box 6184, Madison, WI 53716-0184.

South

Florida

Florida Bicycle Safari—Early November; 430-mile loop in central Florida. Group size: 450. Three-day, 200-mile version also available. Contact: 11510 E. Colonial Dr., Orlando, FL 32817.

Georgia

BRAG (Bicycle Ride Across Georgia)—June; 350–400 miles. Group size: 2,500. Contact: 887 Ryan Ln., Lilburn, GA 30247.

Missouri

CAMP (Cycle Across Missouri Parks)—June; 400 miles. All nights in state parks or historic sites. Group size: 250–350. Contact: American Youth Hostels, 7187 Manchester Rd., St. Louis, MO 63143.

Show Me Bike Tour—June; about 300 miles. Group size: 200–350. Gymnasium accommodations when possible. Contact: 22807 Woods Chapel Rd., Blue Springs, MO 64015.

Oklahoma

Oklahoma Freewheel—Early June; 400–450 miles; route varies year to year. Group size: 1,500–2,500. Contact: Tulsa World, P.O. Box 1770, Tulsa, OK 74102, Attn. Freewheel.

Tennessee

BRAT (Bicycle Ride Across Tennessee)—Late September; 450 miles, with most nights spent in state parks. Group size: 500. Contact: Program Services, Tennessee State Parks, 701 Broadway, Nashville, TN 37243-0446.

Texas

Lone Star Bicycle Tours—Not a specific event but a touring company, this organization sponsors one or more tours each year in Texas and occasionally neighboring states. Group sizes are usually small (50 riders was the limit on one recent trip). Contact: Lone Star Bicycle Tours, 1507½ Nueces, Austin, TX 78701.

Texas Chainring Challenge—early June; 400 miles in Texas hill country. Group size: 500. Contact: Longview News-Journal, P.O. Box 1792, Longview TX 75606.

West

Arizona

Grand Canyon to Mexico Almost Across Arizona Bicycle Ride—Early October; two routes, 8 or 9 days, 560–580 miles, converging in southern Arizona. Group size: 125 per group. Contact: P.O. Box 40814, Tucson, AZ 85733.

California

Double Cal 600—Mid-May; rugged, 600-mile, 8-day, figure-eight route beginning and ending in Sacramento, crossing state twice, featuring Lake Tahoe, Sierra Nevada, Napa Valley, and San Francisco. Group size: 100. Contact: North Sacramento Rotary Club, Attn.: Bike Ride, P.O. Box 15083, Sacramento, CA 95813.

Sierra to the Sea—Late June; 400-mile point-to-point course from Mother Lode country of Sierra Nevada foothills to San Francisco. Be prepared for possible heavy traffic, temperatures of 100°+. Group size: 100. Contact: Almaden Cycle Touring Club, 6559 Camden Ave., San Jose, CA 95120.

Colorado

Ride the Rockies—Late June; 450 miles through the Colorado Rockies. Expect several passes with elevations well over 10,000 feet. Group size: 2,000. Fills by lottery in late winter. Contact: Ride the Rockies, The Denver Post, 1560 Broadway, Denver, CO 80202.

New Mexico

Pedal the Peaks—Late June; follows and extremely mountainous 450–500 miles through northern New Mexico. Contact: 2878-H W. Long Circle, Littleton, CO 80120.

The Santa Fe Trail Bicycle Trek—September-October; 1,080-mile route follows the historic Santa Fe Trail between Kansas and New Mexico as closely as possible by paved, public roads. Group size: 50. Can be done in segments or in its entirety. Contact: Willard Chilcott, 885 Camino Del Este, Santa Fe, NM 87501.

Nevada

OATBRAN (One Awesome Tour: Bike Ride Across Nevada)—Late-September; 425 miles east-to-west paralleling route of Pony Express trail. Group size: around 100. Contact: LGFT Productions, P.O. Box 5123, Lake Tahoe, NV 89449.

Oregon

Oregon Bicycle Ride—Mid-August; 500 miles, east to west across Oregon. Group size: 275. Contact: 1324 NW Vicksburg, Bend, OR 97701.

Cycle Oregon—Mid-September; 450-mile sampler tour of Oregon. Often very mountainous. Group size: 2,000. Registration includes portable hot showers and nightly entertainment. Contact: P.O. Box 40268, Portland, OR 97240, or phone 1-800-CYCLEOR.

Utah

Pedal for Power Bicycle Tour of Utah—Mid-August; 500-mile loop through northern Utah. Group size: 100. Contact: Intermountain Consumer Power Association, 8722 So. 300 W., Sandy, UT 84070.

Tour of Southern Utah's National Parks—Mid-September; 230-mile loop, with full days off in Zion and Bryce national parks. Group size: 45. Contact: c/o Carl Ehrman, 3247 Bon View Dr., Salt Lake City, UT 84109.

Washington

Washington State Sampler—Early July; challenging loop through Washington State includes Mt. Rainier and North Cascades. Group size: 100. Contact: CBTS, 1402-73rd, Everett, WA 98203.

Wyoming

RAW (Ride Around Wyoming)—June; 450-mile loop. Group size: 100–200. Contact: 18 Paradise Dr., Sheridan, WY 82801.

Cycle America

In addition to these, one ambitious organization, Cycle America, has conducted as many as two dozen rides per year in the U.S. and Canada, including a 12-week sequence that can be combined into a summer-long 5,050-mile cross-country trek from Bellingham, Washington, to Portland, Maine. Riders are invited to take as many or as few segments of the cross-country route as they desire, or to come back summer after summer to gradually complete the entire trek in a series of shorter installments.

Other popular routes are the Oregon Coast and the Canadian Rockies.

Group size: 100–300 per segment. Contact: Cycle America, P.O. Box 29, Northfield, MN 55057.

Adventure Cycling

Another source of touring information is the Adventure Cycling Association (formerly Bikecentennial), which has mapped thousands of miles of cross-country routes. For self-contained touring, these superb maps make for easy route finding. The popularity of the routes also increases the chances of meeting other cyclists along the way. The organization also offers an assortment of van-supported tours and guided, self-contained tours along segments of its trail network, usually paced at about 45 miles a day. Some go all the way cross-country. For information, contact: Cycle America, 150 East Pine Street, P.O. Box 8308, Missoula, MT 59807-8308.

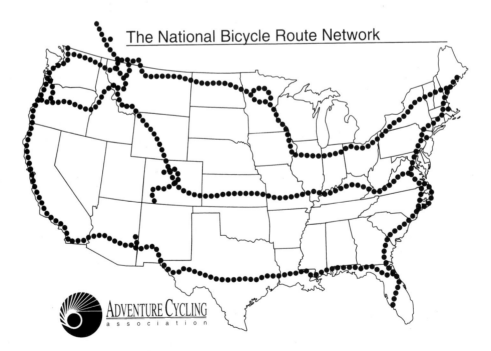

The National Bicycle Route Network